TELE~~VISION~~

PO~~I~~

Classics in Communication and Mass Culture Series

Arthur Asa Berger, Series Editor

TELEVISION
AND
POLITICS

Kurt Lang
Gladys Engel Lang

With a new introduction by the authors

Transaction Publishers
New Brunswick (U.S.A.) and London (U.K.)

Library of Congress Catalog Number: 2001041531
ISBN: 0-7658-0889-7
Printed in the United States of America

Library of Congress Cataloging-in-Publication Data

Lang, Kurt, 1924-
    Television and politics / Kurt Lang and Gladys Engel Lang.
        p. cm.
    Rev. ed. of: Politics and television re-viewed / Gladys Engel Lang. 1984.
    Includes bibliographical references.
    ISBN 0-7658-0889-7 (pbk. : alk. paper)
        1. Television in politics—United States. 2. United States—Politics and government—1945-1989. I. Lang, Gladys Engel. II. Lang, Gladys Engel. Politics and television re-viewed. III. Title.

HE8700.76.U6 L36 2001
324.7'3'0973—dc21   2001041531

CONTENTS

INTRODUCTION TO THE TRANSACTION EDITION
Fifty Years of Politics on Television

The media environment has changed since television first began its coverage of major political events. Smaller and lighter equipment allows television to go almost everywhere while satellite transmission has transformed it into a truly global medium. News and information have been made available around the clock, first on CNN, and then on several other networks. More people have more access to more television than ever before. And, by speeding up the news cycle, the Internet has greatly reduced the tyranny of deadlines, thereby handing the news media, their sources, and the public figures they cover the ability, whenever they feel so impelled, to respond almost instantaneously to political developments in any part of the planet. The world has shrunk and events unfold ever more rapidly.

These changes have made a difference. All of us are living an ever greater part of our lives at a distance. Whether or not we are aware of it, more and more of what we see or hear of public life as well as the form in which it reaches us is being shaped by technologies managed by professional specialists. The images so relayed make up a significant part of the political "realities" to which citizens respond.

It was the power of the televised image to communicate "reality" that initially aroused our interest in mass communication half-a-century ago. Television was then still in its infancy and what has since been institutionalized under the rubric of media research in its early adolescence. In the interim, studies have proliferated. Archives are bursting with data. Media analysts, or whatever one calls the practitioners of this new profession, have sharpened their research tools and vastly increased their capabilities for processing and retrieving information in ways we could hardly have anticipated. If our studies—employing methods that today might be dismissed as "primitive"—retain relevance, as apparently they do in the judgment of Irving Louis Horowitz, Arthur Asa Berger, and others at Transaction Publishers, this is due primarily, we believe, to the continuing interest in our use of site-specific observations to raise broader issues about the immediate and long-range effects of television on political life.

This introduction affords us the opportunity to spell out briefly, but more systematically than in the studies republished in this volume, the thinking that guided our research. We also use it to reflect on the cumulative effect of television on political institutions by reviewing the coverage of political events since: political nominating conventions, televised presidential debates, election night coverage, and the impeachment and trial of a president—in the form of four mini-essays, each of which can be viewed as a sequel to a corresponding chapter in the original book. The fifth, about live video coverage of the battle fields in the Gulf and Vietnam Wars, links in a loose way to "MacArthur Day in Chicago" and may invite the reader, we hope, to consider how different the public view of him might have been if that celebrated hero's retreat from Bataan had been covered "live" on TV. In no sense, however, is this introduction intended as an historical overview of the most recent research literature on the televising of political events.

A Sociological Approach

In referring to the effect of communication, we have in mind a response that depends, not just on the communicator or sender of a message or messages, but on the subjects targeted by the communication. Without some response to the message—even one unintended—no communication takes place. Everyone recognizes, at least in this limited sense, the interactive nature of all human communication, whether it be words uttered in conversation or the world-wide dissemination of a news story via television. But sociologists do not look only at how individuals respond to a message or at how their responses are influenced by variations in content, by how it is packaged, or by the memories, knowledge, sophistication, attitude, and general mind-set of the recipient. Their interest extends beyond these essentially psychological aspects of communication to the society-wide implications for communication systems and the practices prevalent in it. These include, in the political realm, the influence of television on the course of events along with the mutual accommodations between political institutions and those responsible for their coverage.

Nobody has a crystal ball for divining the future. Of course, we can always track trends and make extrapolations with reasonable success. But there are alternative approaches. The one we have frequently employed is the case study. It involves the selection of events as observation sites on how television affects, or more precisely, intrudes, into politics. We think of these events as "critical:" the presence or role of television becomes problematic in the sense that conventional standards of conduct offer inadequate guidance. This can happen because the event is unprecedented or because it creates new options or because it moves political actors to make risky decisions. As a consequence, participants act more deliberately. They map strategies; they adapt or innovate. One gets a richer picture of how television affects behavior by studying reactions on these non-routine occasions. At least that was our premise in improvising the mass observation of the ticker tape parade welcoming General Douglas MacArthur upon his return from Japan after his summary dismissal by President Harry S. Truman as Supreme Commander in the Pacific. That same premise underlay our study of the first political conventions ever conducted on television before a mass audience and, ten years later, of our study of the first televised debate between John F. Kennedy and Richard M. Nixon. On occasions like these, we aimed to position ourselves and our observers to gather fugitive data in a natural context before it would be irretrievably lost. We remind you that at the time there were few resources for the study of events as they were happening. The success of our early efforts, later dubbed "firehouse research," depended very much on volunteer help, largely from fellow students at the University of Chicago, who deserve equal credit and to whom we owe a lot of thanks.

Nowadays things are very different. Communication researchers, most of them well trained in methodology and with access to data bases and more powerful diagnostic tools, are less inclined to take seriously small studies based on less than scientific sampling procedures. Meanwhile, the instant polling that has become routine for the past two decades offers a previously unimaginable day-to-day record of public reaction to just about every controversy and major campaign event. We ourselves have come to depend more and more on the masses of data from the

numerous polls now conducted on a routine basis. Although highly useful in tracking some movements of public opinion, they often fail—
because of the narrower journalistic or political purposes they serve—to
uncover a lot of meaningful information, which makes them a less than
complete substitute for the yield from mass observation of an event and
from detailed interviewing of major actors shortly afterward.

To characterize our approach along a conceptual dimension: we prefer to take as our unit of analysis the collective reaction to an event
rather than the cognitive structures of individuals. Events can be viewed
as composites made up of multiple actors just as organizations are. The
participants have different perspectives. A detailed case study is capable
of yielding insights about the process by which the television coverage
affects what people see but only if one reconstructs the interactions between the political actors and the journalists managing the coverage.
Insofar as inferences about the course of events and more long-term
institutional adaptation do not hinge entirely on statistical significance,
our methodology can be characterized—but only in this limited sense—
as qualitative.

Our focus in these studies has been on how television functions as
part of the press—or of the media (now the preferred term)—where
responsibility for day-to-day operations rests in the hands of professional journalists. Accordingly, the framework within which we analyze
the relation of television to politics connects five points of observation:
(1) politically relevant actors and their "input;" (2) the character of
television as defined by its technology and the perspectives of the people
who manage it; (3) the image of political reality as refracted by television; (4) the television perspective as a reference group; and (5) its
influence on the course of events and on political institutions. We are
aware, of course, that this leaves out other connections of media organizations to the government when they protect their business interests by
lobbying Congress and/or administrative agencies like the FCC. It also
ignores the political ties of some executives to political leaders and parties. These important topics we have left for others to study.

Political Actors. The logical starting point for an analysis of political
communication is what politically active persons, groups, and organizations do and say. The category covers heads of government, party leaders, administrators, interests groups and all their spokespersons, as well

as political operatives, lobbyists and, more sporadically, the public when its members vote, protest, or demonstrate. All go to some lengths to make their voices heard but, if it seems politic, will try to keep out of sight. Insofar as politics—in the opinion of Murray Edelman[1]—consists of symbolic action aimed at defining reality to one's own advantage, political conflicts turn into rhetorical conflicts conducted in the media, today mostly on television. The more visible a figure, the greater the power imputed to him or her. Access to television is a political resource— a means of generating public support for one's cause—unless it casts the actor in an unfavorable light. To protect themselves against such un- wanted exposure, politicians attempt in their public appearances the kind of "impression management" so aptly described by Goffman,[2] while simultaneously working to prevent access to the more restricted forums in which so many of their critical decisions are made. One cannot fully understand the role of television without penetrating these inner regions.

The Character of the Medium. The capability of live television to convey actuality to a dispersed audience through a combination of sound and moving images is indeed impressive, but nevertheless subject to constraints. For one thing, television imposes its own *visual structure* on the coverage. No matter how fast camera crews are able to move, their mobility will forever remain less than infinite. A moving camera, no less than one fixed in place, including the one with a zoom lens, still has to point to some part of the scene. Whatever comes into sharp focus is inevitably blown up; all else, if not totally out of the picture, can only serve as background. Nor does the employment of multiple cameras fully solve the problem. Television, even when using a split screen, can carry only so many pictures from so many points of view at one time. It imposes a structure by the way it splices together the visuals and epi- sodes covered by the camera. The juxtaposition of two speakers may suggest a conversation that never took place while the sequencing of unrelated events can lead viewers to infer a causal link. Selected replays have similar effects.

And while we typically think of television as a visual medium, the visual splicing is complemented by an *interpretative commentary* to as- sist viewers in making sense of complex, possibly confusing, events to create a story line. Telling citizens what they are seeing or hearing does more than just remove ambiguity. It provides a frame within which viewers interpret what is transmitted. For example, Chinese television carried many visuals of the 1989 demonstrations in Tiananmen Square. Viewers all over China had the opportunity to see pictures of demonstrators and of their clashes with the military and police as well as the party leadership's negotiations with student leaders. Thus they were made aware of what was going on but, primed by the commentary, took away quite a different impression from the visuals than viewers outside China when shown with a different sound track. Trying to make the official response appear reasonable, Chinese commentary harped on two themes: (1) the party's willingness to consider student demands but with no mention that Zhao Ziyang, soon after purged, had been overruled on negotiations; and (2) the threat to national stability posed by the violent confrontation the leadership had itself provoked by its intransigent response.[3] This official view prevailed as long as people lacked information to disconfirm it.

Most professional communicators who decide, collectively, what is to be shown and how it is to be framed, cannot fully control the phenomenon of *reciprocal effects*. Television is far from an unobtrusive witness: it can even intrude directly as when, for example, John Chancellor, a veteran reporter, disregarded a directive to clear the floor during an unruly moment at the Republican convention of 1964. He was summarily arrested and, as he was being led from the floor by two policemen with the cameras on him, he was able to broadcast his own arrest. "Playing up" to the camera—whether by a member of the public or a public figure—is often misread as a spontaneous response, though it rarely is. The presence of the camera invites cheers or expressions of anger from an otherwise calm and sedate crowd. It is hardly unusual for a political figure to stage an appearance or hold a press conference for the benefit of the camera or for the appearance of witnesses at televised hearings to be scheduled to make the evening news. Neither are protesters planning a street demonstration unmindful of television. More long-lasting yet are the adjustments that institutions have made over time to the presence of television, learning to keep intra-party differences out of camera range. If party nominating conventions have lost their original function, this is, not entirely but certainly to a degree, because they have accommodated to television.

The Television Perspective. For these and other reasons, our view of the world from the window opened by television is a refracted image of the slice of reality to which we might otherwise not be privy. Refraction inheres in the technology, but the particular angle of vision rests on the decisions and choices within news organizations about how an event is to be reported. Whether refracted or not, what happens on television on certain occasions defines what happens to just about everybody. Thus, Dayan and Katz[4] describe a category of media events that does not originate within the studio but whose coverage is pre-planned in conjunction with official sponsors. These events break into normal routines and preempt program time to create a special "sense of occasion." This category includes televised debates and elections, along with coronations and conquests, where the emphasis is on their common celebratory and ritualistic aspects. One can consider all of them political, but only in the sense that all of them—even contests, because they are regulated to begin and end according to accepted rules—function as unifying experiences.

Saturation coverage, especially of live events, invites public participation not only in celebrations, but in controversies. All have a gestation period. Even one-day occasions are preceded by buildups. The reality as refracted in the news over time creates expectations that have to be met and out of which the significance of the critical moment is constructed. The power of television to rivet public attention is undisputed. So is its input into the construction of the more contentious issues of the time. We prefer the term refraction over bias because the final product that emerges develops through interaction among participants with different interests. Newsmakers, too, have somehow to accommodate to the norms that govern the operations of the news media. Both may have their own biases, but neither functions autonomously from the other or from the public.

Media organizations must navigate a number of contingencies. The first is a matter of logistics. By and large camera crews position themselves where they can get the best pictures. But they also encounter manmade obstacles. They may be denied entrance or forced to negotiate for something less. Additionally, whether or not these become problems, television crews usually favor the more well-known figures and, when seeking clarification through interviews, turn to sources with whom they have already forged links. This is a way of reinforcing their own credibility. Television, even if it assumes the role of an adversary by putting the spotlight on problems authorities would prefer to sweep under the rug, leans toward reflecting the world from an establishment perspective.

A second distorting factor has to do with timeliness. Insofar as news organizations compete, the closer to a deadline a story breaks, the greater its chances for getting on the news, crowding out earlier news and other possible background. But timeliness also means focusing on what is timely in terms of a news cycle. For example, a demonstration that coincides with a peak of general media attention to an issue is bound to receive more television coverage, regardless of size, than a demonstration involving an issue that is not yet or no longer is germane. Thus, in 1991, when the Gulf War was at issue, television took note of many small Washington protests that would normally have appeared too trivial to merit media attention.[5] When there is coverage, the cameras have an uncanny proclivity for singling out any disruptions in an essentially peaceful parade. Threats to public order, no matter how mild, seem always to be high on the media agenda.

Third, some differences of opinion can be unduly magnified when a reporter, chasing after news, encounters a newsmaker equally eager for a story that both can turn to their advantage. The two engage in a tacit transaction unseen by anyone. The newsmaker gets a platform in exchange for something that can go into the evening news. The reporter can push things farther by using the newsmaker's statement to solicit a televised response from the other side. Television news thrives on controversies that they themselves may have aggravated by their mere presence. Yet, they are hardly disinclined to keep the dispute going by eliciting forceful statements from persons they deem newsworthy.

The more general point is that television reporters, as much as their colleagues in the print media, fall back on a limited number of scripts to make sense of a complex and often ambiguous reality that no one can fully comprehend. Some scripts are standard; most are embedded in professional norms; some derive from presumptions of what the audience wants and/or understands; and some express prevailing social values. Throughout much of the Vietnam war, for example, television—not necessarily by design—covered the war as a normal military operation. In doing so, it fostered and lent its prestige to a version of events that, after the war, proved unfounded. Conversely, in dramatizing American prowess during the war in the Gulf, television exaggerated the extent to which the operation achieved its political objective.

TV Coverage as a Reference Group. Televised "reality" matters. It matters all the more because, as a general rule, we find what we have witnessed more convincing than what we are told. The eye perceives directly. The vivid visuals, live or recorded, that appear on the television screen have an authenticity that eludes the spoken report, despite the fact, as we have documented in more than one context, that even live coverage is refracted and edited. But the power of the visual image is most evident in the closeups of political figures, on which so many people rely for their estimates of character, though there is no scientific evidence that one can accurately assess character by "reading" faces.[6] What every one "sees" becomes the common point of reference by which a political figure is judged.

Undisputed is the ability of television to rivet attention on certain personalities, events, and topics. Its importance in this respect is magnified by what Davison[7] has aptly termed the "third-person" effect: not how we ourselves react to the coverage, but how we think—with or without evidence—others will react. The effect operates in a circular manner. Citizens, themselves unswayed by what appears on television, are moved to act by the response they impute to an unknown multitude. This helps explain not only the prevalent concern about the content of television in general and efforts to control it, but also why the "newsworthiness" of an individual or incident is very much influenced by prior television coverage. Political leaders, at least in the short run, act with their eyes as much on television as on the voters in an election that may still be months or years away. The television coverage takes on the function of a reference group for those who must play up to it and even for those who work to keep the cameras away.

Outcomes and Trends. Outcomes are not always predictable. Yet we can cautiously predict that those political figures who approach television as a potential ally rather than avoiding it will probably come out ahead, but only so long as they avoid too blatant posturing before the cameras. On the other hand, "letting the public in" is not always the right thing. Public scrutiny can tie the hands of negotiators seeking a mutually acceptable compromise. Audiences are prone to react with distress to graphic depictions of violence on the streets or on a military battlefield. How much openness fosters sound solutions remains problematic.

In some areas, the boundary between what should remain privileged and private and what the public has a right to know has clearly shifted. In testimony before a jury or court nothing germane to the issue is ever out of bounds. But can we tolerate the same lack of restriction during a proceeding that is televised and plays to a much wider audience? The decision by the Senate Judiciary Committee to open hearings on the nomination of Clarence Thomas to the U.S. Supreme Court broke new ground. Both Thomas and Anita Hill, who had accused the nominee of sexual improprieties, were put into highly embarrassing situations. To salvage his nomination, supporters of Thomas called witnesses who impugned the accuser's character. These hearings, as televised, could only detract from the dignity of the proceedings. They also diverted public attention from the more serious business of examining the qualifications and judicial temperament of a person being considered for one of the country's most powerful appointive positions.

Television has also personalized politics. Being considered a viable candidate has come to depend less on the backing of a party organization than on the ability to project one's self via the media. Being telegenic, together with a carefully crafted campaign, can catapult a virtual unknown into prominence or guarantee victory to a respected establishment figure. Unquestionably, character has always been important, but two aspects, neither entirely new, have been accentuated. Citizens lacking in insider knowledge are invited by the closeup to scrutinize gestures and mien, thus forcing the candidate to find ways of projecting sincerity. Second, and from the standpoint of the individual citizen, the television personality of a politician becomes as relevant, and possibly more relevant, than his/her record and what s/he stands for. And while effective political leadership has always depended on character, we have seen a decisive shift of attention away from estimates of competence to assessments of trustworthiness. The answers to "whom do you/they trust?" weigh more heavily than ever in the selection of candidates and in the electoral choices of citizens.

A somewhat disturbing trend has been the growing distrust of major institutions and government, a trend that coincides more or less with the expansion of political television. Correlations do not prove a causal relationship. One can, as always, find other explanations for the decline in public trust. These include lingering memories of official duplicity during the war in Vietnam, during Watergate and other scandals, and during the investigation of the secret arms deals under the Reagan administration; a general frustration over the rate of progress in such important areas as civil rights, education, drugs, healthcare, and so forth; the inability to fashion effective campaign finance reform to take the money out of politics; and the decline in social capital exemplified by the fact that so many Americans end up bowling alone.[8] We ourselves were led by our early studies of political conventions to conclude that the coverage aggravated for a good many, but far from all, viewers the *disparity* between what they were in a position to observe for themselves, and feelings that their interests, as citizens, were being inadequately represented. The video experience of these viewers, if it had any effect, was to undermine rather than raise people's sense of political efficacy and their confidence in political institutions and parties—attitudes that discourage voting and keep those who do go to the polls from voting a straight ticket and/or sticking to the same party from one election to the next.

Last but by no means least television has expanded the circle of attention from the locality to the nation and from the nation to the international arena. The trend was in evidence as early as 1952. As chronicled in Chapter 3, the backers of Dwight Eisenhower, by playing to television, focused national attention on a dispute within the Republican Party of Texas. Because at the time that party had no real local roots, leadership had almost always been up for grabs. Ordinarily the internal dispute over which set of delegates to seat at the convention might have been settled behind closed doors. Enacted live on television, its significance caught the attention of the nation and effectively paved the way for Eisenhower's nomination. Similarly, since the advent of televised politics, the Iowa caucuses and New Hampshire primary, which have been the first to select their presidential delegates, are watched not only by "insiders" as weather vanes of things to come, but by interested citizens throughout the country. On still another political front, when network television covering the civil rights protests focused on Southern policemen brutally assaulting peaceful marchers, many whites were compelled to recognize that segregationist practices, however firmly entrenched in local custom, had ceased to be an entirely local concern. Pictures of brutality and disaster in far away places have not yet displayed a similar capacity to move a world-wide public to action. Perhaps in the future?

Conventions

The year 1984, immortalized by George Orwell, was also the year in which the major networks abandoned full coverage of the party nominating conventions. For us, having cut our eyeteeth as media researchers on the conventions of 1952 (the first time they were nationally televised), the time seems ripe for a look back at the changes that have taken place in the interim. These historic media events (see Chapter 2) had served as a proving ground for producers, reporters, and camera crews, along with party leaders, candidates, and their strategists. On the one side there were the networks, CBS in particular, disclaiming all responsibility for making a good show out of the conventions; on the other, there were the political organizations that, ever since, have been doing the job for them.

It has become apparent that the most important cumulative, long-range effect of televising the nominating conventions has been to change their nature and purpose. They have lost their main *raison d'être*, which was to select candidates to head the party ticket. For decades now, that outcome has been a foregone conclusion, with little chance that the proceedings would generate any genuine news. An occupant of the White House seeking a second term rarely faces much opposition from within his own party. And, over the course of time, the center of gravity in the nominating process has irreversibly shifted away from the conventions to the state primaries, where voters can directly state their preferences for a standard bearer of their party. By 2000, both Gore and Bush, neither of them an incumbent president, arrived at their conventions with enough delegates won in primaries to be assured nomination and to pre-select their running mates. Bitter convention battles fought out on television surely had something to with this shift in the nominating process away from control of the national party machinery (see Chapter 3).

The presence of television cameras at the conventions has also had a more direct effect on the character of the proceedings. With network coverage now limited to prime time, conventions have become choreographed and sanitized. They have been rid, as much as possible, of any reference to such potentially divisive issues as abortion or gun control. Party managers now regard the conventions as little more than spectacles explicitly produced for television. Speeches are pared down to the bone and delegations are polled off-camera with no bystander public looking on. As the Democrats had learned the hard way in 1968, intraparty disputes are best settled where the camera cannot record them. Has anyone who watched it ever forgotten the televised confrontation between those backing Hubert Humphrey, designated by Lyndon Johnson as his successor, and the anti-Vietnam delegates behind Eugene McCarthy, with police and protesters battling on the streets of Chicago at the very moment that ugly words and ugly confrontations inside the hall were being broadcast "live?"

By 1972, with the Republicans headed for a certain victory, they had already totally scripted their convention. Democrats had still one further lesson about the power of television to learn. That year, in order to minimize controversy, which had so hurt the party image in 1968, they amended the rules for delegate-selection and democratized procedures to produce an unwanted result: the disruption of its schedule. Delays prevented Senator George McGovern, the Democrats' presidential choice, from being "introduced" to the delegates and to the nationwide audience whom they hoped would be watching until after midnight, by which time most viewers had tuned out.

Thus, it was only after 1972 that both conventions evolved into one big commercial for the party, its candidates, and its platform. Leaders of both parties were careful to pre-schedule the highlights for peak evening viewing and not to allow anything to interrupt the smooth progress of the proceedings, which were now supplemented with flattering films of the soon-to-be crowned candidate—of his upbringing, his earlier struggles, his accomplishments, and his love for family—all ostensibly for the benefit of delegates in the hall but, in fact, to catch the attention of the huge number of reporters in attendance and to make the best possible use of the free air time the convention gets as a *bona fide* news event. By 2000, the most memorable moment of the Democratic convention, for the media, turned out to be the long and apparently spontaneous kiss that Gore bestowed on Tipper, his wife, on his way to the podium just as she finished introducing him. Convention managers work to provide opportunities for photos such as this one, suitable for replay throughout the coming campaign. What the networks were transmitting in 2000, as in prior years, was a political spectacle tailor-made to jump-start the home stretch of a year-long, or longer, race to the White House.

Although no longer deemed so worthy of coverage in depth as they once were, conventions still serve some political purpose. Even if not televised, they would still survive as occasions for rallying and reward-ing the party workers, handing them marching orders, boosting morale for the upcoming campaign, and creating a historical narrative—a story line—to take home to their constituents. In this age of personalized politics, conventions have gained additional value as an opportunity for a presidential candidate to present himself (or herself, some day) to the nation. This may seem less necessary today. The candidate will already have been introduced on countless occasions—in televised stump speeches, on talk shows, in the televised debates with challengers in the primaries, and on other staged-for-media occasions. Still, a political "truth," sus-tained by public opinion polls, now guides planning for these conven-tions: no matter how many times the candidates may have previously appeared on television, it is only at convention time that members of the public begin to pay serious attention, to think about what s/he is like and what s/he stands for. A corollary to this belief is a bit of conventional wisdom: whoever leads in the polls a week or two after the conventions will in all likelihood win the election. So it becomes of utmost impor-tance that the televised proceedings give candidates (and the party) an upward bump in the polls.

Quadrennial conventions, in short, are not just pseudo-events that exist only to be televised.[9] They retain their function as a ritualistic expression of party unity and as a place for transacting some party busi-ness—like writing and adopting the platform on which to run. That kind of convention would still be newsworthy, but the coverage can no longer be justified as a window on the nominating process—the concept that had inspired television news in its commitment to carry them live and in their entirety. This same concept also created delight in the coverage as an exercise in democracy. From then on the television networks told the nation, every citizen would have the chance, as never before, to observe for him/herself how candidates are chosen and to arrive at an informed judgment about these choices. Interest in the political process would increase and so would electoral participation.

However, changes in the character of conventions undermined the rationale that once moved broadcasters to provide live gavel-to-gavel coverage. Citizens, experiencing similar disappointment, were finding fewer reasons to watch. The year 2000 saw the audience for any part of the *live* coverage of the conventions at a historic low. The prime time telecasts of the Democratic convention reached a mere 28 percent of TV-households, about five percent fewer than in 1996; the audience for the Republican convention, down by two percent, had fallen to 26 percent.[10] However, the validity of these ratings, as an indicator of interest and exposure, has become less clear. Viewers today have so much more choice about what and when to watch than they had when all available channels were fixed on the conventions. Now that the major networks have limited their coverage to the highlights scheduled for prime time, this leaves cable as the only source for following the *full* proceedings live. This is indeed a limitation. But anyone unable or unwilling to watch them at this time has another chance later during rebroadcasts in the evening or early next morning. The ubiquity of tape recorders has made it possible for people to watch selectively and according to their own schedules what they themselves have taped off the air. Continuous replay of highlights on news programs makes it even harder to say just what having "watched the conventions" actually means.

Furthermore, the more selective the viewing, the greater the refraction. Pictures do not entirely speak for themselves. As we were able to document in 1952, viewers watching the same pooled coverage of a crucial floor vote but on different networks arrived at dissimilar interpretations. Commentary and a pattern of cut-aways peculiar to each network introduced refraction into the image of events. Viewers responded accordingly (Chapter 3). There are signs that the viewers of televised events have become even more dependent on the television perspective. They are inundated with interpretations of such convention highlights as the acceptance speech even before they have themselves been able to view it. Awareness of the extent to which their perceptions are framed by the reportage is incomplete.

Narratives of political conventions since 1952, mostly by political insiders or journalists, have yielded insights too numerous to summarize. The volume by Byron Shafer does, however, deserve special mention. The study by this political scientist parallels our own interest insofar as he focuses on the transformation of these political proceedings when conducted under the glare of television. When the major networks cut back on their coverage, he writes, they "produced what was in essence a 'bifurcated convention,' with one version for participants and another for viewers—a large and growing disjunction between the two."[11] To reiterate our earlier observation about nominating conventions: They still have a function in the life of the parties and in campaigns but they perform it in a different way. As media events they are less important than such other political crowd-attractions as televised debates between presidential candidates or impeachment trials. These changes in the convention, which have taken place over time, add up to an intriguing example of institutional adaptation to a new medium.

Presidential Debates

Televised presidential debates have been major campaign events. Held in prime time, they are usually viewed by more people than other political extravaganzas like party nominating conventions, presidential inauguration ceremonies, or State of the Union addresses. The average audience for all debates from 1976 to 1992, estimated from Nielsen ratings, was 67 million, with a record high of 81 million in 1980 for the first debate between President Jimmy Carter and Governor Ronald Reagan. Since then, audiences, though still huge, have for the most part been declining. In 1992, due to the presence of Ross Perot as a third participant in the race between President George Bush and Bill Clinton, the Democratic challenger, nearly 70 million tuned into what was billed as the "critical" second debate between them. The spurt was only temporary. Viewing sank to a new low in 1996, when only 36.3 million tuned in to the second debate, presumably because Clinton, now running for re-election, was by then far ahead in the polls and near everybody expected him to win the debate as well. Four years later, the audience had still not recovered despite the fact that Vice-President Al Gore and Governor George W. Bush were locked in an extremely close race. Audiences for their last two of three barely exceeded the audience four years earlier.

No candidate is legally required to participate in these televised encounters. Neither Lyndon B. Johnson, who succeeded Kennedy, nor

Nixon in 1968 and 1972 felt that he had much to gain from such confrontations, so both steadfastly refused to engage their lesser known opponents. Not so Gerald Ford, America's first unelected president, who, in his campaign for another term in office, must have felt under strong pressure to heed requests for such a televised encounter. He was the first incumbent but not the last to subject himself to this ordeal.

Since then, although hardly mandatory, debates between presidential candidates have no longer been altogether optional. They have become integral to the process by which seekers of the highest electoral office present themselves and their programs to public scrutiny. While candidates find it hard to refuse, debating carries its own risks. Both Carter in 1980 and the elder Bush in 1992 lost their second terms to opponents credited with far better communication skills. In spite of the pressure for televised presidential debates, some of the networks, now numbering five plus cable channels, have begun to back away from full live coverage. In 2000, Fox Network stuck to its regular program schedule with "Dark Angel," a science fiction serial, agreeing to telecast the debate later on tape. NBC gave its affiliates a choice between the first debate and the American League baseball playoffs, for whose television rights it had paid handsomely. During the third debate, the candidates had to compete for audience attention with an American League championship game on NBC, which is why it turned out to have the second smallest audience ever. In the absence of a legally binding preemption of program time, programs in competition with the debates can only increase as channels proliferate.

Even though televised debates have lost the novelty they had in 1960, they continue to act as magnets on political communication researchers. That they are scheduled makes them easier to study than most other campaign events. The volume entitled *The Great Debates*, within whose covers Sidney Kraus assembled diverse studies and commentary on the Kennedy-Nixon debates, set a trend others were to follow.[12] We now have a slew of surveys, rhetorical analyses, communication experiments, and discussions of the policy implications and political effects of these debates too numerous to detail. We confine ourselves to a single question: What have we learned about the cumulative effects of televising these confrontations over the past forty-plus years?

Many studies affirm what candidates, strategists, and most voters believe: that the debates can make a difference in the electoral outcome, especially if it turns out to be very close. The campaign of 2000, when Gore and "W" Bush met in three debates, provides a case in point. Some, but not all, of the viewers interviewed before each debate showed a slight but hardly definitive movement toward Bush when re-interviewed immediately after. Later polls also showed Gore to have recovered whatever ground he had lost. In the first debate, on October 3, the two men stood at their lecterns answering in turn questions put to them by Jim Lehrer, the respected host of the hour-long evening news program on public television. The rules forbade the candidates to ask questions of each other. They were to limit their responses and rebuttals within the brief time span the two had agreed on in advance. This format did not allow for any genuine exchanges between them nor for much spontaneity.

A more informal format was tried in the second debate a week later. The candidates sat around a table facing the moderator and adhered to a format that allowed for some give-and-take between them. This second debate was widely thought to have been somewhat of a debacle for Gore, who in attempting to counter criticism that he had appeared over-aggressive in the prior debate, deliberately held back. This time his behavior was judged overly accommodating. In a post-debate phone survey by Gallup for CNN and USA Today of 529 viewers, all previously interviewed, 60 percent of the likely Bush voters said watching the debate had made them "more certain" of their electoral choice compared with only 46 percent among likely voters for Gore. The same percentage (4 percent) of both groups said it had made them less certain. One percent reported having switched their preference from Bush to Gore and two percent from Gore to Bush. The rest reported that watching the debate had no effect on their vote intention.

The last debate, on October 20, was a town-hall affair before a studio audience of undecided voters, a group generally affronted by negative campaigning. Both candidates made some effort to be on their best behavior. After the debate, there was little agreement on who had done better, but neither is there, even as of this writing, much agreement on who really won the election. As far as we can judge, the last debate served mostly to reinforce impressions left by the previous two.

As to the effect of debates on this and other outcomes, some caveats are in order. First, a candidate can recoup as Gore apparently did in the two-and-a-half weeks between the last debate and election day. Second, there is little evidence to sustain the oft-repeated belief that a single gaffe can lose not just a debate but an election as, for example, Ford's statement during a debate that Poland was not under Russian domination. Neither is there much evidence that an electoral victory can be achieved by a single verbal masterstroke as the one with which Reagan (in 1984) supposedly put to rest the senility issue once and for all. Alan Schroeder describes Reagan's performance in the first debate as "so disconnected that he caught his competitor off guard."[13] He had missed cues, flubbed lines, lost his place—possibly a harbinger of his later victimization by Alzheimer's. But in the second debate, he had responded to a panelist's query of whether he was too old to handle the presidency with the now famous ploy: "I will not make age an issue of this campaign. I am not going to exploit for political purposes my opponent's youth and inexperience." Observers surmised—as did Mondale himself—that "the biggest barrier to Reagan's reelection was swept away in that moment."[14] But what is their evidence? After all, Reagan already had been safely ahead before this debate and his supporters did not seem to mind voting for the oldest president ever to stand for reelection. With this one-liner, carefully crafted in advance, the president was only following a well worn two-pronged debate strategy first employed by Kennedy in 1960, and by others since, to project their candidate's human warmth and to give journalists something to write about. Reagan succeeded on both counts as Mondale never did.

A third caveat concerns the power of visuals. So often have clips of the first Kennedy-Nixon debate been shown that even the youngest school child must believe by now that Kennedy won the presidency because he was so much more telegenic than Nixon. Kennedy was indeed a master performer and a sharp debater as well. But he helped himself at least equally by coming across as "presidential," as fit for the office to which he aspired. Belief in the power of the visual image is, moreover, sustained by claims, repeated over the years, that those who saw that historical debate on television judged the youthful looking Kennedy the clear winner while those who heard the two on radio favored Nixon. That is the legend. It may come as a surprise that it has remained unsupported, at least until recently, by any empirical evidence beyond a survey of very dubious validity conducted by a market research firm right after the debate.[15] James Druckman, a political psychologist, sought to make up for this lack with an ingenious experiment. He recruited college students too young to have had prior historical knowledge of the political emotions surrounding these debates. Half of the students were randomly assigned to watch a videotape of the debate; the other half listened to a sound tape. The two main findings were that radio listeners were more likely to name Nixon the winner and that visuals did make a difference in the evaluation of the performance and character of the two candidates.[16] Compelling as these findings appear, they do not necessarily apply to a population as involved and interested in questions at issue as in the campaign of 1960. It is at least possible that the political facts relevant at the time mitigated any effect of the medium on how listeners and viewers responded to the original debate. We have no way to test this possibility.

In any case, in judging the effect of a debate, one must always take into account not only what the candidates say or how they appear, but the context in which it takes place. Certainly, political strategists learned early on how much of their effect depends on expectations. What worked against Nixon in the first debate was his reputation as a formidable debater. Was he not, after all, the highly experienced vice-president who had bested Khrushchev when they met in Moscow in what came to be known as their "kitchen debate?" And so, as his campaign posters proclaimed, if he could stand up to the Soviet leader, he could surely stand up to this young Senator, who may have known how to build a political machine but was as yet untested on the national stage. But while the Kennedy performance in the first debate exceeded expectations, Nixon had fallen short, which had adverse consequences for his campaign (Chapter 4). Ever since, political managers, weary of such a political trap, have played the "expectations game." In addition to coaching and rehearsing their candidate, they maneuver to keep expectations low so that, when exceeded, even a lackluster performance can be made to look like a victory.

The campaign of 2000 illustrates how this game can work. The journalistic take on Gore was that he would prove by far the better and more experienced debater, relying on skills he had demonstrated in the Senate, as vice-president in the Clinton administration, and especially as a campaigner, first in 1992 and again in the run-up to his nomination. To be sure, not all the epithets used by reporters to describe his style were exactly flattering. He had been pictured as robotic, programmed, android, and appearing to talk down to people.[17] But he also was known to be in command of the facts and to have scored, and scored decisively, in debates during the primary season against former Senator Bill Bradley, an equally erudite opponent. On these occasions, so ran the consensus, he had come across as energetic and aggressive, but seemed best able to convey his personal charm when directly conversing with his opponent. "W" Bush, in his much fewer appearances on national television, had shown himself a faltering impromptu speaker. Many reporters were struck by how strangely uninformed he was on some elementary aspects of foreign affairs. His penchant for mispronunciation and garbled syntax had become the stuff of comedian jokes on the late-night TV shows. In short, most commentators expected Gore to outperform Bush.

Low levels of expectations of his performance moved media critics to award Bush high marks just for having held his own. He had avoided serious gaffes and not otherwise stumbled. Many credited him for not being quite as uninformed as they had anticipated. He had, at the first opportunity, shown himself able to rattle off the names of a number of small countries, names he had quite evidently memorized for recitation. From all appearances, "W" won—or, at least, Gore lost—the "game of lowered expectations." In the days immediately following, as the high points in the debate were replayed and the pundits had their say, there developed a consensus that Bush had "won."

Two articles from a news magazine illustrate how expectations affect reactions. Before the first debate, according to *Time*,[18] "Gore started dreaming of delivering a knockout blow in the debates. That, aides say, is why the Vice-President came out swinging and lecturing and exaggerating in Boston two weeks ago. 'He was pumped up,' says a rueful Gore adviser. 'He thought he could put Bush away that night.' Last week's upheaval in the Middle East might have given Gore another opening had Bush not surprised even some of his own advisers with his *adequate* [italics ours] handling of the foreign policy questions that consumed half of Wednesday's second debate. Bush showed how far he had come since failing a reporter's pop quiz on world leaders in the run-up to the primary." Another version of the same view by Howard Fineman appeared in *Newsweek*.[19] "So far Bush is ahead on points in a debate season that was assumed to be his moment of maximum peril.... By branding Bush a 'babbling bumbler' after the first debate, the Goreans lowered expectations for Bush further and he impressively exceeded them. In the latest *Newsweek* poll, Bush inched ahead, 45 percent to 43 percent, among likely voters who see him as more honest, more likable and leaderly. 'Let's face it, our guy is not going to win the popularity contest,' a top Gore aide said."

We expect that President Bush, should he run again, will have to debate his challenger, but this time with a persona shaped by four years as an incumbent. His performance may well improve, but, expectations having changed, we can be certain that it will surely be judged by a different standard.

Election Night Coverage

Election night coverage is sure to stir contention in case of a "wrong" call by broadcasters. In the election of 2000, whose outcome hung in balance for five weeks, some smoldering issues resurfaced, largely because early network projections of the outcome in one state had to be rescinded as more returns rolled in. Later on election night, with the national outcome still very much in doubt, the networks made a second call, moving the state of Florida, which they had initially given to Vice-President Al Gore, into the column for Governor George W. Bush. Its 25 electoral votes would have sufficed to put either candidate over the top. These projections, especially when taken together, amounted to a blunder far more serious than the premature call ABC-news made for Nixon in 1960 before all polls had closed even in the Eastern states.

Winning Florida had been identified as crucial for either candidate. Within roughly an hour after polls in the state had closed—except in its small western panhandle—all five networks, using exit polls and returns from selected precincts, had called Florida for Gore. NBC/MSNBC was first at about 7:50 EST, with CBS and CNN following in less than a minute. Then Fox News Channel followed at 7:52 and, ABC ten minutes later. Around 10 p.m., by which time returns from states farther west were confirming an exceedingly close count, more complete and more accurate information from Florida moved the networks to retract earlier calls. Some four hours later, well after midnight in the East and late in the evening along the Pacific coast, each of the networks, within five minutes of each other, awarded Florida to Bush, but even these projections did not end a long night of see-sawing. Before early morning, the networks had once again to recant what had looked like a Bush victory. Returns coming in pointed to a race whose outcome was still too close to predict.

Some Republicans in key positions in the House of Representatives were quick to seize on these premature calls as evidence of "probable bias." W. J. "Billy" Tauzin of Louisiana, chair of the House Energy and Commerce Committee in the new congress, called a press conference, in which he charged the networks with having misrepresented the trend when they awarded Florida and other closely contested states to Gore on the basis of very incomplete returns while inexplicably delaying projections favorable to Bush. Glossing over the fact that, for most of the night, the actual tally of electoral votes on TV had shown Bush leading Gore, Tauzin maintained that the "biased" calls for the Vice-President with polls still open in parts of Florida and in most Western states not only had deprived Bush of a more decisive victory but contributed to the defeat of some California Republicans running for congress.

In later congressional hearings Tauzin hammered the same theme, namely that projections based on models used by the Voter News Service were biased against Republicans but graciously allowed that the bias may have been "unintentional." However, he did not back away from his claim that the networks had favored Gore by awarding him states earlier than they should have. The networks countered with detailed reports. While admitting errors, they nevertheless emphatically rejected the charge that in their predictions they had favored one or the other of the two candidates.

Claims that large numbers of persons in line to vote have defected when networks reported returns before polls closed have never been validated, certainly not by our own study of broadcast effects in the 1964 election (see Chapter 5) nor in 1980 when Jimmy Carter conceded even before polls had closed in all states.[20] In 2000, it seems ludicrous to suggest that declaring a winner in Florida when the only polls still open were in counties with about five percent of the state's vote had an *undue* influence on the outcome. Surveys cited in support of this charge have been based either on unsustainable statistical assumptions or on second-hand reports from people about what others had told them, not on personal observation at the polls or accounts of people's own behavior. How many prospective voters would have been listening to or watching returns within the barely ten minutes left to go to the polls? And how many of this obviously small number, given their interest in the outcome, were likely to have decided, on the basis of what they learned, not to cast a ballot in a state with a hotly contested Senate race? But, so runs the counter-argument, in an election as close as that in Florida, which was awarded to Bush on the basis of his 537 lead in the official count, a small number of votes that ordinarily would not matter could have made a decisive difference. Indeed, they *could have,* but their potential effect on the outcome seems trivial in comparison to deficiencies in the Florida electoral system that kept voters from having their presidential preference counted.

The possibility of election-day slack in states across the nation has to be evaluated in the context of general findings about non-voting and, especially, of our own observations about the 1964 election, in which an incumbent Lyndon B. Johnson buried Senator Barry Goldwater in a landslide. Early projections from Johnson's sweep of states in the East did nothing more than confirm what campaign coverage and pre-election polls had already led most voters to expect. In 2000 things stood rather differently. The two contestants were known to be in a very tight race, and the networks, in spite of repeated gaffes, did not officially proclaim a winner until hours after polls everywhere, including Hawaii, had closed. In other words, the 2000 election fits into the Type 5 election (Chapter 5). There was no upset. Election day saw most voters acting on understandings they had all along.

Holding the election coverage responsible for either man's defeat rests on still another shaky assumption: that the deterrent effect was concentrated among citizens about to cast their vote for the ultimate loser. Moreover, the tally of electoral votes remained close enough throughout election night that, wherever the candidates were running neck-and-neck, *all* partisans would have been intent on voting and to have their votes counted. Even in states so clearly headed for the Democratic or Republican column that the outcome was unproblematic, one's vote could still be valued as a means for expressing one's partisan convictions and/or as meeting a citizen's felt obligation to make full use of one of the more cherished privileges of American citizenship. There had actually been some vote trading between voters in essentially uncontested states who cast their vote for a third-party candidate with no chance to win in exchange for a vote in a state where a vote might elect the future president.

Despite these caveats, perceptions often count for more than the lack of demonstrated effect. Two facts are undisputed. In 2000, as in earlier years, polls showed majorities quite strongly against projecting any result before polls everywhere in the country closed.[21] Second, many residents on the Pacific coast and beyond have long *felt* effectively disenfranchised in presidential elections by early definitive returns from the East. Whether this attitude will, over the long run, reduce turnout is almost impossible to ascertain given the number of factors that affect turnout. A third less clear fact stems from the nature of the election-night experience, which—since the advent of the radio news broadcast—has fit the contest category as defined by Dayan and Katz.[22] The audience keeps score, awaits the end, and then participates in the ceremonial concessions and victory speeches meant to bridge partisan divisions. Will the television coverage on election night, we asked back in 1964, "now breed new controversies centering on returns—about how they might have influenced the election or how such returns might be manipulated in the future?"

The five-week contest over the Florida vote count feeds anxieties. Nothing could have been more divisive than the protracted post-election political and legal maneuvering by the two parties, much of it unfolding before the cameras. The Bush camp accused Gore of unwillingness to concede an election that, according to network anchors, he had evidently lost. Gore countered: he wanted nothing more than to see every vote tallied. There were other charges of irregularities of the kind one frequently hears in close elections. One can, of course, argue that the election night coverage did not create this controversy; rather, it was the razor-thin margin between victory and defeat coupled with flaws in the electoral system, and television in the weeks after the election did nothing more than offer the two parties a platform from which to make their case. Up to a point this is indubitably true. Any election this close will be followed by recounts, contests, challenges, charges and counter-charges. One need only recall the Tilden-Hayes debacle in the wake of the 1876 election or how the Republicans in 1960, far from graciously accepting Nixon's defeat, mounted a ferocious challenge focused on the 9,000 votes by which Kennedy had carried the state of Illinois. But in neither case did the candidates and their political advisors have to contest the election with television spotlighting their every move, as was the case in 2000. Hence, few people remember that Nixon's concession the day after the election was a conditional one, predicated on the continuation of present trends in the vote count.

Insofar as anchors were projecting what was about to happen before it actually happened, the live coverage transmitted a refracted view of events with some influence on political actors as well as on the public. John Ellis, a cousin of Bush, who also happened to be head of the election desk at Fox News network—the first to call Florida for Bush (at 2:16 a.m. EST)—had stayed in constant touch with the Bush brothers, "relaying early vote counts as they showed up on his screens."[23] His superiors had no knowledge of this violation of accepted journalistic practice. The Gore campaign seized on it as evidence of bias by a network owned by the politically conservative Rupert Murdock. But other news desks, spurred by the competition, were not far behind in making the same call. Dan Rather of CBS coupled his with a pronouncement that it was tantamount of Bush's winning the presidency, a view in which he was hardly alone. The networks collectively left the impression that the election was over when, in fact, it would not be for weeks or, in a sense, for years.

The people around Gore were apparently drawing the same conclusion—that Bush would win in Florida—from tallies available to them. What else could have induced their candidate to place a call to Bush in which he reportedly offered his congratulations on winning the election? But, based on others' reading of the returns, they had second thoughts. The public concession, anticipated by the networks, did not follow. That Gore should have reneged made him look like an ungracious loser, an impression that became a cornerstone in the strategy of the Bush camp during the controversy, for which election night coverage set the stage.

The count in Florida was close enough to qualify for the recount state law mandated for an outcome decided by less than five percent of the vote. But more than corrections of routine errors turned out to have been involved. Already on election night, television had drawn attention to the strange result in Palm Beach, a county with many Jewish voters and a Democratic stronghold, who had given conservative Pat Buchanan more votes than any other Florida county. No one expected such a result, and Buchanan himself conceded that it could not have been an accurate reflection of these voters' preferences. The oddity had apparently been caused by a "butterfly" ballot with names on both sides of a middle row of the perforations on which voters were to punch their preference. Gore's name appeared on the left, opposite to that of Buchanan on the right. One could easily misplace a punch meant for Gore next to the name of Buchanan. In the days after the election, several voters spoke on television about having been confused. But nothing could be done to correct such voter errors.

Another set of problems, one capable of remedy by a hand-count, had to do with the rejection by tabulating machines of punch-cards. Some votes for president were not read because the perforations voters were to punch out with their stylus had not been pushed hard enough. The same voter error could have been caused by a misalignment of the ballot. Chads hanging on ballots when voters turned them in may have led to still more rejections of votes when enough chads fell off to clog a tabulating machine. Voters made other mistakes. Some punched the right hole but then, to make doubly sure that their vote had registered as intended, entered the same name in the space for write-in candidates, which the machine would read as an invalid double vote.

A hand-count could have corrected an undetermined but not negligible amount of ballots mistakenly invalidated as "undervotes" or "overvotes." Since more counties with Democratic than Republican majorities were still using the punch-card system, the Gore team was convinced that a more accurate count by hand would overturn the outcome. To make their demand for such a count appear legitimate, they decided to limit it to four counties from which irregularities had been reported. Bush, who was still ahead, had nothing to gain from any recount. All he needed was to hold on to his slim lead as tallied in the original count. These transparently antagonistic interests led to a two-front battle: first, on the legal-administrative front over which ballots should be counted and by what method and, second, in the court of public opinion where appearances count for a lot.

On this second front, fully played out on television, the Gore team worked to persuade the public that correcting a very imperfect vote count was an absolute necessity. Every citizen, his spokespersons kept emphasizing, had a right to have his or her vote counted but, due to flaws in the system, many had been effectively disenfranchised. What Gore and his lieutenants had to overcome were public perceptions that pressing for a recount was nothing more than an attempt to "steal" an election that Bush had already won. The Bush team, headed by James Baker and backed by Jeb Bush, the brother and governor of Florida, argued that Gore, once ready to concede, was now calling for a hand-count in which election clerks were somehow to "divine" voter intent and would keep doing so until it somehow put him ahead. Spokespersons for both sides made full use of television to repeat their favorite mantras but with one difference: the communication director for Bush, now in retreat to his ranch in Texas, laid out the schedule of her boss as if he already were the president-elect.

Things came to a head when Katherine Harris, the Secretary of State of Florida active in the Republican campaign, insisted on certifying the results immediately after a full count of absentee ballots. Gore, who needed time for the hand-recount, went to the courts to force a delay. This drew a new charge: The Democrats were taking the election out of the hands of millions of voters and giving it to the seven unelected justices of the Florida Supreme Court, who had agreed to hear the appeal of a lower court's ruling. Nor did the Republicans fail to remind the public that all these justices owed their appointment to a Democrat governor. The arguments before the court and its decision were televised and helped foster the erroneous impression that it was the Democrats who were seeking redress in the courts when in fact the Republicans had first turned to the legal system to stop the hand-recount in Dade County, thereby causing most of the delays that worked against Gore. Equally frustrating to the Democratic effort was their own dependence on the courts as a counter-weight to Republican control of the electoral apparatus in Florida.

The Democrats failed to capitalize fully on other issues. One had to do with regulations concerning absentee ballots, which both sides expected to favor Bush. The ones from overseas had to be postmarked and arrive by election day. When Democratic canvassers sought to check which had fulfilled these requirements, Republicans ambushed them by charging that the Gore team, notwithstanding its insistence that all votes be counted, was pushing for the disenfranchisement of American men and women serving their country abroad. Democrats retreated, even though, as a lawyer for the Democrats National Committee put it, the election officials were merely "being asked to apply the rules, whether to an overseas employee of an oil company or a member of the military."[24] Reports of significant undervoting in the poorer district of Duval County, a county that had gone for Bush by a lopsided majority, came too late to be included in the protest lodged by the Democrats, on which everything hinged. On the other hand, there were no legal remedies short of invalidating the election to correct errors attributed to the "butterfly" ballots in Palm Beach County or to make up for the favoritism shown by election officials in one county when they filled in required voter registration numbers missing (because of a computer error) from absentee ballot applications of registered Republicans without offering the same service to Democrats.

The question of whether televised returns made any difference defies a simple answer. We do know that Americans had been paying a good deal of attention on election night and that audiences for all-news cable networks increased significantly during the controversy, then dropped to less than one half to about one quarter of these highs once the election was settled. And yet, at least according to one survey at the time, only seven percent of respondents described themselves as "fascinated" by the coverage of the controversy with another 37 percent "interested." More than a majority claimed to be either bored or fed up, many complaining that the legal and political controversy was receiving too much coverage.[25]

Television did not reveal adequately, and probably could not have, that the hand-counts were being conducted in the presence of lawyers and observers from both sides. Republicans on the Palm Beach recount team, a Democratic stronghold, were reported, but not shown, to be challenging so many ballots that they created a bottleneck. Any on which volunteer enumerators could not agree were put aside for later consideration by a three-person canvassing board. Their numbers ran into the thousands. There were reports of disruptions of the hand-count operation in heavily Democratic Dade County. As if this were not enough, the electoral apparatus under a Republican governor imposed all kinds of delays on a challenger who had to convince the multitude of interested citizens that he had legitimate grounds for dragging out the final determination of the winner. The Bush team, on the other hand, needed only to concentrate on getting the unofficial results validated and certified. The immediacy of the television experience worked to compress time. Had no winner been "called" in any state, and certainly not in Florida, until after the various counts were complete, the public would have been less impatient about the drawn-out recount.

Two days after the election, by which time serious problems with the vote count had already surfaced, respondents in a national sample were asked what was more important: "getting matters resolved as soon as possible so we know who our next president is or making certain to remove all reasonable doubt that the vote count has been fair and accurate?" Respondents by a 72 to 25 percent majority opted for a fair and accurate vote count. This majority shrank to just over 50 percent as impatience grew. When queried directly in a Gallup poll, taken December 2 to 4, whether they were "willing to wait at least a little while longer for a final resolution to the presidential election situation or [thought] the presidential election situation has gone on too long already," only 36 percent expressed a willingness to wait.

Television may not have had a direct influence on the outcome of the 2000 election. After all, the dispute did end in the courts and not in the court of public opinion. Live coverage of the three hours of legal arguments allowed by the Florida Supreme Court, previously denounced by Republicans as stacked with Democrats, could hardly have convinced party loyalists that its decision, split as it was, had not been politically motivated. Besides, the court's approval of the hand-count in the four Florida counties, on which the Gore camp had focused its efforts and hopes, was soon overruled on appeal to the U.S. Supreme Court. In a history-making split decision, five conservative justices voted to stop the recount with four liberals writing stinging dissents. Unlike Florida, where cameras had followed the court case, there was no live coverage of arguments before the highest court. The justices had refused to budge from their prior ban on cameras. Only the announcement of its decision, uncharacteristically at ten minutes to three on a Saturday afternoon and in time for Sunday editions, was covered live and replayed on the evening news.

In removing the last obstacle to a Bush presidency, the Supreme Court may have settled the legal issue but not the doubts about who had really won the election. This issue, which underlay the legal maneuvering, was never convincingly de-politicized as were the quasi-judicial televised proceedings before the House Judiciary Committee during the Watergate controversy (Chapter 6). Why wasn't it? One reason, obviously, is that the court was so sharply divided. We hypothesize as an additional reason—in our judgment—that repeat appearances on television, live and in replays, of spokespersons for the two sides overshadowed whatever legitimacy the robed justices may have bestowed on the decision. The public debate was framed less by the opinions rendered by the justices than by the video clips—of lawyers arguing for their clients, of communication directors putting a spin on events, and occasionally of voters and/or election clerks reporting on their experiences on election day or in counting votes.

What people saw over these weeks was eroding their faith in the fairness of the electoral system. In the first poll on this point the public had been fairly evenly split. Democrats were inclined to accept the Gore version and Republicans to reject it. After the Supreme Court decision, only 32 percent of the respondents in a national poll responded "yes" to the question: "Now that the (2000 presidential) election is finally settled, do you think we got a fair and accurate vote count in Florida, or not?" A full 60 percent said "no;" an additional eight percent expressed no opinion on the question.[26]

So widespread was the perception that the election outcome was tainted that it cast doubt on the legitimacy of the Bush presidency. How long this short-term effect lasts will depend on how he conducts himself in his office and on the problems with which his administration will have to cope. Apart from their partisan significance, the facts brought to light in Florida are not exactly reassuring. Memory of the all too evident flaws in the vote count are bound to feed into beliefs, already prevalent among a large part of the public, that whether or not one votes makes little difference—which serves as a justification for not exercising one's franchise. Given the many other factors that deter people from voting as well as the massive campaigns—by the parties, by public interest groups and others to get people to the polls—it seems highly unlikely that anyone will ever be able to demonstrate the effect of the election night coverage with statistically reliable evidence.

Whether institutional reform of the electoral process will be a result of the 2000 controversy is debatable, Virtually everyone seems agreed on the need for a technologically more up-to-date system for counting ballots. By early February 2001, ex-presidents Jimmy Carter and Gerald Ford consented to act as honorary chairmen of a National Commission on Federal Election Reform soon to be appointed. A score of election reform proposals were floating around in Congress and in the capitals of fifty states.

Meanwhile, the premature calls of the Florida outcome have rekindled interest in measures intended to lay to rest once and for all the issue of election projections. Within days of the Supreme Court ruling, Representative Edward Markey of Massachusetts had introduced another uniform poll closing bill. In a joint-appearance by the heads of four networks and the manager of the Associated Press before the Committee headed by Representative Tauzin, all five endorsed some kind of uniform poll closing measure. The problems caused by early projections, they contended, were up to the government to fix. What chance such a bill has of passing both Houses of Congress remains unclear as of this writing. Even if enacted into law, it would not force the media to forswear the rush to judgment as soon as polls close but it would cut the ground under charges that broadcasting early returns affects electoral outcomes.

Lawmakers in a number of states have confronted the issue, now back on the political agenda, in their own way. One legislator in Mississippi, as reported by the AP on February 15, 2001, proposed a $1,000 fine on anyone who published election results before polls closed. North Dakota and Massachusetts were also exploring how to restrict early news of election results. The legislatures in Connecticut, Georgia, Maine, Nebraska, and Oklahoma had received proposals for a variety of measures to keep exit pollsters hundreds of feet from voting booths.

Congressional investigation into this apparent fiasco prompted the networks to put their election night operations under internal scrutiny. Despite denials that competitive considerations had any part in the timing of projections, some had second thoughts. ABC reported that it might be prepared to insulate its decision desk, which has the last word on calls, from all reports about what other networks are doing. Other recommendations bore on the strengthening of internal communications, the tightening of procedures for calling a state, and, above all, creating a more precise vocabulary for distinguishing between a result and a projection, which is an estimate, and reporting these estimates with appropriate qualifiers. All agreed that the criteria for making a call had to be toughened, that there should be more reliance on actual returns, that networks should wait for polls to be closed before announcing winners, and that great care must be taken never to make a call as long as any polling place in a state remains open. There was further agreement that, in order to prevent a recurrence of 2000, the model on which predictions were based had to be refined to take into account possible anomalies in voting patterns, the ever larger absentee vote, and response rates to polls that are barely over 50 percent. Some hinted at a withdrawal of support from Voter News Service, the consortium responsible for the exit polls and the model from which networks made their predictions. CNN went so far as to recommend the commissioning of "an academic institution to conduct a parallel national exit poll to provide journalists and the public with better information on voting patterns."

These recommendations, inspired as they are by an urge to do better, only underline the fact that televised returns have become as integral to the electoral system as the official vote counting machinery. Political actors, public officials, reporters, and members of the electorate pay attention to the election night coverage. We need to think about how this may affect the way we conduct our elections.

The Impeachment of a President

In 1972 the idea that an American president under fire from congress might face impeachment or be forced to resign was unthinkable—even unspeakable. As late as spring 1973, when a California Representative reacted to Richard Nixon's first televised attempt to "get out the facts on Watergate" with a call for a formal inquiry into precisely that possibility, the Democrats' floor leader "Tip" O'Neill dismissed the motion as "a bit premature." Of course, Nixon was never impeached. Faced with the probability that he would be removed from office, he resigned. The nation took it in stride. No more than two of ten Americans, and possibly as few as one in ten, were unhappy with the outcome, and even that minuscule minority, though perhaps disillusioned, accepted the resignation as inevitable and necessary. Few were vengeful or bitter.[27] The live televising of the main Watergate events leading up to this truly extraordinary outcome had played a crucial role in ending the long controversy on a unifying note.

So it was that by the time that William Jefferson Clinton took office in 1992, the idea of a president being removed from office was no longer considered far out. Before this president-elect could even be inaugurated, there were calls for his impeachment. The language of Watergate had worked its way into the ready vocabulary of politicians and the media. Since Watergate, every controversy related to the White House had become "gates," thus recalling the long controversy that had so shaken the nation and undone one presidency. There were Travelgate, Whitewatergate, Filegate, and in the end, Monicagate. Not only did such code words evoke images of crimes—but of crimes that might be impeachable.

Thus, when the House of Representative on October 8, 1998 approved an inquiry to ascertain whether there was cause to impeach Clinton, most Americans were no longer totally unfamiliar with the procedures for removing a president from office. Whether they themselves had actually watched most of the televised events that led up to the resignation of Nixon, or had merely read or heard about them, just about everyone knew something about impeachment. Mainly, their knowledge was limited to two things: a president had to be found guilty of acts that amounted to "high crimes and bribery," and the process had to be fair. Otherwise, the country would never accept the removal of a duly elected president.

By the time the House began its inquiry in November, a clear majority of Americans did not judge Clinton's actions serious enough to warrant so drastic a step. Nevertheless, on the 9th, 10th, and 19th of November, the Judiciary Committee of the House (HJC) held hearings. The members asked the president to respond to 81 questions, which he did on the 27th in writing. Four more days of hearings were held in December, at the end of which the Committee, voting along party lines, approved four articles of impeachment to send to the full House. Two were turned down. With its approval of the two others, the House had impeached the president. As the next step, the case had to go to the Senate for trial. Presiding over the Senate when it convened on January 7 was Chief Justice William Rehnquist in full regalia. Since most of the facts bearing on the charges were uncontested, the trial could proceed without testimony. Both Democrats and Republicans agreed that there would, in effect, be a two-week trial. Upon its conclusion, they would then decide whether or not to call witnesses. They never did. In the end, Clinton escaped conviction by a narrow vote almost completely along partisan lines.

All these hearings, arguments, and votes were televised but watched mostly on cable. C-span had carried all of them live from gavel to gavel. On the day of the House debate, followed by the vote to impeach and the Clinton response to it, CNN, which in addition to C-span had also covered them all, averaged 1,823,000 homes with 2,386,000 viewers. These figures exceeded CNN's 24-hour average in 1998 by 380 percent. The Fox News Channel audience was up by 300 percent and MSNBC by 200.[28] Several of these numbers set new records. Meanwhile, anyone without cable could follow these events on public television or tune in to replays carried by the regular networks.

In spite of these impressive figures, attention to the proceedings was rather sporadic. Audiences reached their peak of 5.3 million households when President Clinton addressed the country shortly after the impeachment vote in the House. Most of the audience apparently found the proceedings less compelling than a dozen other news events that year. When CBS cut away from the HJC hearings to a National Football League game between the New York Jets and Buffalo Bills, it quadrupled its audience. While the public might have paid attention to the more surprising turns in these events, they lost interest once the Committee had voted out articles of impeachment, knowing full well how the House would vote.

The impeachment and trial of Clinton were in many ways unprecedented, but that the shadow of Watergate hung over both calls for explicit comparison. The HJC and its vote were essentially replays of the hearings on Watergate. But there were some differences in the way they were covered. In 1974, the three commercial networks, taking turns, together provided 43.3 hours of coverage over seven days from July 24 to July 30, including the final vote with which the Committee approved three out of five articles of impeachment against Nixon: his obstruction of justice, his abuse of presidential power, and his contempt of Congress.[29] In a further contrast to Watergate, the recent televised proceedings against Clinton had not been preceded nearly a year before by highly dramatic hearings by a special committee of the Senate. The testimony from a parade of star witnesses—like John Dean, telling his tale of complicity, and of "villains," like H. R. Haldeman and John Erlichman, Nixon's two closest aides, or the colorful and unforgettable Gordon Liddy, the most unrepentant of the Watergate burglars—prepared the ground for Nixon's final demise when it became, so to speak, inevitable.

Second, during the televised HJC hearings in 1998, there were no last-minute revelations, like the release of the tape of Nixon's incriminating conversation. The blue dress with the tell-tale stains had surfaced months before and Clinton himself had already admitted his involvement with Monica Lewinsky, albeit reluctantly, in a deposition filled with prurience, the videotape of which had been televised. Much the same can be said of the lengthy X-rated report Independent Counsel Kenneth Starr made to the committee and of his answers to questions by members of the committee and the counsels for the two sides.

Third, altogether unprecedented was the live televised coverage of the trial by the Senate. Viewers everywhere could follow it and, if so inclined, judge for themselves the fairness of a proceeding that ended in the acquittal of the president. Some videotaped testimony and arguments by some of the nation's most skilled and admired lawyers should have been riveting for anyone with interest in politics.

Most important—and here we repeat ourselves—the televising of the HJC hearings in 1974 had provided the public with a model or standard by which to judge this effort to remove a president. Conducted in full publicity, these earlier hearings had raised expectations by demonstrating that such a proceeding against a president could be fair, impartial and, if not apolitical, at least not patently politicized. According to experts who followed them, nearly all—93.1 percent, to be exact—of the arguments advanced at that time had been framed in constitutional legal terms. Partisan and political rhetoric had been practically nonexistent.[30] The five Republicans who had already endorsed three articles of impeachment against Nixon reflected their own ambivalence. They knew that they could be committing political suicide: One of the five, noting that some voters in his congressional district would be hurt deeply by his decision, assured them that he "had enough pain for them and me."

The public response to the impeachment and trial of President Clinton was in stark contrast to the removal of Nixon. Clinton's rating in the political realm exhibited a remarkable resilience. The public refused to regard his dalliance with a White House intern—even if he lied about it—as an impeachable offense. Even as the impeachment inquiry opened, all readings of opinion from polls showed at least 60 percent judging it as insufficient to warrant his being impeached and removed from office. The mid-term congressional elections (1998), widely billed as a referendum on impeachment, bear this out. Democrats did better than expected. Public opinion remained steady throughout the course of all the rhetoric in the HJC, all the speeches on the floor of the House itself, and right through all the legal arguments during the trial in the Senate. Opinion was also two-to-one against resignation, and it never shifted.[31]

We need not look very far to understand why the televised proceedings involving Clinton failed to move the public as they did during the Nixon inquiries. To begin with, the HJC vote, as well as that of the full House, except for a few crossovers, was strictly along party lines. As a result, the public perceived the Republican majorities in the House, and later in the Senate, as a bunch of zealots intent on damaging Clinton. The behavior of Henry Hyde, chairman of the House committee, contrasted sharply with that of Peter Rodino, his predecessor, whose management of the committee during Watergate had been universally praised. Rodino believed that the committee, and especially its chair, had to be judged fairly, and so, from the beginning of its inquiry had taken great care to nurture an image of fairness. Henry Hyde, too, had been aware of this imperative but was never able to project an image that he was truly impartial. Even though he did manage, before the hearings, to portray himself as a kind, even-handed, avuncular chairman, that assessment quickly ran into trouble when it was revealed that he, like Clinton, had been involved in an adulterous affair. He explained it as a "youthful indiscretion" when he was 40-something. There were other blemishes on his record. Just as Hyde and his committee were preparing to charge the president with having obstructed justice with his perjured testimony about his relationship with Lewinsky, the media reminded the public that Hyde himself had strongly defended Oliver North's obstruction of justice in his testimony in the Iran-Contra case. Not surprisingly, when the HJC voted in a straight down-the-line party split to impeach Clinton for obstruction, the public did not expect Hyde and the other Republican leaders to manage the upcoming Senate trial in a non-partisan manner.

Small wonder that, following the House vote on impeachment, 60 percent of the respondents to a New York Times/CBS poll thought that the Republicans had voted "mostly to damage Clinton," while only 36 percent believed that the charges in the report of the independent counsel to the committee had been sufficiently serious to warrant a formal investigation.[32] By the time the Senate trial was under way, a similar 60 percent were still questioning the motives of Republicans. The number who saw them as "impartial" was a paltry 28 percent, too small to gain legitimacy for so drastic a measure as the removal of a president.

Also feeding public skepticism was the low assessment of Kenneth Starr, the independent counsel who had diligently pursued the case against Clinton. Opinion had turned against him long before the televised debate began. In September 1998, months before he made his televised charges before the committee, Starr's negative ratings were already twice as great as his positive. Much of the public had come to view him as anything but an impartial investigator. To begin with, he had been authorized to look into the role that the Clintons may have played—before his presidency—in a real-estate development scheme called Whitewater that had gone bankrupt. He was also to investigate the disappearance of some files and the dismissal, early in his administration, of several White House employees in the episode that became Travelgate. But when his long but faltering investigation chose to focus its full attention on the president's relation to Monica Lewinsky, the public objected. By a two-to-one majority, it regarded this as a private, personal matter. This view "persisted unchanged throughout 1998—even as more and more information became available and as the news media pursued the story at far greater length and in far more detail than the public ever desired."[33]

The Senate trial was later described by a well-respected judge and legal scholar, but certainly no friend of Bill's, as a "travesty of legal justice. Although most of the senators pretended not to have made up their minds, their public comments during the course of the trial indicated otherwise."[34] More and more senators began announcing how they would vote as the trial moved toward its conclusion. The number able or willing to rise above partisanship was embarrassingly small.

In sum, the televising of the impeachment and trial could only have reinforced previously held opinions. A majority had arrived at a decision long ago that the all too apparent misconduct of the president did not rise to the level of a high crime that would justify his removal from office. Hence, they saw the charges against him as politically motivated. Which raises some key questions: Did Clinton, like Nixon before him, believe that he had to win "the battle for public opinion" to save his presidency? And had he, indeed, been found "not guilty" mostly or primarily because he managed to win that battle?

In our study of Watergate, we concluded that Nixon might not have lost his battle except for the "smoking gun," that is, the tape that turned up before the House even had a chance to impeach him or the Senate to put him on trial. For Clinton, the alternative would have been censure, a way of avoiding impeachment that was never officially considered by Congress. Michael Kagay, on whose analysis we have repeatedly drawn, thinks that the polling evidence shows that the public believed in some kind of punishment—preferably censure—for Clinton's reckless behavior but, even then, support for censure would have depended on what Congress would have decided to censure him for. In the larger sense, Kagay concludes, public opinion was a major factor in Clinton's survival. People were ready to distinguish the man from the president, to separate the private zone from the public zone. And because they continued to perceive Clinton's opponents as mainly partisan, they continued to award him high job approval ratings. The televised impeachment and trial could only have reinforced these perceptions.[35]

The Televised Battle Field

If war is a continuation of politics by other means, to paraphrase Clausewitz, then it behooves the military to manage it with an eye on the political effects. How a military operation appears can be as important as gains on the battle front, losses inflicted on the enemy, capture or destruction of its arsenals, or damage to its logistic and industrial support structure. When a government shackles the media, truth becomes the first casualty of war. But even without direct censorship, the image conveyed to the public has the capability to convert what could have been perceived as an American victory, judged by military standards, into a defeat. At least this is what Peter Braestrup,[36] critic of the media coverage of the Vietnam War, concluded about the Tet offensive launched by the Vietcong in 1968. Whether he was right or wrong, the specter of Vietnam still haunted American political and military strategists some two decades later when Iraqi troops invaded the small oil producing principality of Kuwait at the head of the Persian Gulf.

President George Bush reacted at once. His demand for immediate withdrawal was backed by the United Nations, which voted for sanctions to force Saddam Hussein, the Iraqi head of state, to comply. Over the next five-and-a-half months, during which Hussein showed no such inclination, the U.S. put together an alliance for a massive military build-up in neighboring Arab states. The deadline for military action was set for January 15, 1991, when Iraq was subjected to a bombardment by planes and missiles, unprecedented in its intensity and followed by just a few days of ground warfare that inflicted tens of thousands of casualties on a militarily inferior enemy. None of the minimal number of American deaths during these operations had resulted from enemy fire. The contrast between this limited loss in the Gulf and the over fifty-thousand Americans who lost their lives during the years of protracted and inconclusive warfare in Vietnam could not have been greater.

What concerns us here is the equally great contrast in the way television covered the battle field. There was no overt censorship in Vietnam. Before the turning point marked by the Tet offensive, briefing officers had succeeded in getting the official generally optimistic view across to the press. On the relatively rare occasions during which television crews had ventured into a danger zone, they tended to keep American casualties out of their visuals. After Tet, as the media began to resonate the policy differences within the political elite, more such clips were shown and televised reports were coupled with comments about ending the war.[37]

Still, regardless of how "responsibly" television may or may not have covered combat operations in Vietnam, many military—as well as civilian—leaders felt strongly that television had been far too critical, thereby contributing to the erosion of public support for the war. So it was that during Desert Storm, named for the attack that ended the war, the military did what it could to avoid a repetition of Vietnam. There were to be no pictures of body bags or graphic depictions of the brutality of warfare. Reporters were organized into pools and chaperoned to visit only the sites that the military wanted to publicize, keeping them at some distance from the front. A few managed, nevertheless, to make it there. The video clips of the actual battle field mostly featured Iraqi prisoners of war and burning enemy equipment.

American viewers experienced the Gulf War more as a media event than as a deadly struggle. Television tracked the progress of military operations by transmitting the nightly briefings, all of them upbeat, by General H. Norman Schwarzkopf, the theater commander. During Vietnam, such briefings by commanding officers had almost never been televised. The purpose of these viewer-friendly shows during the Gulf War was, first of all, to demonstrate the willingness of the military to share information and, second, to present the air war as a surgical operation, meant only to punish Saddam Hussein and not aimed against the Iraqi people. News organizations were handed video clips of "precision" strikes, dramatic portrayals of their impressive accuracy. The strongest evidence of danger to American troops came in reports of Scud missile attacks from Iraq on Saudi-Arabia, and also on Israel, where cameras transmitted pictures of damage and civilian casualties. Yet, the emphasis in these video reports was on the number of enemy missiles successfully brought down by American Patriot anti-missiles.

Small wonder that the only heroes remembered of this first television war were its generals, Schwarzkopf and Colin L. Powell. A woman pilot, singled out for her injuries, enjoyed mere moments of fame. In this new age of televised war, displays of unusual courage and extraordinary deeds count for less than what the whole world is able to watch.

The extent to which the contrast in conflict coverage was due to official restrictions or to the differences in the nature of the two wars is hard to gauge. American troops in Vietnam had been involved in years of ground combat whereas Desert Storm was fought mostly at a distance. Once ground troops went on the attack, it took them just 100 hours to rout the enemy army. Of some interest in this connection is the analysis by Oscar Patterson of a random sample of 847 news stories on the three major networks from 1968 to 1973. He estimates that, despite significant rule violations during the coverage of Vietnam, the majority of information *would* have been acceptable even by Gulf war standards.[38]

The specifically new communication feature in 1991, one definitely not encountered in Vietnam, was the near continuous coverage of the war by CNN, especially the "live" video reports by Peter Arnett from Baghdad, which may have contributed as much as the briefings to convince viewers that television had kept them well informed. In a national survey by the Princeton Survey Research Associates between March 14 and March 18, 1991 (shortly after the official cessation of hostilities), 72 percent of the respondents thought TV "had worked harder [than newspapers] to get the news in the Gulf;" a mere 11 percent saw it the other way around. In this same survey, 91 percent had a favorable evaluation of network television news[39] and gave CNN the largest share of the credit. Asked which network "did the best job in covering the War in the Gulf," nearly twice as many opted for CNN as for the three other networks combined.

Video coverage imparts a sense of actuality. One could hardly be less than overawed by the wave of pictures showing Scud missiles on their way to their targets or of Iraqi missiles intercepted by anti-missiles, by the live reports from Baghdad, by the visuals of bomb damage to civilian air raid shelters in that city, by the coverage of the liberation of Kuwait, by the authoritative briefings by General Schwarzkopf and his skillful use of maps, visual aids, and other paraphernalia to explain the military situation. Does it come as a surprise that, after Desert Storm, an overwhelming number of Americans rated the various aspects of video coverage as either "excellent" or "good?"—and this despite the fact that most were aware that at least "some" information had been withheld from them. They seem not to have minded the omissions. In fact, 83 percent, when directly asked about restrictions by the military on news reports, considered them "a good idea;" a mere 13 percent thought there should have been "less censorship" of Gulf news. Similarly, it did not seem to matter very much to the minority (36 percent) who knew about restrictions that forbade reporters "to go out on their own to cover the fighting (in the Persian Gulf)" or that, because their movements were restricted, they had to "cover the war through press pools organized by the military." Nearly all of those aware of such restrictions regarded them as more or less in the public interest. The slice of reality they had witnessed with their own eyes seems to have satisfied their curiosity.[40]

The direct effects on the public of televised coverage of events in the Gulf or in Vietnam, as distinct from the effects of the events themselves, are impossible to pin down. Hallin, for one, takes issue with the contention of critics of television that network news was opposed to and helped lose Vietnam. He reminds us that public support had already been falling before Tet.[41] Polls do, indeed, confirm this. But this same trend could also support the alternative view, that opponents of the war were so emboldened by televised reports that they could turn them into an effective argument for bringing it to a quick end. We simply lack the rich data needed to resolve the issue. Noteworthy nevertheless is that, according to polls, public trust in the military *as an institution*, though not in the military leadership, emerged from the Vietnam experience surprisingly intact. Was this because of television? A national survey taken in 1972 just after the election and before the signing of peace in January, 1973 contains the one bit of direct evidence we have been able to locate. Heavy viewers of television news (who said they watched "every night" or "several times a week") had higher regard for the military (69 vs. 59 percent) and showed greater support for military spending (69 vs. 58 percent) than light viewers. Although the relationship holds in the presence of control variables for political ideology, party identification, education, number of news sources, and interest in politics, the differences are small. One cannot convincingly assign them to the viewing experience.[42]

Desert Storm did not, however, last long enough to give an opposition much time to mobilize. Television, with its saturation coverage, presented a sanitized view of the violence while the magnitude of the victory made obsolete earlier congressional calls for postponing a military response in the hope that sanctions might yet work. It raised confidence in the military and approval of the president to unprecedented highs. Here again one faces the question: Did the television coverage promote this "rally to the flag," which is, after all, the common response to foreign crisis?[43] On such occasions, political differences tend to be muted and information more tightly controlled. In a post-victory survey by Morgan, Lewis, and Jhally, support for President Bush's decision to use military force was 76 percent among heavy television viewers but only 47 percent among light viewers. The more people had seen of the war, these authors contend, the more they remembered the "misleading" imagery and the less they knew about the background and the facts of the war.[44] That argument is plausible inasmuch as persons with little interest in public affairs are more likely to rely more on television and to take a less critical view of the distant events carried directly into their living rooms.

Finally, there is the effect on the conduct of coercive diplomacy. American television had no camera crews in Kuwait to cover the Iraqi invasion and hence no visuals to stir up anger. The threat to the oil supply sufficed to persuade President Bush to seek support from other heads of state for his strong stand. Propagandists did their part with atrocity stories. Nevertheless, American leaders remained apprehensive about home-front reactions to pictures of battle scenes. The fear, not just of casualties, but of casualties on television, goes a long way toward accounting for the controls that the military imposed on the movement of reporters. A military strategy aimed at inflicting unacceptable damage on the enemy while minimizing risk to our troops helped secure near unanimous approval. Air strikes and missile attacks at a distance relieve both perpetrators and reporters from having to face up to the suffering these cause and, when missiles from Iraq put American troops and Israeli civilians at risk, the television—except for Israel, where some damage was shown—focused on the interceptors to the near-exclusion of the deathly power of these missiles.

One of the truly remarkable aspects of the Gulf war was the live video transmission from Baghdad, which Hussein not only permitted but probably encouraged. The pictures were monitored by the American military to supplement other reports on the effects of the American bombardment just as Iraqis watched the briefings by Schwarzkopf. But the video presentation of a bombed hospital in which an undetermined number of civilians had lost their lives became a cause of embarrassment that the Iraqi government sought to exploit. To counter this evidence of an air war less discriminating in its targeting than had heretofore been claimed, military leaders re-examined their rules of engagement and probably made some effort to prevent a recurrence. The world-wide television audience functioned as a third party, whose tacit support or neutrality was a potential asset in this as in other disputes. How things might look to viewers was probably a consideration, though surely not the only one, behind the decision not to push the pursuit of fleeing troops too far beyond the border of Iraq and not to track Hussein to his lair and topple his regime.

World-wide television is becoming the wave of the future. The Internet and electronic mail now make possible citizen mobilization across boundaries and on a scale none of us had even dreamt of a generation before. These subjects, clearly beyond our purview, remain for other scholars to agonize over using new methodologies along with some true and tried old ones.

Gladys Engel Lang
Kurt Lang
March 20, 2001

NOTES

1.   Murray J. Edelman, *Politics as Symbolic Action: Mass Arousal and Quiescence* (New York: Academic Press, 1971).
2.   Erving Goffman, *The Presentation of Self in Everyday Life* (Garden City, NY: Doubleday, 1959).
3.   Personal communication.
4.   Daniel Dayan and Elihu Katz, *Media Events: The Live Broadcasting of History* (Cambridge: Harvard University Press, 1992).
5.   John D. McCarthy, Clark McPhail, and Jackie Smith, "Images of Protest: Dimensions of Selection Bias in Media Coverage of Washington Demonstrations, 1982 and 1991," *American Sociological Review*, 61 (July 1996): 478:99.
6.   Siegfried Frey, *Die Macht des Bildes: Der Einfluss der nonverbalen Kommunikation auf Kultur und Politik* (Bern: Hans Huber, 1999).
7.   W. Phillips Davison, "The Third-Person Effect in Communication," *Public Opinion Quarterly*, 47 (Spring 1983): 1-15.
8.   Robert D. Putnam, *Bowling Alone: The Collapse and Revival of American Community* (New York: Simon & Schuster, 2000).
9.   Daniel J. Boorstin, *The Image; Or What Happened to the American Dream* (New York: Atheneum, 1961).
10.   Based on Nielsen ratings for major networks without cable.
11.   Byron E. Shafer, *Bifurcated Politics: Evolution and Reform in the National Party Convention* (Cambridge: Harvard University Press, 1988), 261.
12.   Sidney Kraus, ed. *The Great Debates: Background, Perspectives, Effects* (Bloomington: Indiana University Press, 1961). See also, George F. Bishop, Robert G. Meadow, and Marilyn Jackson-Beeck, eds, *The Presidential Debates, Media, Electoral, and Policy Perspectives* (New York: Praeger, 1978); Sidney Kraus, ed. *The Great Debates:Carter vs. Ford, 1976* (Bloomington: Indiana University Press, 1979); Kathleen Hall Jamieson and David S. Birdsell, *Presidential Debates: The Challenge of Creating an Informed Electorate* (New York : Oxford University Press, 1988); James B. Lemert *et al.*, *News Verdicts, the Debates, and Presidential Campaigns.* (New York : Praeger, 1991); and.Alan Schroeder, *Presidential Debates: Forty Years of High-Risk TV* (New York: Columbia University Press, 2000).
13.   Schroeder, *Presidential Debates*, 107.

14. David Broder, cited in Schroeder, *Presidential Debates*, 41.
15. For a full review of the disputations over this project and its implications, see Sidney Kraus, *Televised Presidential Debates and Public Policy*, 2nd edn. (Mahwah, NJ: Erlbaum, 1999), 208-212.
16. James N. Druckman, "The Power of Images: The First Kennedy-Nixon Debate Revisited." Paper presented at the annual meeting of the International Society of Political Psychology, Seattle, July 2000.
17. Schroeder, *Presidential Debates*, 117-18.
18. *Time Magazine* (October 23, 2000): 58.
19. *Newsweek* (October 23, 2000): 39.
20. Seymour Sudman, "Do Exit Polls Influence Voting Behavior," *Public Opinion Quarterly*, 50 (Fall 1986): 331-39; Percy H. Tannenbaum and Leslie J. Kostrich, *Turned-On TV; Turned-Off Voters: Policy Options for Election Projections* (Beverley Hills, CA: Sage, 1983).
21. In a survey conducted under the auspices of the *Freedom Forum* (April 3-27, 2000) 51 percent disagreed strongly and another 17 percent somewhat with the statement that "Television networks should be allowed to project winners of an election while people are still voting."
22. Dayan & Katz, *op. cit.*
23. *New York Times* (November 15, 2000): A-26; Hendrik Hertzberg, "Talk of the Town: Pieties," *The New Yorker* (November 27, 2000): 70.
24. Cited by Richard T. Cooper, *Los Angeles Times* (December 24, 2000): 1.
25. CNN/USA-Today Poll (November 26-27, 2000).
26. CBS/New York Times polls (11/19/2000, 11/26/2000, 12/9/2000, and 12/14/2000).
27. Gladys Engel Lang and Kurt Lang, *The Battle for Public Opinion: The President, the Press, and the Polls During Watergate* (New York: Columbia University Press, 1983), ch. 6.
28. Nielsen ratings.
29. Lawrence Lichty, "Unpublished Monitoring Notes," cited in Lang & Lang, *op. cit.*, 311.
30. *Ibid.*, 312.
31. Michael R. Kagay, "Public Opinion and Polling During Presidential Scandal and Impeachment," *Public Opinion Quarterly*, 63 (Fall 1999): 460.
32. *Ibid.*, 457.
33. *Ibid.*, 454.
34. Richard A. Posner, *An Affair of State: The Investigation, Impeachment, and Trial of President Clinton* (Cambridge: Harvard University Press, 1999), 127.
35. Kagay, "Public Opinion," 461.
36. Peter Braestrup, *The Big Story: How the American Press and Television Reported and Interpreted the Crisis of Tet in Vietnam and Washington* (Westport, CT: Westview Press, 1977).
37. Daniel C, Hallin, "The Gulf War as Popular Culture and Television Drama," in W. L. Bennet & D. L. Paletz, eds. *Taken by Storm: The Media, Public Opinion, and U.S. Foreign Policy in the Gulf War* (Chicago: University of Chicago Press), 149-63.
38. Oscar Patterson, III, "If the Vietnam War Had Been Reported under Gulf War Rules," *Journal of Broadcasting and Electronic Media*, 39 (Winter 1995): 20-29.

39.   Cf. also Zhongdang Pan, Ronald E. Ostman, Patricia Moy, and Paula Reynolds, "Audience Evaluations of U.S. News Media Performance in the Gulf War," in B. S. Greenberg *et al.*, eds. *Desert Storm and the Mass Media* (Creskill, NJ: Hampton Press, 1992), 213-31.

40.   *The People, the Press and the War in the Gulf: Part II* (Times Mirror Corporation, 1991).

41.   Daniel C. Hallin, *The "Uncensored" War: The Media and Vietnam* (New York: Oxford University Press).

42.   C. Richard Hofstetter, "Watching TV News and Supporting the Military: A Surprising Impact of the News Media," *Armed Forces and Society*, 5 (Winter 1979): 261-269.

43.   Richard A. Brody, " Crisis, War, and Public Opinion," in W. L. Bennet & D. L. Paletz, eds. *Taken by Storm: The Media, Public Opinion, and U.S. Foreign Policy in the Gulf War* (Chicago: University of Chicago Press), 210-27.

44.   Cited in Gabriel Weimann, *Communicating Unreality: Modern Media and the Reconstruction of Reality* (Thousand Oaks, CA: Sage, 2000), 311.

PREFACE

In this book we examine some ways in which television, through its live coverage of major political events, has shaped public images of politics and political personalities and, in so doing, has influenced the nature and course of political life. It is a much changed and updated version of our *Politics and Television,* which was based largely on our own studies, first published in 1968, and allowed to go out of print only in 1982. Where the studies in that book took readers through election night 1964, the present volume not only takes them through some major events of Watergate and the Carter-Ford debates but also develops the implications of all these events for that critical year 1984, and beyond.

In the years since *Politics and Television* appeared, there has been no end to books on the subject. Mass communications research has become a thriving industry. The major themes we advanced to challenge the conventional wisdom are now *à la mode.* Thus it is now widely taken for granted that, contrary to McLuhan, the medium is *not* the message, that television has no inherent capacity to convey ... "reality" ... or the ... "truth" ... that even with the new and powerful means of visual and audio transmission, communication systems are still human systems. No longer is it necessary, as it once was, to demonstrate that indeed, there are significant media effects, to argue that the "minimal effects" theorem tells only a small part of the story. The focus of empirical inquiry has shifted away from factors that blunt the direct influence of specific communications on individuals in the audience, it has turned toward the role of television in creating a symbolic environment through which people largely experience the political world.

Why then resurrect these studies of the past? First, we believe they constitute a kind of history of political television worthy of attention. We are convinced of the value of a backward, perhaps nostalgic, look at events that many readers are too young to have experienced and that the rest of us no longer remember very well. There is something intrinsically interesting about every one of these events: the ballyhoo and ticker-tape parade that greeted General Douglas MacArthur's homecoming from Korea after his dismissal by President Truman for challenging civilian authority; the bitter fight over a loyalty pledge demanded of delegates who, four years previously, had defected to the Dixiecrats; the way Kennedy succeeded in making himself appear presidential in the first-ever televised debate between national candidates; the first serious concern over the implications for the electoral process of the network practice of projecting winners while voting is still in progress; the tension-packed TV blockbusters of Watergate—the Ervin Committee hearings, the impeachment debate, the unprecedented resignation of a president— carried live to record audiences; the breakdown in the audio transmission of a nationally televised debate that held two men, a President and a President-to-be, captive before the assembled nation for 27 minutes.

With the passage of time these televised events will survive only in the mythological versions that journalists find it convenient to construct. Our documentation may serve as a partial corrective and help set the record straight. That, however, is not the chief aim of this book. We like to think of our studies as more than historical accounts, as demonstrating the utility of treating events as the concrete precipitants of more invariant communication processes. The relation between politics and television is best observed in problematic situations when collective definitions are in flux or when established communication practice proves inadequate.

Our main purpose goes beyond the pinpointing of specific media effects. As media sociologists we have, throughout these studies, used our sociological imagination (or theory, if you prefer) to converse with the data generated from focused observation, small sample surveys, and content analysis. In this way we can draw inferences about the cumulative and long-range effects of television. We take some satisfaction in how well the individual studies have stood the test of time. Their updating for this edition required hardly any substantive change. We did some polishing of language to accommodate new linguistic usage or to clarify what now strikes us as a poorly stated argument. Looking backward, we feel vindicated in our reliance on methods that all too many scientists still dismiss as soft but which, we insist, are viable if guided by an adequate theory. No data ever speak for themselves; it takes a theory to prompt a revelation. We have used a theory but refrained from any pretentious display of abstractions. We have tried to stay clear of such neologisms as might interfere with our direct conversations with the data.

As in the earlier book, nearly all the material draws on (but does not simply reprint) work previously published by the authors. Chapter 2 is a revision of the essay that won the Edward L. Bernays Award of the American Sociological Association in 1952 and appeared in abbreviated version in the *American Sociological Review*, February 1953. Chapter 3 draws heavily on an article in the *Public Opinion Quarterly*, fall 1955. Chapter 4 on the Kennedy-Nixon debates is essentially a rewrite of the article that appeared in that same journal in summer 1961. Chapter 5 on the late voter phenomenon is based, in good part, on a study that appeared in *Voting and Nonvoting: The Implications of Broadcasting Returns Before Polls Are Closed* (published by Blaisdell Publishing Company in 1968). The chapter on Watergate is a spin-off, developing a theme suggested but not spelled out as part of our book, *The Battle for Public Opinion: The President, the Press, and the Polls during Watergate* (published by Columbia University Press in 1983). Finally, Chapter 7 on televised debate dilemmas draws from two articles on the Carter-Ford encounter. One appeared in the fall 1978 issue of the *Public Opinion Quarterly*, the other in *Journal of Communication* (Autumn 1978). A much more detailed version of the latter appeared in Sidney Kraus (ed.), *The Great Debates: Carter vs. Ford* (Indiana University Press, 1979).

Special acknowledgments for help with individual studies go back a long way and have been, over the years, gratefully given in the appropriate places. We repeat here again our thanks to Professor Bernard Rosenberg, who first suggested to Ivan R. Dee of Quadrangle Books that we weave certain of our works together in book form.

Preparation of the manuscript was expedited by the support staff at the National Humanities Center, where we have been privileged Fellows during the academic year, 1983-84. Here, in this pleasant milieu, we managed to snatch enough evenings and weekends away from our fellowship project to finish this manuscript.

Finally, it was Ithiel de Sola Pool, of MIT, who gave the first version of this book a generous review in *Public Opinion Quarterly* and hoped it would set a trend. He was a scholar with vision and a fine human being. The world of communication research, which is our world as well, will deeply miss him.

Research Triangle Park,   —Gladys Engel Lang
North Carolina   Kurt Lang

1

The Television Image

With the advent of film and radio, mass communications became a distinct area of sociological inquiry. Sociologists had long been concerned with the ways in which a reasonable consensus of opinion, necessary to the functioning of a pluralistic society, could be maintained or achieved. The apparent ease with which images and ideas could be rapidly disseminated to a widely dispersed mass audience both interested and frightened them. Should control over the content of mass communication fall into the hands of a few persons, there were, it seemed, only vague limits to their power to mobilize mass sentiment in any direction, whether for good or for evil. That these media had an impact on political life, they they played an important part in the shaping of political imagery, and that they would bring about changes in political institutions was pretty much taken for granted. Students of mass media sought to pinpoint these effects, documenting in particular in what manner and under what conditions they occurred.

A sharp reorientation was soon to take place. By the time television arrived on the scene as the mass medium *par excellence* sometime in the early 1950s, most research specialists were playing down the persuasive power once attributed to the mass media.

First of all, political events had a way of confounding common-sense assumptions about the ability of the mass media to engineer consent. Al Smith, governor of New York and Democratic candidate for president in 1928, had been the first political personality to star on radio; yet hadn't he suffered a stunning defeat? Subsequently, both Franklin D. Roosevelt and Harry S. Truman were able to win despite the overwhelming opposition of the press. Was this because of the good use they made of radio to counter newspaper influence? A systematic study of presidential campaigns in the United States indicated that a candidate's support by a majority of newspapers had not as a rule spelled the difference between victory and defeat.[1] By the same token, Eisenhower's 1952 victory in the first presidential campaign with nationwide television coverage was a personal triumph and hardly a simple and direct consequence of the new medium. An analysis of public opinion polls taken in 1947 and 1948 showed that the general's popularity, including the wish to see him President, had clearly antedated the coming of television.[2]

If Eisenhower apparently won the 1952 election before the campaign even began, didn't the opportunity to display the famous personality on television contribute to his margin of victory? Again the evidence was essentially negative. Comparing persons who in following the campaign relied most heavily on television with those who relied more on some other mass medium (newspapers, radio, or news magazines) showed that television fans were, if anything, slightly more Democratic in their leanings. The difference was minor and probably not attributable to the use of television.[3] Another study compared voter turnout and the two-party distribution of the presidential vote in Iowa counties covered by television with other Iowa counties not yet within receiving range of the signal. There was no significant difference in electoral behavior.[4]

Every time a new medium appears on the scene, we seem to expect revolutionary changes. The optimists stress its potential for education, the pessimists the possibility of abuse. For every expectation, so it appears, there is an equal and opposite expectation. Exorbitant claims are balanced by dire predictions, but most commentators agree that all things will never be the same again.

One need only recall earlier moments from the history of communications. The era of religious conflict ushered in by the translation of the Bible into the vernacular coincided with the spread of cheap and efficient methods of printing that made it possible to put a copy into the hands of every literate believer. No one could be quite sure what would happen if each man were to become his own judge of the Word. Toward the end of the eighteenth century in Britain, where the freedom of the printed word had long been proclaimed (though not always honored in practice), the opening to the press of parliamentary debates posed a similar problem about the effects of so much informed opinion. And so it was with the coming of the mass-circulation newspaper. Hailed as an instrument of education, it also suffered the charge that its circulation stunts played on the lowest passions. The excesses of yellow journalism, the propaganda of atrocity in World War I, and the ballyhoo of the 1920s readily come to mind. Radio raised new hopes, but Hitler's extensive use of it as his preferred medium of propaganda also left an indelible memory. Hence, the arrival of television, though it coincided with a period of relative political quiescence, was coupled with the imagined rise of Madison Avenue as the seat of dominant power. Although television could be used for elevating the political consciousness of the public, many feared that politics would now be marketed much like toothpaste. Anything could be sold with the appropriate formula.

Social scientists specializing in mass communications research were more cautious. Research efforts, begun before World War II and reaching fruition in the postwar decade, pointed to the limits of mass media influence—and the effects of television were subject to the same limits. Studies showed that individual responses to particular messages transmitted by the mass media were shaped by personal dispositions and competing influences. Mass communication effects, as Joseph Klapper summarized these findings, always occur together with a whole host of mediating factors, which all together help reinforce pre-existing tendencies.[5] Changes in attitudes, beliefs, and behavior directly traceable to the mass media are the exception rather than the rule. This is because exposure is highly self-selective; people pay attention primarily to content that already interests them and that is congenial to their point of view.

This selective exposure, it was said, had been made possible by the pluralistic structure of the mass media in the United States. Yet even when people do expose themselves to contrary or unfamiliar points of view, their interpretations of a message are often different from those intended by the sender. A final limitation on the media influence resides in the situation in which the response takes place. Whether or not people follow through on the intent of a message depends at least in part on available opportunities for doing so and on whether this response is condoned or proscribed by significant persons in their immediate surroundings.

The upshot of all these findings was to temper exuberance about the educational potential of the mass media and, at the same time, to calm fears about the deleterious effects of propaganda. At least it could be stated with some confidence that these hopes and fears received little support from research. Yet there was still some unease, even among those who themselves were documenting the minimal effects attributable to the mass media. Like others, they continued to talk privately—and sometimes to act publicly—as if they still somehow believed in the potency of the media. In 1952, the faculties of the great universities including some of those whose work was constantly cited to illustrate the relative unimportance of mass media influences, waged a battle of newspaper ads in support of Stevenson or Eisenhower. Lacking final answers, they clung to the belief that the mass media were perhaps more influential than they would otherwise wish. Outcries against television performances—like the famous 1952 speech in which Vice President Nixon invoked the name of his dog Checkers, or Senator McCarthy's behavior during the so-called Army-McCarthy hearings in 1954—as well as the enduring and enthusiastic acceptance accorded to George Orwell's *1984* vividly supported the researchers' suspicions that perhaps research did not tell them what common sense revealed was there to be told.

This uneasiness about the conclusions of most research was voiced by the late Eugene Burdick, a political scientist, when he was assembling a collection of essays on voting behavior. In 1956, he wrote to the authors:

> The volume [I am preparing] will contain chapters on almost all of the recent voting studies including the Berelson-Lazarsfeld-McPhee volume, the Michigan Survey Research Center work[6] and some British material. One thing that stands out in all of this, however, is the relative insignificance of the mass media in influencing the voter's

decision. . . . It occurs to me that much of the alleged impotence of the mass media may be due to the fact that the studies were not specifically set up to catch this aspect of voting. I judge (from what I have heard) that you think the mass media may have a much more decisive impact than most scholars believe.

In our answer we tried to set down our reasons for not sharing the conclusion many researchers had adopted at that time. Failure to pinpoint the effects of the media, we wrote, lay:

in the researcher's expectation that there must be some particular and, moreover, short-run change traceable to a particular exposure (or exposures) or to some particular medium. In short, we tend to be disappointed when the mass media "reinforce" rather than "convert" or when television, for example, appears to have no immediately discernible impact on those directly exposed.

It follows further from this expectation that observations are usually conducted when some particular response, e.g., casting a vote, is demanded. Studies on the effects of the mass media on voting are conducted during campaigns, when people know that they are being propagandized, whereas certain media materials not ostensibly part of the campaign may constitute the crucial test. We also object to the new trend which sees personal influence as dominant everywhere. A recent book[7] is supposed to show that "personal influence" [the influence of one person on another] is more important than "mass influence" [the influence of the mass media on the person]. This focus on the ubiquity of personal influence overlooks the fact that any lasting impact the mass media do have occurs within the context of relations and pressures that exist independent of them. The "opinion leader" [the person who influences others] often acts only as a transmitter of news or information, usually of something that has already become the focus of some interest, however vaguely defined, because it has been carried by the mass media. While this transmittal function of "opinion leaders" is usually recognized in a footnote, the fact that the influencee cites the influencer [opinion leader] as the source of his information is interpreted as proof for the relative importance of personal influence.

We went on to give Burdick our own view:

The mass media structure issues and personalities. They do this gradually and over a period of time, and thus this impact seems less spectacular than the shift or crystallization of a particular vote decision. We cannot help but believe that, indirectly, by creating a political climate, a sense of urgency, an image of parties and candidates, etc., they do influence votes.

Our view was more than wishful thinking or unwarranted suspicion. It was based, in part, on what our own research had been demonstrating. In that research we were concerned less with the specific responses of individuals to specific messages than with the way political events were being structured and influenced by the presence of a new medium. The issue was not, to paraphrase John Dewey, so much that communications affect the political community, but that society exists only in communication.[8] Television might provide a new kind of social experience with implications for the political process. The nature of this experience had to be studied.

The Age of Television

The era of radio passed so quickly that its impact on political life had hardly been considered when the "new age of television" arrived.[9] Who still remembers the major milestones of television firsts, in which the dramatic potential of that medium for disseminating public events was initially revealed? Politics without video is inconceivable to anyone today.

The discussions of mass media experts in the early 1950s, when nationwide coverage first became a reality, centered on the front-row seat that television gave every viewer. Enthusiasts believed that television, because it enlarged the viewers' social world beyond belief, enabled them to become intimately acquainted with persons and places to which they would never, without television, have access. As one pioneer producer we interviewed in 1952 put it, "TV is something in the nature of a transportation medium. It takes the viewer to the scene of the crime. It is like being there. The viewer is there and sees what it is like."

Television, as a new means of transport, provided the means for direct participation without the need for physical movement. In this way, television was said to have transformed the mass society into a mass neighborhood. Television's personalities entered the daily lives of people and involved them in interactions that have been called "para-social."[10] The characters in TV serials and hosts of other programs became significant social personalities with whom interactions were sustained. Public participation, via video, in the political life of the country would have a similar para-social character.

What were the major events that first aroused our interest in political television? In 1950, a Senate subcommittee's investigations into organized crime were televised. Witness after witness from gangland was paraded before the TV camera and subjected to questioning by Senator Kefauver and his chief counsel, Rudolph Halley. The committee's investigations brought to the national consciousness the prevalence of organized crime. One investigation of the public response to the hearing indicated a high degree of emotional arousal and indignation, but when it came to doing something to remedy the situation, this study indicated that only a small minority of persons were sufficiently motivated to take even modest political action, such as writing "to their congressman.[11] Could it therefore be said that the presence of the television cameras had no effect? Hardly. Crime and corruption became one of the major issues in the 1952 elections, and Kefauver, thanks to television, emerged as its chief opponent to become a leading contender for the Democratic nomination and, in 1956, ultimately to be nominated for vice president. His chief counsel was elected president of the New York City Council, winning against the Democratic machine.

In 1951, television's role in another event made us question the allegedly automatic reportorial accuracy of video reporting. On April 11, in the midst of the Korean War, President Harry S. Truman's summary dismissal of General Douglas MacArthur as commander-in-chief of the American forces fighting a desperate battle stirred up a national furor. MacArthur was a World War II hero. The White House communiqué relieving him of all his commands clearly stated the reason for dismissal: Through his public statements, MacArthur had repeatedly invaded the field of policy making, the prerogative of the President. The statement concluded with deep regret that

"General MacArthur is unable to give his wholehearted support to the policies of the United States government and of the United Nations in matters pertaining to his official duties." In other words, he was dismissed for insubordination and not for technical incompetence.

MacArthur's departure from Japan, a week after his dismissal, and his homeward journey after 14 years of continuous service abroad were more like a triumphal march than a voluntary acceptance of the President's supreme authority. A reporter and a historian, in describing the mood of the country, said it was doubtful "if there has ever been in this country so violent and spontaneous a discharge of political passion as that provoked by the President's dismissal of the General and by the General's dramatic return from his voluntary patriotic exile."[12]

These events had little to do with television. Viewers in this pre-Vietnam era had not yet become accustomed to battlefield close-ups on the nightly news. But from the moment MacArthur reached the continental United States, television cameras accompanied him on every public appearance from his first landing in San Francisco, where he received a hero's welcome, to his stops in other cities, large and small. The press reports, including television newsreels (this was before videotape), of his reception gave an impression of mass hysteria and an active outpouring of political outrage. The authors were then residing in Chicago, and MacArthur Day as celebrated there was thought to offer a unique opportunity for a systematic study of crowd behavior and of the role of the media of mass communication, particularly television, in this kind of event.

Our main goal was stymied. The air of curiosity and casualness exhibited by most members of the crowd was a surprise to every observer reporting from the scene. Yet those watching the televised welcome saw pretty much what they had expected to see. What intrigued us was: Why should "reality" as experienced over television have diverged so much from the "reality" of personal participation in the event? Those who participated in the study could no longer believe that reportorial accuracy was intrinsic in the technical capabilities of television.

The MacArthur Day study has sometimes been cited as proof of *deliberate* distortion by news media.[13] This interpretation misses the point. In Chapter 2 we offer a more detailed account of the findings and an explanation of what we called "unwitting" bias. The existence of this form of bias has since become axiomatic but at the time the press was reluctant to acknowledge it.

With our interest once aroused by MacArthury Day, it was natural that we should turn our attention to the presidential campaign as it was shaping up for 1952. Both political conventions were to receive national political coverage for the first time, and this promised to be the first campaign in which both parties would make a major investment in television.

The 1952 Republican convention turned into a two-way contest, with Eisenhower gaining a narrow victory over Senator Taft. The convention "proved" to ABC commentator Elmer Davis, that "it was no longer possible to commit grand larceny in broad daylight"—in other words, in front of the glaring eyes of the TV cameras. "Larceny" referred to a dispute over the seating of contested delegations from three Southern states; the resolution of the dispute turned out to be crucial for the outcome, because the successful challenge of credentials enabled Eisenhower to get enough additional delegates to be assured the nomination. But whether and how television affected the public response and, through it, the decision of the convention was the $64,000 question. We discuss the answer in Chapter 3.

A more deliberate effort to use television to solicit a public reaction occurred during the campaign and made us wonder about the supposedly terrifying capacity of the television camera to reveal the truth and to expose disingenuousness of every sort. Thus, Adlai Stevenson, the Democrats' nominee, who never could resist a joke, especially on himself, insisted after the 1952 elections that he had lost the election but "clearly won the bosom-beating and public stripping contest of last fall." The issue he raised, however, was a serious one. It concerned the successful defense by Richard M. Nixon, in front of television cameras, of the private fund set up for him by some California supporters.

In 1952, "the mess [created by the Democrats] in Washington" had become one of the major themes of the Republican campaign. Yet in the middle of the campaign the success of this strategy was jeopardized. Some enterprising reporters had unearthed a possible scandal involving their own vice-presidential nominee: 76 Southern Californian businessmen had, it was reported, set up a secret fund on which the senator could draw, purportedly to meet the expense of office. As this news snowballed, pressure mounted for Nixon to withdraw from the ''anti-corruption'' ticket. Eisenhower was reported to be collecting facts and pondering a decision. When it was announced that Nixon would offer a full explanation in a half-hour television broadcast, the event became front-page news and gave Nixon the largest television audience ever for any campaign speech.[14]

Nixon's half-hour program was produced by an advertising agency. For the first fifteen minutes he sat behind a desk and spoke directly to the audience. In simple and measured words, he told about his personal ordeal in having his honesty and integrity questioned when he had a big mortgage on his house and his wife was wearing a cloth coat, not a fur coat. During the second fifteen minutes he moved out from behind his desk and stood talking to the audience; the camera, at appropriate moments, revealed Mrs. Nixon looking at her husband as he addressed the television audience. The broadcast concluded with an unprecedented appeal to the public to wire and write the Republican National Committee, as the chief authority over his campaign, whether or not he should be dropped from the ticket.

The press reported an avalanche of letters, telegrams, and telephone calls overwhelmingly in favor of Nixon. The national committee said its mail ran 350 to 1 to keep him on the ticket. Senator Nixon flew to Wheeling, West Virginia, where Eisenhower publicly embraced him with the words, ''You're my boy.'' As a result of this speech, Nixon had not only turned to his (and his party's) advantage what could have been a disaster for both, but he had also gained in stature. He had become a public figure in his own right, not just another running mate. To many he was a hero, and his speech stimulated new interest in the flagging campaign. It also generated public accountings of finances and explanations of income taxes paid by the three other national candidates.

Regardless of whether the Nixon speech won the Republicans additional votes, its impact on images could not be denied. The Oxford Associates reported that among their panel of television viewers in Ohio, Democratic voters were more ready to concede that Nixon acted ethically in using this fund than were Republican voters ready to grant that Governor Stevenson had done no moral wrong in soliciting funds from anonymous donors to supplement the low salaries for Illinois public servants and thus lure competent men into his administration.[15]

Many commentators pondered the symbolism Nixon used to make his appeal. One such person was the arts critic, Gilbert Seldes, who some months later asked, "Did the camera panning over to Mrs. Nixon add the image of 'Whistler's Mother' (the pose was similar) to the verbal emphasis on 'Pat' and March 17 as her birthday?" Nixon talked of a little cocker spaniel, which he had accepted as a gift for his children. He made use of other market-tested symbols to convey his personal honor and love for his country. To this he tacked on a routine campaign speech, in which he attacked his opponents and gave effusive praise to General Eisenhower who was listening and said to be trying to reach a decision on Nixon's place on the ticket.[16]

Nixon himself, after resuming the campaign trail, marveled how a person from the humble background that was his could run for high office and when attacked could go on television and radio, where all he had to do was tell the truth. Thus an issue of political morality was transformed into one of personal honesty. Press comment about how the "man in the street" reacted revealed this only too clearly:

> The people who own dogs like I do are for Nixon. That story about the dog for his children made me love him.
>
> Nixon was so utterly sincere that no one could doubt his honesty.

Or a deviant reaction:

> I think he told a lot of lies. He's just too young to be in there.

While there was much criticism of Nixon's unscrupulous use of theatrics, his "soap-opera" appeal, the low level of intelligence at which he had pitched his defense, and the use of show business methods in politics, no one could deny that his political technique had been effective. But what about the more basic issue of "appealing" one's case to the great American "jury," when there were no rules of evidence? Was television's capacity for revealing the truth so inescapable that no one would mistake the rehearsed speech for spontaneity? And what kind of precedent did this new use of television set for standards of political debate in the future?

In transferring true and tried propaganda techniques to a medium whose effects were so immediate, there might result what Walter Lippmann called "mob law by modern electronics." Many of us shared his misgivings over the new partnership between television and public life and, like him, we and others were disturbed while watching, reacting much as we would some 20 years later to then-President Nixon's last battle, waged largely over television, for his political life. His "Checkers" speech was the first portent of things to come. Wrote Lippmann in 1952:

> The charges against Senator Nixon were so serious that for five days General Eisenhower reserved his own judgment on whether to clear him or condemn him. Why? Because the evidence, the law, and the moral principles at issue are none of them simple or obvious. . . . They have to do with matters which can then be decided only by some sort of judicial process. How, then, can a television audience be asked or allowed to judge the matter before General Eisenhower finished his inquiry and reached his conclusion? . . . What the television audience should have been given was not Senator Nixon's personal defense. That should have been made first before General Eisenhower. What the television audience should have been given was General Eisenhower's decision, backed by a full and objective account of the facts and of the points of law and of morals which are involved.

The question of the television personality in politics was raised by another event relating to the end of the era of McCarthyism. The televised Army-McCarthy hearing, in which the Wisconsin senator attempted to bulldoze with reckless charges several members of the defense establishment, held the country's attention in 1954. These hearings certainly coincided with the turn in the senator's fortunes, and television is still cited as the major cause of McCarthy's downfall and his censure by the Senate. In front of the pitiless TV cameras, it is alleged, McCarthy revealed himself to the public not as a patriot but as the demagogue he actually was.

We know of no evidence to support this simple an explanation. McCarthy's standing in the polls began to slip only after the Senate moved to take action against him. Hence, whatever role television played in the destruction of the myth of McCarthy's invincibility, it certainly did not create a mass aversion against his antics before the cameras. Had not the Nixon episode shown that important issues could be sidestepped without this resounding to the detriment of the candidate? After the hearings, powerful political forces in the Senate and on Capitol Hill were finally stirred to action. McCarthy's public performance was among the actions they used to discredit him. The Nixon speech, by contrast, was not only a smoother performance, but as campaign oratory it was less open to challenge.

The Army-McCarthy hearings also marked the first time that one of McCarthy's charges met an immediate challenge from an opposing counsel. This happened during an interchange with lawyer Joseph Welch that had all the markings of a courtroom drama. When McCarthy persisted in an attempt to damage Welch's reputation by destroying the reputation of a young member in his law firm, Welch told both a stunned McCarthy and the nation, "Until this moment, Senator, I think I never really gauged your cruelty or your recklessness."

The "instant reply" was subsequently built into the televised presidential debates. In the first of these, in 1960, Richard M. Nixon was paired against John F. Kennedy. Sixteen years passed before two other presidential contenders—Gerald Ford and Jimmy Carter—debated before the cameras. Our studies of these confrontations, reported in Chapters 4 and 7, show again how responses to a politician's television personality are influenced by political convictions. If this is so, we can infer that the dramatic impact of Nixon's "Checkers" speech on millions of viewers—we made no study of our own of this incident—was less a product of what he said than a reflection of Eisenhower's great appeal to voters. Many persons, Republicans and Democrats alike, did not want to see the general embarrassed politically and hence were ready to exonerate Nixon as long as he offered them a rationale for doing so.

A final and basic issue concerns the impact of television, as a medium of political communication, on the functioning of government institutions. After 1960, pressure built to make televised debates between presidential candidates a routine part of the political process. There were demands for permanent modification of the equal time provision to enable the networks to accommodate such debates without undue loss of revenue. Yet, with no permanent change in the FCC regulations, these televised encounters, as late as 1980, had to be disguised as bona fide news events covered by TV rather than broadcast as the staged-for-TV events that they actually were. This official deception created a dilemma for politicians and journalists alike when the first Carter-Ford debate was suddenly interrupted by a technical failure (Chapter 7).

Important innovations in communications technology have changed the ritual of election night and raised serious questions about the impact of election day broadcasts on the democratic process. By 1964 the broadcasting of presidential election returns to the public while polling places in some states are still open had become the controversial issue which it continues to be in the 1980s. This is the sujbect of Chapter 5.

Television and Public Events

The studies in this book are not limited to the electoral process. They cover other political events that have made television history, including the major television events that made Watergate history in the 1970s. The excitement over the events themselves is gone. We can recapture for ourselves only with difficulty our own sense of involvement at the time the studies were in process. Nevertheless, we believe that they are not just history and of purely academic interest. Since they all touch on rather general issues, they are, to that extent, not dated. A concern with the effect of television on images of politics, of politicians, and of political moods is the common theme that ties all of them together.

If these studies of the "television image" diverge in many respects from usual studies of perception, this is because we have treated the viewers not solely as observers who are the target of certain messages, but also as participants in the events they observe over video. Through the empirical study of major televised events we have sought to understand: What is the nature of participation in televised public events? How does it affect the viewer's imagery of the political process and, indirectly, his or her political behavior? How have politicians and political institutions accommodated themselves to this electronic political participation? What are the processes involved, and what long-term changes are the result?

To characterize our interest in these events as sociological is to distinguish it, first of all, from that of the journalist (or historian) who offers a meaningful account of what transpired during a particular event. But our orientation also sets us apart from those researchers whose primary concern is with documenting and measuring a particular effect as precisely as possible—What candidate was helped? Who won the debate? And so forth. Knowledge about how high audience ratings are achieved or how attitude change is maximized is important for the effective use of television by political actors. These instrumental uses of television are themselves only a small part of the myriad relationships between television and politics. We naturally assume that every televised event has some kind of effect; our idea has been to so conduct the study of any event that, once it is over, we can depict and analyze in some detail *whatever* effects turn up. This has sometimes taken us in new and unanticipated directions. Insights obtained from attempts to assess and understand the impact of any one event have then become the starting point for an entirely new line of inquiry.

This is not to say, however, that our inquiries were altogether without focus. Rather, they have been guided in a general way by several early and popular assumptions about the effects of television, effects assumed to be intrinsic to the medium though not usually subjected to direct scrutiny. These effects refer, in one way or another, to the intimacy, simultaneity, directness, and completeness of the view of public events afforded by television.

(1) Many people have voiced the opinion that television, because it affords a close-up view of personalities and events, creates a sense of familiarity with public figures, political activities, and distant places. This type of face-to-face contact is presumed to have resulted in a sense of intimacy and personalization of politics.

(2) Again, by adding sight to sound, television is said to have done more than combine a newsreel or movie with radio broadcasting. Where the coverage of an event is live, visual simultaneity provides a dimension of experience that is like being transported to the scene. This unique characteristic of television results in the viewers "being there" and allows them to participate directly in public affairs.

(3) A third consequence supposedly follows from this characteristic of the medium per se: Because viewers can see "for themselves" and the camera "does not lie," a supposedly authentic picture of public events is disseminated. The public no longer must rely on a third party to report what goes on. Viewers can formulate their own judgments without danger of being victims of others' biases or interpretations.

(4) As long as there is full coverage, the vantage point provided by television is alleged to result in a fuller, richer, and more complete picture of what is taking place than that conveyed by other media. "Watching over TV" may not only be as good as "being there"; it may in fact be better.

No one study could possibly have answered all the questions these assumptions raise about the role of television in politics. But if some of the effects inferred from the technological capabilities of the medium have proved real, this may have been less the direct result of technology than of the fact that people came to *believe* in these effects. Accordingly, the assumptions that have governed the "use" of television may have been real in their consequences because members of the audience, mass communicators, and political actors have acted "as if" certain qualities inhered in the coverage. Certainly, television has become an increasingly important element in the looking glass image through which political actors assess their appearance to a larger public. We deal with this point more explicitly in the final chapter.

NOTES

1. Frank Luther Mott, "Newspapers in Presidential Campaigns," *Public Opinion Quarterly*, 7 (1944): 348-67.

2. Herbert Hyman and Paul B. Sheatsley, "The Political Appeal of President Eisenhower," *Public Opinion Quarterly*, 17 (Winter 1953-54): 443-60.

3. Angus Campbell, Gerald Gurin, and Warren E. Miller, "Television and the Election," *Scientific American*, 188 (1953): 46-48.

4. Herbert A. Simon and F. Stern, "The Effect of Television upon Voting Behavior in Iowa in the 1952 Presidential Election," *American Political Science Review*, 49 (June 1955): 470-78.

5. Joseph T. Klapper, *The Effects of Mass Communication* (Glencoe, IL: Free Press, 1960).

6. These were two, by now classic, studies of the 1952 presidential election.

7. Elihu Katz and Paul Lazarsfeld, *Personal Influence* (Glencoe, IL: Free Press, 1955).

8. See John Dewey, *The Public and Its Problems* (New York: HOlt, 1927).

9. A term first publicized by Leo Bogart in his book by that title (New York: Frederick Ungar, 1956).

10. Donald Horton and R. Richard Wohl, "Mass Communications and Para-Social Interaction," *Psychiatry*. 19 (August 1956): 215-29.

11. G. D. Wiebe, "Responses to the Televised Kefauver Hearings: Some Social Psychological Implications," *Public Opinion Quarterly*, 16 (Summer 1952): 179-200.

12. Richard H. Rovere and Arthur M. Schlesinger, Jr., *The General and the President* (New York: Farrar, Straus, 1951), 5.

13. See, for example, remarks made during the Corning Conference included in Eugene Staley, *Creating an Industrial Civilization* (New York: Harper, 1952), 82.

14. The speech was carried by 194 stations of the Columbia Broadcasting System and by the 62 station hookup of the National Broadcasting Company's television network. NBC estimated, without making an audience count, that the program was "possibly" seen by 25 million people. Mutual Broadcasting estimated that 90 percent of the nation's 45 million radio homes were tuned in.

15. Miami University, Department of Marketing, *The Influence of Television on the Election of 1952* (Oxford, OH: Oxford Research Associates, December 1954), 177.

16. Some of Gilbert Seldes's comments are contained in *The Public Arts* (New York: Simon & Shuster, 1956).

2

The Unique Perspective of Television

MacARTHUR DAY

Since Admiral Dewey, in 1899, was "spontaneously" invited to a hero's welcome by cities throughout the United States, such receptions have become traditional. Through such ceremonies America pays tribute to its great heroes, its men of achievement. Promotion helps along the enthusiasm. Silas Bent documented in his book, *Ballyhoo*,[1] how some crusading newspapers in the 1920s raised the mobilization of enthusiasm to the status of an art, how celebrities were induced to lend their names to receptions, and how community organizations and local governments cooperated. Once this had been done, the mass of spectators needed to contribute only their presence and vocal power, throw ticker tape, and snatch up insignia.

The homecoming of General Douglas MacArthur in 1951 offered a chance to revive a custom last practiced when other military leaders of World War II returned some six years before. There would not be another until the next decade when returning astronaut John Glenn received his due for being the first American to orbit the earth. But in the spring of 1951, cities—big and small—eagerly seized the opportunity to ask the general to honor them with a visit. On April 16, Democratic Mayor Martin H. Kennelly extended Chicago's official invitation. It was in this same spirit that on the next day, following a plan by a WGN radio commentator, Chicagoans could hear whistles, firecrackers, and church bells—or so one read in the newspapers on

April 18—exactly at the time the plane bearing MacArthur touched American soil in San Francisco.

Yet there were other overtones to MacArthur's triumphal return. In the two weeks between the general's dismissal and his reception in Chicago on April 26, the press featured stories indicating widespread public indignation. State legislatures passed resolutions of their trust in the general and their condemnation of the President's action. In Congress there were some unusually vitriolic attacks on Truman and his backers. For instance, a Republican senator applied the epithet "pygmies" to those who had tried to "bring down this tower of strength and deserving idol of the American people." Three senators actually came to blows during one of the more heated exchanges. Meanwhile, news reports from every section of the country told of effigies of Truman and Dean Acheson, his secretary of state, hanging from trees. This was, after all, at the height of McCarthyism. Tempers appeared stretched to the breaking point in a country divided over the issue of a sell-out to communism.

Developments were clearly moving toward some climax when, upon reaching Washington, General MacArthur made a memorable address to a joint meeting of both houses of Congress, at the close of which he promised that like an "old soldier" he would "fade away." The speech was reported to have had an "electrifying" (what a buzzword) effect on the nation. Few thought it a contradiction of this avowed self-effacement for MacArthur to go on to a triumphal homecoming in New York. Then, after nearly a week of relative obscurity, he emerged again to receive what Chicago promised would be an ear-splitting welcome, second to none. The MacArthur odyssey was obviously rife with political significance.

MacArthur Day in Chicago included the following events, all of them televised: MacArthur's arrival and greeting at Midway Airport; a motorcade and parade through the city, with a stop at the Bataan-Corregidor Bridge to lay a wreath in honor of the war dead; the resumption of the parade through the heart of Chicago's business district; and an evening rally at Soldier Field, where the general gave a speech. Chicagoans could participate as spectators at any of these events. They could likewise view any or all of them on television. The number along the parade route together with those who viewed the event over TV must have added up to a sizable proportion of Chicago's population. It was a genuine public event.

The Study

The idea of systematically studying what was to happen on MacArthur Day came up in an advanced seminar on crowd behavior that Dr. Tamotsu Shibutani was then conducting at the University of Chicago. The suggestion met with a spontaneously warm response. Because there were fewer than 72 hours between suggestion and event, we were in some haste to formulate hypotheses, design procedures, recruit fellow graduate students as volunteer observers, and make all the concrete preparations necessary for an investigation of this sort.

The study was, by design, open-ended, an effort to explore rather than test specific propositions. Our aim was to get maximum coverage of the event. To this end we assigned volunteer observers so that no important crowd-observation spot in the general's itinerary was neglected. There were 31 observers so distributed that some were able to cover the day's events from more than one station. An observer could, for instance, witness the arrival at the airport and still arrive in Chicago's Loop in time to see the downtown parade. The resulting coverage thus was based on some 43 perspectives.

Observers received instructions that called special attention to the need to discriminate in their reports between their own subjective feelings and what they were able to observe about others—who said and did what, how, where, and when.

In addition, two persons monitored the TV coverage, the audio portion of which was also recorded on tape. Because of our interest in television, observers on the scene were asked to take special note of anything indicating possible television influences on the event, such as action directed toward the TV cameras or staging for the benefit of TV.

When we compared the various observers' reports, it became strongly evident that the MacArthur Day reported by persons on the scene was rather different from the MacArthur Day as it appeared to the televiewer. This contrast between the two perspectives of

MacArthur Day led us to inquire into possible causes and, from this basis, to assess the role television played in the presentation of public events and its significance in politics generally.

The Pattern of Expectations

As a rule, the mass media prepare the ground for the way an event is seen. MacArthur Day was no exception. After a build-up of ten or more days, the crowd that turned out for the motorcade and parade was far from a casual collection of individuals: Its members *intended* to be witnesses to an unusual event. The pattern of expectations became apparent from two sources: statements of spectators (recorded in observer reports) about what they expected and personal accounts of the 31 observers of what they themselves had expected. The latter were recorded on the eve of MacArthur Day.

Both spectators and observers shared the same image. Many of the spectators had *anticipated* "mobs" and "wild crowds." They had expected some disruption of transportation schedules. They had come downtown in search of adventure and excitement. When all overheard and solicited-in-conversation statements of expectations were examined, one-third concerned such wild—perhaps threatening—scenes. Leaving aside another quarter of the remarks alluding to purely personal hopes (being able to see, photograph, wave to MacArthur), the second largest group of remarks emphasized the "spectacle." Table 2.1 sums up what the spectators expected.

Observers' expectations differed slightly in emphasis but not in content from those of the spectators they observed. This difference

Table 2.1 Spectator's MacArthur Day Expectations

Disorderly conduct and excitement, disruption of facilities (due to "crowd behavior," that is, an implicit *threat*)	37%
A chance to hail, photograph the hero (the *personal* anticipation)	27%
Extraordinary magnitude regarding showmanship and turnout	19%
Factual expectation (time of arrival, etc.)	7%
Display of political sentiment	2%
Other	8%
All expectations as evidenced by remarks	100%

can be accounted for, in part, by the observers' "unrepresenta-tiveness" (they had a special interest in participating), and, in part, by the different conditions under which their expectations were elicited. Each of these volunteer observers filled out a personal data sheet before setting forth to observe. As a result of an unfortunate collapsing of several questions into one, the response did not always focus properly on what observers themselves "expected to see." Of those who clearly stated their personal anticipations, two-thirds ex-pected excited and wildly enthusiastic crowds. But it is a safe guess, when we recall the discussion during the briefing session, that the number who expected such crowds was considerably higher. After all, as pointed out in Chapter 1, the main incentive to volunteer was the opportunity to participate in a first-hand study of crowd behavior.

To sum up: Most people expected a wild spectacle in which large masses of onlookers would take an active part and which contained an element of threat in view of the heightened emotions and the power of large numbers.

A more detailed examination of these same data shows that this pattern of expectations was shaped by the mass media. For it is by way of the media that the picture of the larger world comes to sophisticated as well as unsophisticated people. The observers were no exception to this dependence on what newspapers, newsreels and television cameras told them; they were perhaps better able than others to describe the origin of such impressions. Thus Observer 14 wrote:

I had listened to the accounts of MacArthur's arrival in San Fran-cisco, heard radio reports of his progress through the United States, and had heard the Washington speech as well as the radio accounts of his New York reception. . . . I had therefore expected the crowds to be much more vehement, contagious, and identified with MacArthur. I had expected to hear much political talk, especially anti-Communist and against the Truman administration. These expecta-tions were completely unfulfilled. I was amazed that not once did I hear Truman criticized, Acheson mentioned, or as much as an allu-sion to the Communists. . . . I had expected roaring, excited mobs. Instead there were quiet, well-ordered, dignified people. . . . The air of curiosity and casualness surprised me. Most people seemed to look on the event as simply something that might be interesting to watch.

Here are some very similar notations by other observers:

> I had expected—after reading, and seeing newsreels of his reception
> in other cities—tremendous enthusiasm, larger crowds, and louder
> cheering. As it was, I could not quite figure out why people were
> there, unless it was to see how other people acted and in the expecta-
> tion of seeing a magnificent spectacle, of the sort which had been
> promised by the newspapers. The wave of sentiment and excitement
> that passed through this group was surprisingly below what this
> observer had anticipated as a result of listening to the radio broadcast
> of his [MacArthur's] arrival in San Francisco and the parade in
> Washington, D.C. The feeling of participation in a genuinely excited
> crowd was almost absent. Certainly at no point were they carried
> away, nor did they experience or express strong sentiments, except
> in isolated, individual cases.

We wanted to observe the event in its natural context, so this meant
forgoing the use of a formal or even an informal interview, in which
people, especially those with television sets at home, could have been
asked *why* they had forsaken the comforts of home viewing to take
themselves or their families downtown. Because such standardized
data are missing, the *why* cannot be fully answered. But this much
could be ascertained: People expected to take part in an event, the
full flavor of which was to be savored only by direct participation
in it. Conversations recorded by observers provide ample evidence
that spectators, like the observers themselves, inferred a mood, a
feeling of enthusiasm, a throb of excitement. Though they had already
read about it, *heard* about it, or even *seen* it for themselves (on TV
news shows), they felt they could appreciate and share in it fully only
by being present.

As people waited for the parade, many made comparisons between
the advantages of "being there" and "seeing it over television." The
conveniences and intimacy of the family circle were weighed against
the opportunity of taking an active part. Said a father with two
children:

> Sure, it's more fun than seeing it on TV. People are simply too lazy
> to take their kids out; no wonder there's communism.

An elderly woman answered an observer's conversational gambit that he "could have been watching from an office window":

My gosh, how come you're out here! Of course, I could have been sitting home and seeing this much better on TV, but I decided I'd just like to be in a crowd today.

What brought people out? Why were they there? Observers, though instructed to report concrete behavior rather than general interpretations, did at intervals or at the end of the day generalize their impressions. All generalizations on the motivation of the crowd were either of two kinds: that crowds had turned out to see a great military figure and public hero "in the flesh," or—the logical supplement of the first—that they had turned out not so much "to see *him*, as I noticed, but to see the *spectacle*."

No observer generalization supported the official view, stressed by the mass media, that people had come to find vantage points from which to see the man and his family so as to welcome, cheer, and honor him. Yet among the concrete behavior these observers reported there were few isolated incidents which would justify such an interpretation.

Actual incidents, behavior, and statements recorded were most revealing of why people had joined the crowd. Each was classified as lending support to one of the three above-mentioned generalizations as to why people were there—to see a celebrity whose arrival had been widely publicized, to find excitement and witness an unusual spectacle, and to pay homage as an act of hero worship. The results, when tabulated, affirmed observers' impressions:

Interest in seeing MacArthur 48%
Passive interest in the spectacle 42%
Active hero worship (1% not classifiable) 9%

At first glance these figures may seem to contradict the contention that people were mainly anticipating a spectacle, a great show of some sort. But interest in the spectacle did not preclude a secondary interest in seeing MacArthur—the spectacle did revolve around him, and in many ways these two interests were complementary. More important, when these observations are broken down according to the area in which they were observed, it is clear that the crowds in the Loop, the great bulk of the spectators who took part in MacArthur Day, thought of the occasion *primarily* as a spectacle. There in the Loop, in the heart of Chicago, 60 percent of the observations supported the "spectacle hypothesis." Contrast this with percentages in other areas: Black district, 40; Soldier Field, 23; airport, 18; University of Chicago area, 0.

The Unfulfilled Expectation

This probe into motivation helps to confirm the pattern of expectations observed. To this evidence should be added those constantly overheard expressions—which increased as time spent waiting increased and the expected excitement failed to materialize—of disillusionment with particular vantage points. "We should have stayed home and watched it on TV" was the almost universal way in which such dissatisfaction was verbalized. Compared with the spectator's experience of extended boredom and sore feet, alleviated only by a fleeting glimpse of the hero, previous experiences over television had seemed truly exciting and promised even greater "sharing of excitement" *if only one were present.* As these expectations went unfulfilled, unfavorable comparisons with television became frequent. To present the entire body of evidence bearing on the inadequate release of tension and the widely felt frustration would add little of relevance to televised politics. It does, however offer unequivocal proof of a great let-down, a feeling that nothing had really happened.

The observer records show that some people voiced disappointment only because, after waiting so long, they had somehow failed to see MacArthur. Others—and such remarks were frequently part of the small talk in the crowd—thought "they ought to have a band to liven things up a little." "Heck of a parade. It's too quiet." "They should have more music," ventured another; whereas a third person would proclaim, upon seeing the jets overhead, "Yes, that's it. We need more planes for this celebration." Disappointment centered on the failure to provide a show, not only the brevity of the peek at MacArthur. For example a movie-camera-carrying man voiced his hope that "the next time *something* happened," he would have better luck getting pictures. "Was that a parade? Heck, I expected more than that," remarked another disappointed spectator after it was all over.

Not everyone thought the show unrewarding, however. A participant at Soldier Field said, "It was swell. I just love crowds anyway." Those in search of excitement sometimes managed to find it. They "got a bang out of the passing police cars"; they expressed awe at the jets; or they found the throwing of confetti from office windows amusing. The opportunity to express their disregard of traffic authorities by overflowing into State Street just as soon as MacArthur had passed was another source of satisfaction for many.

Those who arrived in a "holiday spirit" were in no mood to be disappointed and ready to substitute other diversion. In one bar, two observers found a group of firemen, who had been called out as auxiliaries, engaging in mutual horseplay and collective ridicule of the entire proceedings and the set-up behind it. Restaurants were crowded, with people forming lines out into the street. Observers indicated that a "fair" proportion of those who were evidently not downtown office workers appeared "dressed for the occasion." Movie seats were, indeed, not to be had within minutes after the parade. Others found solace in the "historicalness" of the event: Its like had never occurred before in Chicago. The crowds on V-E Day (1945) and for Truman during the 1948 election campaign had not been as tremendous, so spectators repeatedly commented. The spectacle, moreover (as one man told an observer), was far more lively than the Shriners' parade a year or so before, though that parade had had "real color." A woman anticipating the high point of the ceremony—at the Bataan Bridge—relived her travels for the benefit of people around her and, in the end, wondered aloud why she had never been to the Mardi Gras in New Orleans. Even those who were most disappointed consoled themselves that the weather had been good.

A Good Show on Television

For televiewers the story was different. Persons who followed the coverage saw and heard very much what they expected. Here is what was shown and described by the announcer, as reported by the monitors:

> The scene at 2:50 p.m. at State and Jackson was described by the announcer as the "most enthusiastic crowd *ever* in our city. . . . You can feel the tenseness in the air. . . you can hear that crowd roar." The crowd was described by the commentator as pushing out into the street with the police trying to keep it in order, while the camera was still focusing on MacArthur and his party. The final picture was of a bobbing mass of heads as the camera took in the entire view of State Street northward. To the monitor, this mass of people appeared to be pushing and going nowhere. And then, with the remark, "The whole city appears to be marching down State Street behind General MacArthur," holding the picture just long enough for the impression to sink in, the picture was suddenly blacked out.

One of our monitors reported her own reaction to this phase of the television transmission:

> The last buildup on TV concerning the "crowd" (cut off as it was abruptly at 3:00 P.M.) gave me the impression that the crowd was pressing and straining so hard that it was going to be hard to control. I first thought, "I'm glad I'm not in that," and "I hope nobody gets crushed."

An observer, on the scene at the moment it appeared from the TV picture that the crowds were surging out into State Street and breaking into the parade, gave the following account of what happened:

> [As MacArthur passed] everybody strained but few could get a really good glimpse of him. A few seconds after he had passed most people merely turned around to shrug and to address their neighbors with such phrases as "That's all." "That was it." "Gee, he looks just like he does in the movies." "What'll we do now?" Mostly teenagers and others with no specific plans flocked into the street after MacArthur but very soon got tired of following as there was no place to go and nothing to do. Some cars were caught in the crowd, a matter which, to the crowd, seemed amusing.

This comparison of the television perspective with that of the participants indicates that the video treatment of MacArthur Day *preserved* rather than upset expectations. Television remained true to form. From the beginning to the very end, the broadcast interpreted what happened in line with expectations. Viewers received no hint of any disappointment or of the let-down experienced by the crowd.

The landing of the plane that carried MacArthur to Chicago graphically illustrates the contrast between the two perspectives. On television, viewers could watch MacArthur's plane land and then follow the general and his family as he was greeted by Mayor Kennelly and other dignitaries. They could see him acclaimed and greeted by "enthusiastic" crowds. But among those actually at the airport, only those fortunate few who spotted where the plane landed were able to catch a fleeting glimpse of the hero, and of his wife, as each emerged. They had to guess at what was going on during the greeting protocol. Said one girl who had been waiting to spot the general, "He's probably babbling or giving a speech." A sizable number of people—including three of the six observers who expected to watch the arrival from the airlines' observation deck—saw nothing at all. This being in the days before the ubiquitous transistor radio, they had no announcer to tell them they were waiting in the wrong place. Only the salvo given in official salute and the cheering that sounded faintly in the distance told them that the general had arrived. People near one observer were saying that "surely he would drive out of the airport their way." But gunsmoke and a plane in the distance were all they saw of MacArthur Day:

> Ours was a disappointed crowd. They were cold. They had been entertained while waiting by the arrival and departure of the aircraft. The waiting period did not seem too long because of this. Excitement built up only a few minutes before twelve. This is the time at which I came to watch the sky closely and figured that there was only one way for an aircraft to land. I had expected an announcement and none had come. The guns brought the message that MacArthur had arrived. Now no one cheered; no one was happy, because the arrival was a disappointment. It meant that we had waited in the wrong place with perhaps a thousand others. The rapidity with which the crowd broke

up was fascinating. . . . Disappointment was expressed by a shrug, by a grunt, and by their rapid departure.

The Structure of the TV Presentation

Television's picture of activity in the Loop was also made to conform to expectations already disseminated over the mass media. Even during the early phases of the telecast, when the crowd was just beginning to gather and little was happening, television personnel were already interpreting the crowd's motivations in accordance with their own preconceptions. Later they seized on anything that could be interpreted as enthusiasm. What television failed to catch entirely was the growing disappointment of the spectators. From beginning to end, television interpreted the event true to formula, that is, as dramatic, as colossal, and as personal tribute.

Visually, the television perspective was different from that of any spectator in the crowd. Making use of its mobile cameras, television could rearrange the event in its own way, using close-ups for what it deemed important and leaving the apparently unimportant for the background. There was almost complete freedom to aim cameras in accordance with news judgments. Moreover, the producer could shift to any camera that appeared to show something interesting. In this way, the technical possiblities of the medium helped to play up the dramatic at the expense of the routine. While the spectator, if fortunate, caught a brief glimpse of the general and his family as they passed, the televiewer found MacArthur the continuous center of attraction from his first appearance during the parade down State Street, at 2:21 p.m. until the sudden blackout at 3:00 p.m. For almost 40 minutes, not counting his 7-minute appearance earlier in the day at the airport and his longer appearance at Soldier Field that evening, the TV viewer could fasten his eyes on the general and on what could be interpreted as the interplay between a heroic figure and his "enthusiastic" admirers. The cheering of the crowd seemed not to die down at all, and even as the telecast ended, the cheering seemed only to have reached its crest. The cameras focused principally on the parade itself, so the crowd's applause seemed all the more ominous a tribute from the background.

The shots of the waiting crowd, the television interviews with persons within it, and the announcers' commentaries had previously prepared the viewer for dramatic developments. With the abrupt ending of the telecast at 3:00, the outcome was left to the inference of the individual. But television had already offered enough clues to leave little doubt about the course things were likely to take.

The daytime coverage of MacArthur Day lasted three hours. For over two of these MacArthur was beyond the range of the camera. This time had to be filled with visual material and vocal commentary. By far the largest portion of it was spent on anticipatory shots of the crowd. Nevertheless, the relative amount of time spent watching MacArthur, as opposed to the time spent anticipating his arrival, was much greater for the TV observer than for the spectator on the scene.

Television used this waiting period to build up the viewer's expectations. The parade schedule (that is, reports on the progress of the still invisible motorcade and MacArthur's expected time of arrival) was reviewed altogether 45 times. Reference to it took up 17½ minutes of the three-hour telecast. And while these references had the character of objective reports and enabled the viewer to maintain an overall picture of the event, they nonetheless contributed to the build-up.

Televised interviews had this same quality of "objective" reporting. They served for the most part to elicit the expectations of spectators, but could not yet show some of their disappointment. The criterion that seemed to govern the choice of interviewees and the choice of questions was in line with the public interpretation. Thus, out of 26 interviews, 8 were with official or semi-official personages, who in their capacity as sponsors presented the welcome as a nonpolitical outpouring of gratitude. Five others were with army men, several of whom had served on General MacArthur's staff. Thirteen were with civilians involved as mere spectators.

Interviews with officials all stressed that on this unique and great occasion Chicago was not to be outdone. Chicago had a Democratic administration, so that "officially" MacArthur Day was entirely nonpolitical and a matter for civic, rather than partisan, pride. The three police officials interviewed on TV emphasized the problems involved in controlling the spectators, as if there were a universal expectation that the crowds would get out of hand. There were additional interviews with Mayor Kennelly, with a representative of the mayor, with the president of the Gold Star Mothers, who was to participate in the bridge-dedication ceremony, with the Father of Prayers at the same ceremony, and with former Mayor Carter N. Harrison, who was emphatic that certainly not since the 1899 visit of Admiral Dewey had Chicago seen the like of this. Among the 13 civilians selected, 4 were veterans who were encouraged to state whether they had ever served under MacArthur—thus, by indirection, stressing a sentimental association with the event. Of these 13, 2 were out-of-towners, a much higher proportion than our observers were able to locate.

As far as the general tone of the interviews was concerned, one observer noted while watching, "None of them really say anything, because the announcer asks questions, answers them, and the interviewees merely nod confirmation."

The descriptions by the commentators (also reflected in the interviews) contributed to the restructuring of the day's events. The magnitude of the event, in line with preparations announced in the newspapers, was constantly emphasized. The most frequent theme was that "no effort has been spared to make this day memorable" (eight references). There were seven claims by announcers that they had "never seen the equal of this moment," or that it was "the greatest ovation that this city had ever turned out." The unique cooperative effort of TV was elaborated on five different occasions and was of course tied in with the "dramatic" proportions of the event.

Categorization and tabulation of every description was impossible. These ranged all the way from guesses about overcrowded transportation facilities and numerical estimates of the crowd to the length of the city's lunch hour and the state of "suspended animation" into which the business had fallen. Nothing, the commentators kept reiterating, was being allowed to interfere with the success of the celebration; even the baseball game had been cancelled. (But the day's activities at a nearby race track were not. When at one point in the motorcade from the airport to the Loop, a temporary traffic block resulted in a "captive audience," an irritated captive remarked, "I hope this doesn't make me late for the races.")

In addition to the factual fill-ins on the parade schedule, who was who, and the focus of the shots, two—and only two—aspects of the spectacle were stressed: One was the unusual nature of the event just described; the other the tension that was said to pervade the entire scene. Even the 11 references to the friendly and congenial mood of the waiting crowd portended something of the change that was expected to occur. Of 9 references to the orderliness, 7 were in the context of "control" and police action; 4 cited the patience of the crowd, as if it were about to end.

With regard to the crowd mood, the general emphasis was on tension and not on patience or congeniality. The announcer was explicit 20 times about such tension, whereas, in contrast, observers' reports failed to affirm that such a mood was in any way dominant. The announcer frequently made use of phrases such as "the air is electric," "there is the feeling you just can't wait," "never such a thrill," and so forth. These descriptions went much beyond what was shown on TV, but as the crowd mood could only be inferred, the announcer had a free hand in making the event appealing to the viewer. When there was little confetti in the air, "people were saving it" so that, the announcer predicted, during the parade it might black out the TV picture. If the crowd was well in hand, the viewer was reminded that in other cities this had not been so. The size of the police detail was repeatedly reported; the many boarded windows were taken as an omen, and the references to the bodyguard, whose presence was routine, took on its own peculiar signficance in such a context. Thus, in addition to direct references, the mood of the crowd was described in many subtle ways. The "happy enthusiasm" and "ardor" (three references) with which the crowd gave its greeting might have brought a sigh of relief to those anticipating "disorder"; and the cheering from the background could be interpreted as an overwhelming demonstration.

The combination of visuals and commentary in the television coverage also had a "personalizing" effect; it put the focus on MacArthur while allowing the background to remain obscure. The TV viewer had an extended opportunity to observe many little details about the general. Through television, the "very famous MacArthur wave" (the personal idiosyncrasy most frequently attributed to him during the telecast) joined the "scrambled-eggs cap" and the "battered trench coat,'' made famous by newspapers, as symbols visually associated with him. The ''already legendary charm and grace'' of Mrs. MacArthur also came in for mention. Yet, even MacArthur, who in the public mind (according to our observers' records) stood for a sober, austere, and heroic figure, could not hide an occasional smile from the camera. The announcers picked this up and interpreted it as the general's personal reaction to the reception. In this same way, his every move was under observation and enhanced by the commentary. MacArthur's gestures became as familiar as those of a film hero. Women could see him as a family man; see him, as a loving husband, kiss his wife during the evening cermonies; and observers noted that these incidents (especially the kiss) received much voluble and favorable comment in gathering places for public viewing. At such points in the telecast, the spectacle was obscured by this personal dimension.

In view of the selectivity of the coverage, with its emphasis on close-ups, it was possible for viewers to see themselves in a *personal* relationship to the general. For instance, during conversation overheard in bars with television,[2] people judged the appropriateness of MacArthur's behavior, his physical fitness (his failure to show fatigue), his family; they searched for a sign of humility or resentment on his face, a hint of gratitude at the reception or outward signs of the egotism and haughtiness imputed to him by his detractors. As the announcer shouted out, ''Look at that chin! Look at those eyes!'', each viewer, regardless of what the announcer meant him or her to look at, could seek a personal interpretation that expressed the real feeling underlying the exterior that appeared on the television screen.

It is against the background of this personal inspection that the signficance of the telecast must be interpreted. The cheering crowd, this ''seething mass of humanity,'' was fictionally endowed by the commentators with the same capacity for a direct and personal relationship with MacArthur as the one that television momentarily established for the TV viewer through its close-up shots. The overall effect of the televised event thus stemmed from a convergence of these two phenomena: the seemingly extraordinary scope, including the apparent enthusiasm of the public, and the *personalizing* influence just referred to. The spectacle was interpreted in a very personal nexus. The total effect of so many people, all shouting, straining, cheering, waving a personal welcome to the general, disseminated the impression of a universal, enthusiastic, overwhelming ovation for MacArthur and all he stood for. The selectivity of the camera and the emphases of the commentary gave the televised event a *personal* dimension, nonexistent for the participants in the crowd. It was a highly unique perspective, in sharp contrast to being there.

Other Exaggerations

Television confirmed expectations that the entire city would come to a standstill on MacArthur Day, but observer estimates of the crowd size and of the extent of disruption cast doubt on media reports that the millions of Chicagoans in the Loop might have been joined by as many as a million others who had poured into the city from the suburbs and adjoining states. For a further check on the discrepancies between the participant and television perspective, we used a number of indices to determine whether crowds and crowding were as expected: passenger statistics (obtained from the Chicago Transit Authority and suburban lines); spot checks in offices, restaurants, and parking lots; and the volume of sales reported by street vendors.

The results all substantiated the finding that MacArthur Day had been grossly blown up by the mass media. The most incontrovertible evidence came from the transit lines. The city and suburban lines reported only a very slight increase over their normal traffic loads into the city. The total increase in inbound traffic on streetcars and elevated trains was only about 50,000 passengers, some of this due to rerouting. The Chicago and Northwestern Railroad, a suburban service, put no additional cars on its trains. It estimated that passenger traffic was between 7 and 10 percent above normal, mainly wives and children joining the normal "male" traffic. The additional load of some 3,000 persons was easily handled within the morning rush-hour schedule. In contrast, the period between 1 and 2 o'clock in the afternoon (when the parade was going on) saw a tremendous increase over the normal load for that hour, but it was a rush *away* from the city. The railroad had advanced its normal rush-hour schedule by three hours, and the trains at the usual rush hour ran as they normally would have during the earlier hours. Obviously, most people who commuted regularly to the city had returned home as soon as their offices released them. These numbers suggested to a knowledgeable railroad official that practically all who saw the parade were Chicagoans. The same story was told by statistics from the Illinois Central, serving the southern suburbs, and from the Chicago Metro Coach Company.

These relatively slight increases in passenger traffic on public conveyances may reflect nothing more than a decrease in the number of private automobiles driven to the city that day. Warnings by the Chicago Motor Club to stay away had apparently been heeded. Our spot checks of parking lots showed that several, normally overcrowded, had a below-capacity load.

Checks at hotels indicated no unusual crowding. The influx from out of town failed to materialize. The YMCA, braced for an unusual demand for rooms, reported vacancies. Observations in downtown offices further confirmed orientations the media perspective did not acknowledge. Among the office staffs sampled, only a small proportion indicated that they intended to watch the parade, even though dismissed early for that purpose. Many office workers simply took advantage of the opportunity to catch up on their shopping or household chores, including some who, on previous occasions, had been outspoken in support of MacArthur and his views.

Business in parade souvenirs was far from brisk. Hawkers, who as professional parade-goers are rather sensitive judges of enthusiasm, called the parade a "puzzler." In spite of their aggressive sales lines, they had made few sales. One observer at different times took samples of fifty persons along one block on State Street; among those walking in the space between those leaning against buildings and those pressed against the curb, there was not a single button. Among those who were evidently spectators, 10 percent wore MacArthur insignia on their lapels. Another observer made extensive spot checks on sales. At the end of the parade, one vendor said "Business is lousy in buttons and flags. Up to now I haven't sold ten buttons," Another vendor said that "business has been fair. Nothing like Lindbergh." Two observers working independently wrote that in their vicinity the price of buttons had dropped from 50 to 25 cents even before the end of the parade.

The purchase and display of patriotic and political symbols is another indication of whether or not people in the crowd meant their presence to demonstrate their solidarity with MacArthur in the controversy that led to his dismissal and return to the States. Besides buttons, pennants, corncob pipes, and head bands, hawkers had "five-star" flags for sale. Of the 50 with which he had started out, one vendor said, he had sold all but 4. Actually, these were Confederate flags, but hawkers and buyers often thought they were pennants especially designed for a five-star general. This is significant in explaining the difference in the atmosphere experienced by our observers and the climate as reported by the mass media. Thus, CBS Washington Correspondent Charles Collingwood, on a regular newscast on April 19, had pointed to the "prevalence of Confederate flags" at MacArthur homecoming parades, which, he said, outnumbered the Stars and Stripes. Collingwood's interpretation failed to recognize that to most people the five-star flag seemed a special and fitting souvenir of the occasion. Instead he assumed that the choice of this symbol was deliberate and deduced from it that the MacArthur demonstrations derived their fervor from the opportunity for the expression of all forms of discontent and dissident views.

Detailed Illustration of the Contrast

The wreath-laying ceremony provides a graphic illustration of the contrast between the television experience and direct participation in the MacArthur welcome. The parade was scheduled to halt at only one spot, the Bataan-Corregidor Bridge. At a tricornered site near the entrance to the bridge, a platform had been erected. Here General MacArthur was to place a wreath under the memorial plaque, make a brief speech, and be greeted by a contingent of Gold Star Mothers. Seven of our observers were witness to the ceremony.

TV perspective: In the words of the announcer, the bridge ceremony marked "one of the high spots, if not *the* high spot of the occasion this afternoon. ... The parade is now reaching its climax at this point."

The announcer, still focusing on MacArthur and the other participating persons, took the opportunity to review the ceremony about to take place. . . . The camera followed and the announcer described the ceremony in detail. . . . The camera focused directly on the general, showing a close-up as he removed his hat and bowed his head during the invocation. He made a few remarks, looked very grave. "Those men who died were mine. I shall always hold them in my heart, inviolate and sacred. To their mothers and families who are here, I can only say that since they fell I have shared their sorrow."

"Thank you, general," added the announcer. . . . There were no shots of the crowd during this period. But the announcer filled in. "A great cheer goes up at the Bataan Bridge, where the general has just placed a wreath in honor of the American boys who died at Bataan and Corregidor. You have heard the speech. . . . The general is now walking back. . . . The general now enters his car. This is the focal point where all the newsreels—frankly, in 25 years of covering the news, we have never seen as many newsreels gathered at one spot. One, two, three, four, five, six. At least eight cars with newsreels rigged on top of them, taking a picture that will be carried over the entire world, over the Chicagoland area by the combined network of these TV stations of Chicago, which have combined for this great occasion and for the solemn occasion you have just witnessed."

During this scene there were enough close-ups for viewers to have a definite reaction, positive or negative, to the proceedings. They could see the general's facial expressions and what appeared to be momentary confusion. They could watch the activities of the Gold Star Mothers in relation to MacArthur and define these as they wished—as inappropriate for the bereaved moment or as understandable in light of the occasion. Taking the cue from the announcer, one could view the entire scene as rushed and out of line with the supremacy of the sacrifices being commemorated. But whether the event was viewed as *solemn* or not, the picture of a general being cheered—the cheer coming from an unseen crowd—while honoring the war dead could not be ignored. The cheer, whatever degree of enthusiasm it implied, had to be associated with the act and the actor just observed at close range by the televiewer. The relationship was a personal one, and the crowd activity, though unseen, was interpreted as similarly personal. It was possible to assume that the observer on the scene was, indeed, experiencing the same occasion.

Actually, this is the way what was meant to be a solemn occasion was experienced by those attending, an experience we call the *crowd perspective*: First, sirens were heard. Motorcycles followed by armed detachments and bands passed by. Observers differed in their accounts of the reception accorded these units in the parade. Notwithstanding the varying estimates of enthusiastic approval, the observers agreed that this was in large measure a response to the imminent arrival of MacArthur. As MacArthur's car passed, everybody pushed and strained to see. Getting a good view was the major preoccupation of the crowd. In one section, people standing on crates, the only ones who could see him at all, served as reporters for the rest.

"There was no loud cheering in our section" when MacArthur passed, wrote one observer. "Most people waved or clapped their hands. Some people in my area didn't do anything but look and press forward." Another observer reported "little cheering, some crowding," and still another—standing some 50 feet from the second observer—indicated that "MacArthur pulled up on us rather quickly, and there seemed to be more straining to see him than cheering. ...There were uncoordinated queries and yells heard. ...[MacArthur] climbed the stairs and received a little more cheering and hand clapping, while the people near me were still trying to find him."

The dedication ceremony, announced as a *solemn* occasion, aroused little of the sentiment it might have elicited under other conditions. According to one observer, "People on our corner could not see the dedication ceremony very well, and consequently after he [MacArthur] had passed immediately in front of us, there was uncertainty as to what was going on. As soon as the word came that he had gone down to his car, the crowd dispersed." Another observer could not quite see the cermony from where he was located, slightly to the east of the bridge. Condensed descriptions given by five observers illustrate the *confusion* surrounding the actual wreath-laying ceremony:

The ceremony was all but over before people realized what had happened. While MacArthur was engaged in the ceremony, the women caught a glimpse of Mrs. MacArthur and her son. "Oh, there she is! She has a purple hat!" one shouted. The little woman beside me now pushed forward, desperately trying to see. She smiled and waved, "There's Arthur with his cap. See him?" "I wish cops didn't have heads," replied another in a jovial voice. As MacArthur was returning to the stairs, he again received an ovation. This time it seemed stronger and more united than before. He waved and some people shouted, "Hi Mac" and "We want Mac." He got into the car and left, as the people strained to add a few inches in order to see the departing family. . . . The crowd began to disperse.

It was difficult to see any of them. . . . MacArthur moved swiftly up the steps and immediately shook hands with people on the platform waiting to greet him. There was some cheering when he mounted the platform. He walked north on the platform and did not reappear until some minutes later. *In the meantime the crowd was so noisy that it was impossible to understand what was being broadcast from the loudspeakers.* Cheering was spotty and intermittent, and there was much talk about MacArthur and Arthur.

A car pulled up with MacArthur in it. Several people got out, one of whom was MacArthur. They all climbed up on this platform. Our view was considerably obstructed. . . . *We could catch glimpses of MacArthur speaking and hear the mumblings from the loudspeakers, but could not understand what he was saying.* . . . After he finished speaking, he walked down the steps and got a big cheer. With many exceptions, the people near me hollered hooray or something of the sort. . . . As soon as the car pulled away, everyone turned and began to walk toward Michigan, evidently hoping to get another look at MacArthur when he passed the corner of Jackson and Michigan.

Many of the people could not see him. . . . *During the dedication ceremony the general was completely out of view.* His words were amplified, but the people about me did not seem to be listening— they wanted to see him.

Those who were not on boxes did not see Mac. They did not see Mrs. MacArthur, but only her back. *MacArthur went up on the platform, as we were informed by those on boxes, and soon we heard some sound over the loudspeakers.* Several cars were standing in the street with the motors running. . . . Some shouted to the cars to shut their motors off, but the people in the cars did not care or did not hear. Thus the motors stayed on. The people in our area continued to push forward trying to hear. When people from other areas began to come and walk past us to go toward the train, the people in our area shrugged their shoulders. "Well, I guess it's all over. That noise must have been the speech." One of the three men who had stood there for an hour or more because it was such a good spot complained, "This turned out to be a lousy spot. I should have gone home. I bet my wife saw it much better over televison."

For those on the spot, the solemnity of the occasion was thus overshadowed by the distraction of trying to catch a glimpse of MacArthur and his family. The distraction might have been less had the spectators actually been able to see the general. But even those who continued to try to hear could not comprehend the inarticulate sounds over the loudspeaker system. Regardless of the good intentions of the planners, solemnity was destroyed by officials in the parade intent on a time schedule and by cameramen recording the ceremony for the larger TV audience and for posterity. The witnesses often could neither see nor hear. But whether they did or not, there were few expressions of intense hero worship with overtones of nativism and political partisanship.

Instead, a crowd of disappointed spectators, cheated in their hopes of seeing a legendary figure in the flesh, was left behind.

Reciprocal Effects

We cite some direct evidence for the way in which television imposed its own peculiar perspective on the event. One observer at Soldier Field could watch both what was going on and what was being televised.

It was possible for me to view the scene [at Soldier Field] both naturally and through the lens of the television camera. It was obvious that the camera presented quite a different picture from the one received otherwise. The camera followed the general's car and caught that part of the crowd immediately opposite the car and about 15 rows above it. Thus it caught the part of the crowd that was cheering, giving the impression of a solid mass of wildly cheering people. It did not show the large sections of empty stands, nor did it show that people stopped cheering as soon as the car passed them.

In much the same way, the television viewer received the impression of wildly cheering and enthusiastic crowds before the parade. The camera selected shots of the noisy and waving audience. But in this case its presence directly provoked the activity on which it focused. The cheering, waving, and shouting was often but a response to the aiming of the camera. The crowd was thrilled to be on televison, and many attempted to make themselves apparent to acquaintances they knew to be watching. Beyond that, an event important enough to warrant the most widespread pooling of television equipment in Chicago video history up to that time gained thereby in magnitude and signficance. Casual conversation among the crowd kept on coming back to being on televison, and this was considered among the greatest thrills of the day.

To the restructuring of the event by the camera (through selection and the sequencing of shots) and the framing by the audio (the commentary and the interviews), we add the third important element: the power of television to generate activity. Its mere presence elicits responses that otherwise would not occur. Although we had not set out to look for this aspect of structuring by TV, almost every one of the observers recorded incidents in which participants in some way addressed themselves to the television audience.

To be on television, even as one among a vast number of people, meant something to most people. They continually nudged each other and grinnned, wondering what kind of image they might relay across the nation.

A camera truck came by with the lens pointing directly at us. The Roman Catholic priest said, "Now we're going to be on television."

Such interchanges were common. Television entered people's consciousness in many ways. Sometimes cameras helped the crowd to orient itself to important happenings they could infer only from the direction in which the TV camera focused. Some people chose their vantage point for the chance it offered to be on TV:

A small group of people gathered around the TV apparatus on the sidewalk, but on the whole the crowd was not deeper there than along the edge of the sidewalk. However, certain arrivals ... were heard to comment to one another that, if we go down farther, we can get into the picture.

More generally, when we say that television modified the event, we have an image of society as a network of personal and mass communication. Any new medium of communication does more than simply transmit knowledge and information. Once it enters consciousness, it affects the relationships among those who use it. These effects are reciprocal. The cheering into the camera and the choice of positions within the beam of the television camera illustrate this kind of effect in its most primitive form. The timing and exact scheduling, the haste with which the various ceremonies—at the airport and the bridge—were run through, and the complete inflexibility of the route suggest the staging of events for the benefit of radio and television time schedules. The event televised was no longer the same event it would have been had television not been here.

The reciprocal effects we were able to document on this occasion were ephemeral. Yet, at the time, the idea that such effects might occur was still somewhat novel. But in the years since MacArthur's glorious homecoming, the deliberate staging or reenactment of political events for television has often become the subject of controversy. One such flagrant violation of the ethical canons of TV journalism took place during the tumultuous Democratic convention in 1968. Urged on by camera men, street demonstrators re-enacted violent confrontations for the benefit of television.[3] But far more important than these improvisations in the pursuit of a TV story is the way that institutions, like the national nominating conventions, in changing their schedules and rules so as to attract audiences, have thereby changed the very nature of these proceedings. Political campaigns, legislative hearings, and even negotiations within and between governments have increasingly made use of the television forum with consequences that may or may not be beneficial. Publicity is a two-edged sword. What course, for example, might negotiations over the 53 American hostages have taken had there been no television to assure their Iranian captors that the eyes of the world were upon them? We will never know.

But of this, we can be sure: The world has changed because the wide and deep penetration of the television image gives events a new "bystander public." This does not mean that watching is the same as being there, only that participation in the event—whether as a spectator at a parade or a protestor at a demonstration—takes on a new meaning because the whole world is watching. Insofar as the political actor's participation in any televised event takes account of likely audience response, the effects of television are indeed reciprocal.

Political Perceptions and the Landslide Effect

The MacArthur Day study challenged the accuracy with which television and other news media portray public moods. News and special events coverage by television provide glimpses of the reality needed for intelligent participation in the political process. This includes the reality of public response to events and issues. However little contact they may have with the "public out there," ordinary citizen and professional politician alike constantly draw inferences about and respond to its dominant moods. Those who see themselves holding an unpopular view proceed cautiously: they are apt to remain silent rather than actively press their opinion on others. Contrariwise, those who perceive themselves, rightly or wrongly, to be in step with the majority are less inhibited.[4] Perceptions about the public temper reflect a climate of opinion, which enters into and, under some circumstances, exercises considerable influence on political activity.

Political actors are even more attuned to what they define as public opinion, especially to what the people in their constituencies approve and disapprove. Few slavishly follow momentary shifts as revealed in political polls. Yet, without such evidence, it becomes, at once, more difficult to predict the probable success of a given strategy and to justify it. Should one embark on a potentially risky course with no assurance that there is untapped support "out there"? Sometimes politicians even find it useful to fabricate overt expressions of supportive public opinion that make the course they are about to follow appear both reasonable and legitimate. What they seek is almost inevitably a simplified measure of public opinion that, in its concreteness, is readily grasped; the concept of public opinion as a collective image to which people are sensitized in different degrees has no statistical appeal. Not only politicians but also the editors and managers of the mass communication agencies, who cater to the interests, the visual images, and the analytic schemes of the anonymous John Q. Public, exhibit the same penchant for the measurable. It appears that they cannot function without resort to some overly simple assumptions, which are then reified. The issue we raise has less to do with the reliability of any one estimate of the state of public opinion (whether it comes from a poll or some similar data base) than with the compulsion to select out from among the many indices one (or a few) that get picked up by the press, are repeated and disseminated, until they take on an authority of their own and elicit responses at the several levels of the polity.

It is in this way that a "landslide effect" can result as media coverage of events and publc responses to that coverage reinforce each other. The kind of video coverage observed during MacArthur Day has the capability of setting in motion a sequence of mutually reinforcing and potentially self-confirming images of where the public stands. By selecting a limited number of manifestations of public opinion as symptomatic of public opinion, the press as a whole helps create a climate of opinion. Reactions to this climate can induce public figures to orient themselves to an image of public opinion rather than to the real opinion, until in the end this refracted image becomes the opinion toward which public figures orient their activities.

The episodes surrounding MacArthur's triumphal return have gone down in history as recorded by television and by print journalists taking their cues from the television coverage. The picture of public opinion conveyed was one of overwhelming support for MacArthur in his confrontation with Truman. Those dwindling few who recall these events will remember that the MacArthur testimony before Congress, which lasted an entire week, to be followed by that of Acheson and Generals Marshall and Bradley, seemed like an anticlimax to the dramatic events in the streets of San Francisco, New York, and

Chicago. Having held the limelight for somewhat over a month, MacArthur actually did go into military retirement. His subsequent attempts to re-enter the spotlight, or efforts by his admirers to force him back into the center of controversy, met with little success. Never again, until his death in 1964, did the general hold national attention as he had for several weeks in 1951. The conclusions we drew from our mass-observation data about the temper of the time appear to have been verified and the picture inadvertently drawn by the news media refuted. The official welcomes received by MacArthur were spectacles rather than political occasions.

To be sure, a false impression of public opinion, such as that created by the television coverage of MacArthur Day, can always be counteracted by other indicators such as polls. Usually these measures appear *after* the events and do not have the same persuasiveness. Moreover, public opinion polls are likely to reflect the effects of media coverage. When people sense that other people are almost of one mind on an issue, they are less likely to register their dissent. Thus, the polls may only add to an existing impression.

MacArthur Day is but one case of a landslide effect that resulted as media coverage of events and public responses to that coverage reinforced each other. Television disseminated an image of public sentiment that was overwhelmingly in favor of the general and, by implication, his politics. This effect gathered force as it was incorporated into political strategy, picked up by other media, entered gossip, and thus overshadowed reality as it was experienced by observers on the scene.

A landslide effect is cumulative; it builds as assumptions about reality lead to acts that reinforce the definition as reality. Newsmen, in planning the coverage of a public event, make certain assumptions about their medium, about what viewers expect, and about what will hold their attention. An industry that puts great stock in audience ratings wants to assure steady interest. So the MacArthur Day telecast was made to conform to the newsmen's notions of viewers' expectations. In line with the assumed pattern, the commentators steered clear of political issues and avoided offending any viewer. Viewers were expecting a dramatic occasion, so drama it had to be, even at the expense of reality. Camera, commentary, and, to some extent, the spectators' consciousness of being on television helped to make the television event dramatic. Two characteristics of the TV presentation enhanced the dramatic impact of what was seen and heard and thereby contributed to the misevaluation of public sentiment.

First, the depiction of the ceremonies mainly in terms of unifying patriotic rather than potentially divisive symbols left no room for the depiction of dissent.

Second, and more important, the television presentation enlarged the viewer's field of vision but not the context in which he could interpret the event. The viewer could see the entire crowd, and, from above, it appeared as an impersonal and overwhelming force hardly subject to the influence of any one person, unanimous in its enthusiasm. Unlike spectators in the crowd who could exchange views with the five or ten people around them, the viewers were completely dependent for their understanding of the crowd mood on what they saw and on what the commentator said. They could be everywhere the general was and see the responses to the general at every point along the parade route. The viewers' was a unique perspective. Riding with the general along the crowded parade route, they experienced the hero's welcome. They saw a mass of humanity pushing and rushing to get near the general. But they never got the true picture from television of what it meant to be a bored and often disappointed spectator who had come out to participate in an exciting and historic occasion.

NOTES

1. Silas Bent, *Ballyhoo: The Voice of the Press* (New York: Boni and Liveright, 1927).

2. Since in 1951 far from all homes had television sets, bars were for many the place to watch television.

3. See Daniel Walker, *Rights in Conflict: The Violent Confrontations of Demonstrators and Police in the Parks and Streets of Chicago During the Week of the Democratic National Convention of 1968* (New York: Bantam, 1968).

4. Solomon E. Asch, *Social Psychology* (Englewood Cliffs, N.J.: Prentice-Hall, 1952) ch. 16; and Elisabeth Noelle-Neumann, *Die Schweigespriale* (Munich: Piper, 1980).

3

The First Televised Conventions

1952

The Republican and Democratic party conventions held in Chicago between July 7 and July 26, 1952 were the first genuine "television" conventions. To be sure, there had been an earlier experimental telecast of the 1940 Republican convention; the Democratic convention held in Philadelphia in 1948 had also received partial coverage, but the audience was limited to those within receiving range of the TV signal—the audience's size was estimated at a mere 1.25 million viewers. Hence, the nominating conventions of 1952 set new precedents in that they were the first to be telecast *in their entirety* over a national hookup and viewed, according to claims by the networks, by some 65 to 70 million people.

These conventions became a proving ground for producers, reporters, cameramen, and politicians. Not one of the networks appears to have fully anticipated the conventions' long hours. Of the three networks, only ABC had committed itself in advance to cover the proceedings from "gavel to gavel"; CBS had said it would carry a minimum of 20 hours of each convention and NBC that it would carry at least 30. Ultimately, all the networks stayed with the proceedings far longer than they had bargained for.

Several sessions lasted into the early hours of the morning; one (during the Democratic convention) went nonstop for 14 hours. No network dared to cut away from the conventions as long as its competitors were covering them. In the end, *all* networks not only offered full gavel-to-gavel coverage, but they also provided briefings before and usually after each official session; they also covered considerable portions of the hearings before the credentials committees, hearings conducted partly before the conventions had officially convened and partly while they were in recess. The entire coverage of the Republican convention on each network amounted to approximately 70 hours; that of the Democratic to 77.

The convention telecasts underline what was at the time called the "miracle" of television—its ability to bring the political arena directly into the home. It was widely agreed that "the television audience saw more of the conventions than the average delegate—who, like the soldier on the battlefield, could only grasp the event which occurred near to him."[1] The networks congratulated themselves on a job well done. Thus, the Radio Corporation of America, some weeks after the conventions, congratulated itself in a large ad:

> "With the aid of television, we had what amounted to the biggest town meeting ever held. . . . sixty million people had front-row seats and got a better picture of what was going on than any delegate or any reporter on the convention floor. . . . Because of television, American citizens will be better informed than they ever were before. . . . They will be able to vote for men and principles, and not for party labels" (New York Times, August 19, 1952).

Television newspeople usually insist that they are doing the same thing as their print colleagues. They think of themselves as reporters covering an event or story. If television differs from other reporting, the difference lies in the opportunity to use the technology of the medium as an ally. The truth is told *through*, rather than *over* the medium. But television has always been something more than simply a passive transmission device. Its presence entered the consciousness of the convention in many ways both before and during the proceedings. Thus, Chicago had been chosen as the convention city with an eye to allowing audiences on both coasts to watch the evening sessions at hours consistent with normal time schedules. Likewise, the conventions were held at the International Amphitheater, in preference to a larger hall, because of its better air conditioning, but especially because of its more adequate facilities for televising. During the convention, the proceedings were altered in a number of obvious and not so obvious ways. For example, the Democrats, having found that officials' activities in focus behind the speaker's rostrum distracted considerably from what any given speaker was saying to the television audience, introduced a screen shutting these activities out of view. The presence of television was invoked by several convention speakers, and campaign managers were happy to have themselves interviewed whenever it seemed to suit their purposes. Many delegates (and press reporters) used TV to keep themselves informed.

The Republican Convention

The convention[2] that met from July 7 through July 11 and nominated General Dwight D. Eisenhower as its presidential candidate was involved in a bitter dispute between two wings of the Republican party. Since Eisenhower was subsequently elected, and re-elected, by a very substantial margin, it is hard to remember how touch-and-go his nomination was, how exciting the balloting at the convention, how intricate the events and maneuvers by which Eisenhower emerged as the victor in Chicago.

The contest at the Amphitheater, whose outcome was witnessed by the TV audience, had been squarely joined for some months. Both Eisenhower and his opponent—Senator Robert A. Taft of Ohio, who had earned for himself the name of "Mr. Republican"—had come to Chicago with sufficient support to sense victory. What transpired during the five days of Republican convention can only be understood as the culmination of developments that had been in process for some time.

Eisenhower had been one of the most popular World War II military heroes, but unlike MacArthur, his popularity had not been linked with any particular political persuasion. His appeal was essentially nonpartisan.[3] He had been widely discussed as a possible candidate for both the Democratic and Republican tickets in 1948. In the spring of 1952, after nearly a year of uncertainty during which it was not at all clear whether Eisenhower would even accept a "draft," he was finally induced to campaign actively for the Republican nomination. His "active seeking of the position" was necessitated by Senator Taft's evident success in a systematic quest for delegates. By early summer the senator had pledges for something like 550 votes of the 604 he would need to win.

The support Taft enjoyed among Republican stalwarts, particularly in the Midwest, had enabled him to wrest control of the Republican party organization from Governor Thomas E. Dewey of New York, the man who twice before, in 1944 and 1948, had suffered defeat in the presidential election. Taft had used his control of the party machinery to install his own supporters as key convention officials. He had successfully installed both the temporary chairman and the permanent chairman of the convention. His friends and supporters predominated among the scheduled speakers and appeared to be in firm control of the Credentials Committee, which had to pass on the right of all delegates to be seated at the convention, and of the Platform Committee responsible for the drafting of the party program.

Taft's opponents saw this success in corraling pledges and delegations and control of the convention machinery as a steamroller. It had to be stopped, and the opportunity to do so seemed to present itself when the Taft forces moved into Texas to round up a delegation that would support their candidate.

It is well known that in these years of a solidly Democratic South, the Republican party in most southern states was almost nonexistent between elections. It surfaced every four years to play a role in the selection of a presidential nominee and, because of its normal shadowy existence, was usually torn by factional strife over who was properly entitled to represent the wishes of the constituencies at the national convention. The Taft forces were able to win out in Texas, even though the Eisenhower candidacy had considerable popular support among a large group of voters who, though previously registered as Democrats, were politically closer to the Republicans and ready to convert if Eisenhower were the candidate. Some of these Democratic cross-overs had spearheaded the Eisenhower campaign in Texas. The issue of the eligibility of the Johnny-come-lately Eisenhower supporters to help select the instructed delegates had already been fought out. The Eisenhower forces had made effective use of the news media to focus attention on a procedural issue that ordinarily would have been of little more than local interest. When a slate of delegates favoring Taft won out, the Eisenhower managers had their issue. They called the outcome a "theft of delegates" and sent Eisenhower into Texas to call for "fair play."

"Fair play" in this context had a very specfic meaning, one that was often lost on the public. The issue was whether members of this disputed delegation (and of other delegations whose credentials were challenged) were entitled to vote upon the credentials of *other* delegates whose accreditation by the Taft-controlled committee might be challenged from the convention floor. Precedent was clear only on their ineligibility to vote on the matter of their *own* seating. However, Dewey and other Eisenhower campaign managers were able to convert this political dispute into a more general issue of political morality. If these disputed delegates could vote on any other dispute, they argued most persuasively, this would not be fair play. By chance, the annual meeting of governors of the then 48 states took place in Texas shortly after the Republican state convention. Under Dewey's leadership, the pro-Eisenhower governors succeeded in soliciting a call from other Republican governors for a fair play amendment to the rules of the national convention. This then set the stage for the video drama in Chicago.

The first convention forum to hear the case of the disputed delegations was the Taft-dominated National Committee. When the committee refused to open its hearings to television, the "Eisenhower commanders simply stood aside while the new but powerful television industry, jealous of its rights, turned its full rage upon the committee. The din was so great that most Americans undoubtedly felt that an effort was being made to hold the hearings in secret. Actually they had always been open to the press. The Taft majority in this case were old-fashioned rather than malicious; one Taft official complained, 'Next thing we know they'll bring a printing press into the committee room.'"[4]

The issue of the "Texas steal" and fair play so effectively dramatized by the Eisenhower forces led to an important concession even before the convention got under way. Of 38 Texas delegates, 16 were conceded to Eisenhower. There were reports that in an effort to avoid a showdown in front of TV cameras, the Taft forces had offered further concessions, in a conference just behind the speaker's platform, just about the time the convention and the convention telecast were to start.

The convention itself was a clear two-way contest that involved two tests of strength, as a result of which the outcome of the one and only ballot for the nomination became successively more predictable. The first test vote came at the televised opening session on Monday, July 7, when Governor Langlie of Washington, an Eisenhower supporter, offered his Fair Play Amendment asking that any delegation contested by more than one-third of the National Committee be disbarred from voting on the seating of other delegations. He spoke at least as much to the television audience as to the delegates on the convention floor. An amendment to this amendment was offered by Taft-man Clarence E. Brown of Ohio, whom some commentators later called the "goat" of the convention for his evident tactical blunder. He only muddied the issue for everyone by calling for the exemption of seven members of the disputed Louisiana delegation whose credentials had not been challenged under the Fair Play rule. After a long debate, the Brown amendment was put to a vote and defeated. The Fair Play Amendment was passed shortly thereafter.

The case of the disputed delegations next came before the convention's Credentials Committee. In fully televised hearings, the Taft forces, having been made to look like the bad guys, gave further ground. Nevertheless, when this committee's final report came before the convention on Wednesday evening during the sixth session, there was a second test of strength. Despite an eloquent speech by pro-Taft Senator Dirksen of Illinois, all decisions on disputed delegates by the Credentials Committee favorable to Senator Taft were reversed by a vote from the floor, and Eisenhower delegates were seated instead.

Eisenhower's nomination on the only official ballot of the Republican convention, following, as it did, the two previous test votes was really a third rather than a first ballot for the nomination. The real turning point had come two days before, with the resolution of the seating dispute that more or less determined who would win. There were, to be sure, other aspects to the dispute that arrayed the Republican Old Guard against those attempting to give the party a new image; it also had elements of confrontation between the traditional isolationist wing of the party with its roots in the Midwest and the newer breed of internationalists. Nor do we wish to downgrade the moral and legal substance of the hotly contested procedural issue. Yet regardless of what the delegates may have meant to signify by their vote (be it their support of fair play at the convention or some other cause), the import of every vote was to move Eisenhower closer to the nomination he sought. To be against fair play on television was, in the words of one commentator, like trying to commit grand larceny in broad daylight. But was it really larceny? In their ability to cast the issue in this light, the Eisenhower forces showed themselves to have mastered the new medium of television. By their manipulation of the television image, they put every delegation under pressure to do nothing that might give the appearance of not playing the political game by acceptable rules.

The Democratic Convention

Ten days after the Republican had concluded their convention, the Democrats opened theirs in Chicago. Meeting from July 21 through July 26, they nominated as the standard bearer of their party, Governor Adlai E. Stevenson of Illinois, who until that time had been practically unknown to the general public outside his own state. The viewer who had followed the Republican proceedings had the advantage of some elementary familiarity with the organization and procedures of a political nominating convention. But this apparent advantage was more than offset by differences in the major plots of the two conventions, particularly by the complexity of the maneuvers among the Democrats, who—it has always been recognized—manage to enjoy themselves more in being politicians.

While the Republican convention was essentially a straight fight between two leading contenders, there were five Democrats (not counting favorite-son candidates) who came to Chicago actively seeking the nomination. At the head of the pack was Senator Estes Kefauver of Tennessee, star of the televised hearings on organized crime and subsequently a winner of primaries in several states, who came with the largest block of committed delegates. Senator Richard Russell of Georgia was the South's candidate. There were also Senator Robert Kerr of Oklahoma and former Mutual Security Adminstrator Averell Harriman of New York, as well as the septuagenarian Vice President Alben Barkley of Kentucky who withdrew his candidacy just before the convention when several labor leaders refused him their support because he was too old. And then there was the candidacy of Adlia Stevenson. Despite his unwillingness to do anything personally to advance his own candidacy, he had never shut the door altogether on a genuine draft and his enthusiastic volunteer followers had set up campaign headquarters on the 15th floor of the Conrad Hilton Hotel.

Whatever happened at the Republican convention could be understood simply by establishing some linkage to the two-way contest between ''Ike'' and Taft. The viewer, on either side, could readily identify the good guys, the villains, and the fence-sitters. Among the Democrats, however, the various lines of division on candidates and issues tended to criss-cross and shift. It was sometimes difficult to fathom the composition of any temporary coalition or to assess the implications of any vote for the fortunes of any candidate. As Richard Rovere put it, ''At the Republican Convention, there seemed to be something like a plausible connection between the candidates and the ideas they were supposed to stand for. Among the Democrats this year, not only at their convention, but during the whole preconvention campaign, the connections existed but they did not seem very plausible.''[5]

Shortly after the convention opened, a group of young Democrats, who came to be identified as the ''liberals,'' began rallying support for a resolution that would require all delegates to sign a loyalty pledge as a condition to their being seated. The avowed purpose was to prevent a recurrence of what had happened in 1948, when in some southern states, the name of President Harry S. Truman, who was running for reelection, had not appeared on the ballot as the Democratic party candidate. But the move was also meant to reduce the influence of some southern conservatives in the selection of a nominee. Delegates likely to bolt to Eisenhower, the liberals reasoned, should not be permitted to stymie the selection of a truly liberal candidate.

The resolution asked that delegates promise to use "all honorable means" to see that the name of the convention's nominee was on their state ballot. This wording was adopted without a roll call in the first evening session on Monday, July 21. Continued protests by some southern state delegations who had voted against the pledge led to a further compromise—a proviso that this pledge would be binding "for this convention only." Nevertheless, Virginia, South Carolina, and Louisiana still refused to sign. Early on Thursday evening, July 24, when the major but not yet the minor nominations for President had been made, the question of the right of these three states to participate in the official proceedings was raised once again and brought to a vote over the seating of the Virginia delegation. The vote was a long and drawn-out affair with many delegations asking to be polled. (Some delegates, it was alleged, wanted to be seen on television back home.) The turning point came after Pennsylvania and Illinois, two key delegations in which Stevenson sentiment was strong, surprisingly reversed their prior vote and decided in favor of Virginia. The trend in the vote, which at first had gone against seating, was quickly reversed as other delegations also changed their vote. South Carolina and Louisiana were seated shortly thereafter.

That same evening, just before balloting for the nomination was to begin, those backing the loyalty pledge moved to adjourn the convention. Although the motion was defeated, the convention nevertheless adjourned until the next day after a fire had started on the convention floor and the fire chief pointed to the hazard caused by the many newspapers and other litter strewn about.

Next day, Friday, July 25, two slow ballots, in which Kefauver, Stevenson, and Russell led the field, occupied the entire morning and afternoon. After a dinner recess, Harriman and Dever (the favorite-son candidate of Massachusetts) announced their withdrawal in favor of Stevenson. The third ballot was likewise a protracted affair, lengthened by continuous requests for polling of delegations. At the end of it, Stevenson was nominated and came to the Amphitheater to deliver his celebrated aceptance speech at so late an hour that the television audience was minimal.

The dispute over the loyalty pledge was the key to understanding the Democratic convention, but it was only during the roll call vote on the seating of the Virginia delegation, on Thursday the 24th, that its precise relationship to the fortunes of the various candidates had gradually become evident. Until then it had been rare for commentators to identify a single candidate with any tactical move. Instead, journalists' interpretations of the seating dispute had relied on such themes as the traditional North-South cleavage, attempts to secure unity at the convention and avoid a permanent North-South split, young and ambitious amateur politicians fighting the old pros, liberals versus conservatives, an endeavor to force party loyalty on those whose affiliation with the national Democratic party appeared to be purely nominal, and improving the chances of electing a Democratic President by advance assurance that the nominee's name would appear on the ballot in all states. Only during the balloting on Thursday night did the stop-Stevenson forces begin to label the move to seat Virginia as a move *by* the Stevenson forces. The motion to adjourn, made moments later, then became a test vote between the Stevenson supporters and a temporary coalition formed by Kefauver and Harriman backers for that evening.

Yet television did not always stress the implications of these events for the outcome of the convention. Not only was there considerable confusion over the significance of what had happened on Thursday night, but the clear ascendancy of Stevenson between the second and third ballots on Friday, while the convention recessed for dinner, remained to many a puzzle. In scrutinizing how some episodes during the Democratic convention were handled by television, we were less interested in the capacity of television to dramatize the role of particular individuals, than in how disparate events could be linked by commentary so as to affect the viewer's interpretation of those events. Through these linkages television structures an event. This symbolic construction of reality occurs even where news personnel are positively committed to objective reportage.

Refraction

The 1952 conventions helped set the style for the televising of future political conventions and other major political events. Then, and ever since, the three major networks—ABC, CBS, and NBC—have pooled their coverage of the main proceedings. Six cameras of the pool were placed inside the hall, three of them facing the speaker's platform and three the crowd within the convention hall. Two other cameras were parked at the entrance to the hall, where they could catch delegates and candidates as they arrived. A single pool director made the decision as to which of the images from the pool would be available to networks at any time.

How such camera selections can result in the refraction of an event has already been discussed in connection with MacArthur Day. We need only reiterate here that a pooled coverage helped make that event witnessed over television considerably different from the same event experienced by participants. During the political conventions, the common coverage extended only to the six cameras positioned so as to cover the official proceedings on the convention floor. In addition to its contribution of equipment and personnel to this pool, each network also came to Chicago with its own contingent of commentators, reporters, and technicians. It was through the deployment of personnel and equipment outside the pool that a network could display ingenuity and initiative.

In the first place, each network developed its own sources of information. Even when two networks were transmitting the identical picture, their interpretive comments might diverge considerably. In the second place, editors in the network studio always had the choice of substituting the video from their own cameras. Thus, networks were free to insert interviews from their studios or from any one of the many hotel suites and lobbies open to camera crews; they could focus on activities and demonstrations in lobbies or outside the Amphitheater. They could scan the convention floor from cameras in their own booths high above the convention floor and zero-in on particular individuals, usually when they were being buttonholed by their own network reporters. With their mobile equipment they could even go right onto the convention floor for special pictures without disrupting the proceedings. For example, NBC put much stock in what it called its "walkie-lookie," a battery operated camera, a newly designed TV version of the familiar walkie-talkie. Equipment was primitive and bulky by present-day standards.

In the precedent-setting televising of these conventions, each network's decisions on how to deploy its own equipment, its commentary, and the extent to which it stayed with the pool and the main proceedings or substituted sideshows, followed a pattern that was both similar to and different from that of the other networks. This pattern reflected the network's policy with each decision a clue to its operating code. Decisions based on cultural definitions of propriety, on shared professional self-images of TV personnel as members of the press, and on the inherent capabilities and limitations of equipment resulted in similarities among the networks. At the same time, different images of the audience (whether correct or not) and differences in organization, skill, resources, and so forth introduced idiosyncratic elements into their coverage. Each network selected different camera shots and filled in with individual comment that stamped its own mark on the finished product.

A quasi-experimental situation that arose during the heated dispute over seating at the Democratic convention gave us the opportunity to study the impact of these decisions on the television image of the event. Our analysis was based on two kinds of data. The first consisted of a record of the TV content of each network, based on tape recordings of the commentary and minute-by-minute descriptions by monitors of the video image. Second, we had comments, recorded blow-by-blow as they watched, which represented what they believed they were witnessing at any particular time. We also had some observers in the galleries of the Amphitheater and at places of public TV viewing (for instance, bars), but our coverage from these vantage points was too spotty to permit any systematic analysis.

The monitoring records provided what was, for us, persuasive evidence that the commentary on the three television networks sharing the pooled video coverage had given, in each case, a significantly different structure to the event. As a consequence, persons watching on each of the networks got a different idea of what was going on and what to make of it. In the following pages we let the reader reach the conclusion with us that the different interpretations reflect an unwitting bias on the part of the telecasters and, further, that this bias can in part be attributed to differences in the telecasters' judgments of their audience.

The period subject to intensive analysis began at 4:56 p.m., Thursday, July 24, and lasted until 1:07 the next morning. Our analysis begins at the point during the roll call on nominations for the presidency when Louisiana, one of the states that had refused to sign the so-called loyalty pledge, yielded to its co-rebel Virginia for a parliamentary inquiry about the status of nonsigners in the convention. A ruling by the chair, that they could not vote unless they signed the pledge, was reversed after a drawn-out roll call characterized by considerable vote switching. Virginia, South Carolina, and Louisiana, the three noncomplying states, were seated during this session, but not until after Senator Paul Douglas of Illinois had started a dramatic attempt to halt the proceedings by moving for adjournment. The verbal fireworks were finally interrupted by a genuine fire on the floor of the convention. Panic was narrowly averted by a Massachusetts delegate who seized the only open mike and "talked the fire out." After it was extinguished, the debate went on but briefly. Notwithstanding a prior defeat of the move to adjourn, just a little while after the fire another adjournment motion was suddenly recognized and quickly gaveled through.

During this period the television coverage of these episodes by the three networks was—as we have indicated—being monitored for visual and verbal content, and almost all of it was audio-taped. (Videotape was still in the future). In addition, monitors were encouraged to record (where and when possible) their own interpretations of what they were seeing and hearing. At the time, the monitors did not consider these periodic interpretations as data that would be subject to systematic analysis. Nevertheless, the use of these comments as data resulted in an interesting observation: *the monitors on CBS gave a significantly different evaluation of the evening's activities than monitors on ABC and NBC.* The question was, what had led to this differential effect?

One monitor's notes, jotted down just after the close of the session at about 2:30 a.m., summarized the conflict in interpretations: all three persons monitoring CBS thought that with this attempt to force an adjournment "Douglas had made a fool of himself." Their resentment centered on the "so-called liberals"—notably Kefauver of Tennessee—who "would do anything to stop Stevenson."

> They saw the roll call on the move to adjourn as a "test of strength" on part of the Kefauver-Harriman forces versus Stevenson. . . . They felt that the move to keep the Dixiecrats out—at this point—was only a political maneuver on the part of the Kefauver-Harriman forces.

NBC monitors were equally resentful, but in a different way. As far as they were concerned, Chairman Sam Rayburn and cohorts had put on a bad show, had,

> shoved the southern states in, . . . They recognized that politics were involved, but never thought of the vote as a simple "test of strength."

A check with monitors of ABC revealed their attention, like that of the NBC viewers, had been focused on the chairman's part in the proceedings. They had viewed the event as the attempt of a "Stevenson-Byrnes coalition against Kefauver" to achieve "unity at any price."

In view of the reasonable homogeneity of backgrounds and outlook among the ten monitors, the resulting differences could not be seen as the influence of individual preconceptions. Recruited from a group somewhat above the usual college age—most of them veterans of World War II, all but one working on or having obtained graduate degrees in the social sciences—they individually rated themselves politically sophisticated. This self-judgment was borne out by an evaluation of their past exposure to conventions, interest in news media, and political experience and knowledge. They were all strongly opinionated in favor of the Stevenson candidacy, with only one favoring Eisenhower over Stevenson among all possible candidates of either party.

Also controlled was the monitors' exposure to earlier telecasts of the Republican convention. All had an opportunity to compare and evaluate the quality of coverage on each network. This enabled them to assess, accept, or discount the particular emphases of each. Again, the explicit monitoring instructions assured a constant and comparable amount of attention from each person. Because during the period analyzed the networks relied heavily on pooled video coverage on the floor, televiewers on the different networks were exposed for the most part to the same visual image. The effects of cutaways, since they were few and brief, should have been minimal.

It therefore seemed a legitimate assumption that significant differences in group interpretations and understanding resulted from a difference in network commentary rather than from camera choices or from distinctive frames of reference with which our monitors approached the telecasts. The inherent open-endedness in each of the episodes during the evening's telecast further supported this view. Being unusually complicated and full of surprising turns, the episodes were open to varying interpretations. The commentary of each network, during the period in question, was meant to fill in the information on convention procedures and backstage developments that might help to understand the developing strategy. The differences in commentary thus reflected the telecasters' conception of what interested the audience and what they needed to know in order to follow.

Yet when we scrutinized and compared the commentary on each of the networks, we were surprised to find that neither the amount of information nor the basic facts differed in any essential way. As a result, we were led to look in a new direction, namely at the manner in which the various televised episodes were *linked* to prior events and to events outside the range of the cameras. The context so created could well account for variations in viewers' interpretations of the same events. The same overt elements could be put together into a number of different configurations.

Here is a schematic picture of how this might occur. First, the *interpretation* given to a particular incident (or the *lack of interpretation*) affects the viewer's focus of attention. Similarly, the *timing of information* also contributes to the formation of a frame of reference into which subsequent incidents are fitted. However, once this *frame of reference becomes crystallized*, it tends to overshadow subsequent information so that new and contradictory information will be ignored. Also, a network's tone or attitude toward the convention can have certain subtle effects. We might call this the *style of coverage*. These elements together encourage viewers to interpret a complex and confusing event in a particular way. This structuring, although the result of certain policies, has results that may not be intended by news personnel or even anticipated by them.

An analysis, episode by episode, of how the events on the Thursday night of the Democratic convention were reported by each network should clarify how the divergent definitions by viewers of these same events were a result of decisions that inadvertently gave these events different structures.

(1) (4:56-7:30 p.m.) *The Rayburn ruling.* The seating fight really began with the calling of Louisiana, which yielded to Virginia for a parliamentary inquiry. Neither state had signed the loyalty pledge. In answer to a request for clarification and after some wrangling, Rayburn ruled that failure to sign excluded Virginia from participation in the official proceedings.

Monitors. During this phase, all three networks let the video carry the story. Monitors' attitudes toward Rayburn had not yet crystallized. Since it appeared that some real issues of the convention were about to be tackled, expectations were high and attention still centered on the delegations and on the impending fracas. Sinister motives were not yet imputed to either side, and the struggle was among political groups with conflicting aims, among whom Rayburn was trying to mediate.

Networks. Orville Freeman, chairman of the Minnesota delegation, immediately rose to protest Virginia's parliamentary inquiry. ABC did no more than identify the person rising. All other ABC comment was restricted to, "This is democracy in action." CBS, even before Freeman spoke, indicated his intention to "make the loyalty-pledge business a floor fight." In contrast, NBC, having cut away from routine floor proceedings for a regular news program, inadvertently missed the beginning of the action. Brought abruptly to the convention floor in the midst of what appeared as an uproar, the NBC viewer's only orientation was this brief introduction:

Rayburn is confused. A row has started. Minnesota and Michigan won't let Rayburn make the rules.

Yet there is reflected in these initial introductions the fundamental outlook of each network. From the outset, the viewer of ABC was led to the *dramatic*, the NBC viewer to the *personal*, and the CBS viewer to the *political* content of any developments. The action centered on Rayburn during this initial phase, and there were frequent close-ups of him on the screen, so interpretations of his facial expressions in line with the tone set by each network were soon suggested to viewers.

A second influence on content was the failure of NBC to depict the beginning of the episode. The confusion resulting from the late start, and the lack of a complete fill-in, was compounded by the commentator's insistence that he shared the viewer's confusion.

(2) (7:30-7:50 p.m.) *Appeal of Rayburn ruling from floor.* After Rayburn's ruling, the calling of the roll of states for nominations continued. When Maryland was called, Sasscer moved to seat Virginia and thus override Rayburn's ruling. Rayburn, in turn, ruled the Sasscer motion out of order, but this was immediately appealed and a roll call demanded on the appeal.

Networks. During this 20-minute period, particular differences in the emphases of the three networks began to emerge. ABC let the action speak for itself by having the pool cameras and microphones bring it into focus. The CBS commentators, on the other hand, interjected constant pointers about the roles and positions of various floor leaders shown on the screen, who, unmentioned, might have escaped notice. Meanwhile, NBC stuck to easily identifiable, personal content, referring repeatedly to Rayburn and the confusion of the moment. For example:

Really getting involved now. . . . It'd take a couple of Philadelphia lawyers to straighten this out now. . . . Rayburn getting assistance again [he was consulting with Cannon, the parliamentarian] . . . big problem now. How does anyone know who is a delegate or not? [during a standing vote on a demand for a roll call]. . . . So many interpretations and motions and points of inquiry now that it's a little difficult to keep them all straightened out.

Monitors. The differences in what was accentuated may appear trivial, but resulting differences in viewer orientation can be documented from the notations made by monitors. As the pool camera lingered over a huddle in the New York delegation, those watching NBC saw the delegates arguing and contributing to the general confusion. CBS monitors perceived the huddle as a conference of floor leaders formulating some undetermined strategy (the nature of which

Table 3.1   Schematic Presentation of Network Emphases During Seating Fight

ABC	NBC	CBS
1. THE RAYBURN RULING (4:56 - 7:30 P.M.)		
Video carries the story, but commentary provides first clue to subsequent differences.		
Drama: Orville Freeman, "This is democracy in action."	*Personalities:* Rayburn "confused"; a row has started (as the camera misses initial motion).	*Political strategy:* Orville Freeman will make a floor fight on loyalty pledge.
2. APPEAL OF RAYBURN RULING (7:30 - 7:50 P.M.)		
Video carries story. Commentary stays out of "drama."	Confusion. Commentator takes role of the viewer.	Commentary identifies floor leaders and their position on seating issue.
3. ROLL CALL ON SEATING VIRGINIA (7:50 - 9:55 P.M.)		
(a) Expectations begin to structure interpretations.		
Principled fight over ruling to seat Virginia.	Is Rayburn fair? Fight over Rayburn ruling on seating Virginia.	Strategy of coalitions between backers of major candidates.
(b) Illinois switch (8:39) holds key to understanding on all networks.		
North vs. South (8:41 - 8:45)	"Hidden pressures" and "peculiar rulings," etc. (8:55)	Stevenson forces support seating, but he disavows complicity (9:19)
(c) Linkage supplied by commentary.		
Quick flashes, no general commentary.	Commentary governed by video coverage of floor.	Commentary is linkage between floor coverage and unseen context.

Table 3.1   Continued

ABC	NBC	CBS

4. NOMINATION ROLL CALL RESUMED (9:55 - 11:45 P.M.)

Overtones in commentary give individual color to broadly similar context.

ABC	NBC	CBS
"Hot news" of Stevenson disavowal of complicity (10:25) Resentment at Arvey-Byrd deal and at Rayburn's tactics. Harriman-Kefauver will try for adjournment, which Rayburn will overrule.	Ill will of "liberals" vs. "Dixiecrats" and "bossism." Recess is move against Stevenson and bossism; Stevenson disavowal (10:40) Senator Humphrey will demand roll call to offset gallery shouting.	Convention leadership expects to finish two ballots tonight. Opposition concedes them strength to do so. "So-called liberal coalition" needs time and will use adjournment move as a "test vote" of strength.

5. THE ADJOURNMENT ISSUE (11:45 - 1:07 A.M.)

Prior context determines ultimate interpretations.

(a) Douglas calls for adjournment.

ABC	NBC	CBS
Clash now open.	Senator Douglas and "liberal" backers fight "pressures."	"Kefauver-Harriman liberal coalition" moves to adjourn.

(b) Meaning of vote on adjournment.

ABC	NBC	CBS
Anti-adjournment votes are mostly from South or for Stevenson.	"Go home" vs. stay and get more accomplished.	Vote to adjourn for Harriman or Kefauver, vote to stay for Stevenson.

(c) Overall interpretation.

ABC	NBC	CBS
Changes in fortunes are indicative of some big (Stevenson-South) "deal" taking place "behind the scenes."	Focus on confusion and emotions on floor suggests arbitrariness of rulings in interest of South and bosses.	Political strategy called for a test vote of strength on the move to adjourn.

they tried to surmise); in other words, it was interpreted as part of the overall contest. Monitors covering ABC evidently failed to take any cue whatsoever from this huddle, for in their attempt to understand the fast-moving proceedings they focused almost exclusively on Rayburn and other convention officials.

In the same way, the standing vote and the uproar that followed the demand for a roll call served to confirm, in the absence of clarification, the picture of confusion previously conveyed on ABC, while Rayburn's temporary hesitation in ruling on the roll call conveyed a personal image of a man taken aback by what appeared incomprehensible. The NBC commentator, taking the role of his audience, explicitly shared the personal bewilderment of the soft-spoken Rayburn with them. He suggested no adequate basis for the subsequent ruling to allow the roll call; no cues were conveyed, so that the decision could only appear arbitrary. But for our CBS viewers the uproar was packed with political significance. Since they could identify the contenders, the picture helped to provide them, even in the absence of specific network interpretations, with indications about possible partisan considerations prompting this particular contest. They scanned the action and the actors for hints about the ultimate alignment in the nominating ballot.

(3) (7:30-9:55 p.m.) *The roll call on seating Virginia.* The roll call from its outset was interrupted by inquiries about the motion, by temporary passing, by drawn-out polls of delegations. During its second hour, when defeat of the motion to seat Virginia seemed almost certain, numerous switches turned the "no" majorities into majorities in favor of seating.

Context of expectations. The expectations and sensitivities built up during the preceding episodes tended to structure the meaning attributed to the voting. ABC and NBC had emphasized Rayburn's personal and official role in the convention and, as a consequence, unwittingly defined the dispute as a principled fight over his ruling. But the CBS commentary, by supplying basic information about the parties to the dispute, had moved questions of political strategy into focus. Thus, a rumor concerning a pending Kefauver-Harriman coalition was reported equivalently on all three networks. Yet only CBS monitors, their sensitivities sharpened to such clues, were able to connect this information with the floor proceedings. The CBS monitors—but none of the others—took the vote of Tennessee, the only southern state solidly against seating, as a clear test for the existence of such a Kefauver-Harriman coalition, even without guidance from the CBS commentary.

The switch (8:39) in the Illinois vote (initially 45 to 15 against seating, then 52 to 8 in favor) signaled, according to all three networks, a significant change in fortune. At this point it became apparent that more was going on than met the camera eye, and all networks ultimately developed a very definite interpretation of just what was going on.

Network interpretations. Until the general switch of votes became apparent, ABC had explained the vote four times as "determining the seating of Virginia." More detailed political interpretation at that point alluded to the contest as North versus South. For instance, spotting Jim Farley at 8:41 (two minutes after Illinois' change), an ABC commentator explained:

> I imagine the confusion and division in this convention hurt Jim [Farley] very severely... Yes, that's Jimmy Byrnes. He's perhaps masterminding the whole affair. It was to anticipate that possibility of a southern revolt led by Byrnes that's caused the North to act as it did.

A few minutes later, at 8:46 it was considered.

> very interesting how many states not connected with the South...Midwest, Indiana, Illinois—where there is considerable southern influence—are going with Virginia. Considerable whispering and *conferring*—you see Missouri, a border state, evenly divided.

NBC repeatedly (six times) stressed the confusion, attributing it to delegates not knowing what they were voting for or to such specific causes as the unit rule and half votes. Or it was simply called "general confusion." The significance of the vote was explained *only* in terms of seating Virginia. Not until some 16 minutes after the Illinois switch did NBC begin to emphasize "possible pressures on delegates to switch their votes" in favor of the seating. There were no fewer than 13 references to such, by inference, hidden forces: "pressure from somewhere"; "peculiar rulings that have been made"; "lots of persuasion used apparently"; and so forth.

The interpretation on CBS was limited, until 9:19, to a reportage of voting procedures, to indications of the trend in favor of passage or defeat, and to two references to the "party unity" at stake. From 9:19 on, the CBS commentary concentrated on explaining (by collating reports from various sources) the reason for the switching:

> [We're going to] try and make some sense out of what's been happening the last few hours.... The Illinois group...changed...and we're told at the suggestion of Jacob Arvey.... The Illinois move

is interpreted as a tip that the Stevenson forces—at least the floor managers for him right now—want Maryland's motion upheld. . . . Stevenson issued a statement that if he [Arvey] did that, he did it without the governor's permission.

According to CBS, Francis Myers, the Stevenson floor manager, had explained that he had been working for the switch because the electoral votes of the South would be very important in the coming election. Other VIPs in the party were mentioned as helping in the effort to seat Virginia. Interviewed by a CBS reporter on the convention floor, Senator Clinton Anderson of New Mexico took credit for having encouraged Senator Russell Long of Louisiana, who had personally complied in signing the loyalty pledge, to cast the entire vote of his delegation in favor of seating Virginia.

The ambiguity of the contest was particularly well suited to bring out differences in the networks' presentation. The underlying issue could be seen as liberal resentment against the more conservative South; or resentment by supporters of the loyalty pledge against a supposedly arbitrary ruling by Rayburn; or an effort to assure Democratic electoral votes in the South; or a test vote by forces behind particular candidates to seat or unseat a delegation whose votes might matter.

Linkages. By examining how the ambiguity of the floor contest was resolved, we can see how the structure peculiar to each style of coverage emerged. Thus CBS relied on the political acumen of its viewers and, wherever possible, tried to supply politically relevant information. The viewer was thus encouraged to see this as a political contest, and the interpretations of CBS viewers reflected this emphasis. Every event was endowed with a meaning that, in principle, at least, was accessible. Where political guidance was lacking, as on ABC, the unfolding convention plot appeared merely as an attempt to bring order out of chaos. Because the workings of the convention were mysterious to ABC viewers, the forces at work seemed sinister and clandestine. In the face of quick but unintegrated news flashes by various ABC reporters, the puzzle took on the semblance of an evolving mystery. The only continuing interpretation referred to a North-South contest.

The contrast in content between CBS and ABC is reflected in the definitions by our monitors. A monitor on ABC saw all the switching after the Illinois vote in terms of Rayburn's efforts to placate the South. Rayburn's straightforward inquiry as to whether any other delegation wished to change its vote (8:48) elicited these comments:

> Rayburn *obviously* extending the roll call to placate the South. He is very anxious about this. Very little fill-in [by commentator] about Rayburn's obvious attempt to keep the three states in [some 13 minutes later].

Whereas on ABC these notions about sinister activities were simply inferred from the lack of explanation and the quick shift of fortunes, the NBC commentator deliberately shared the viewer's imputation of dark forces behind the confused events. Referring to Rayburn, the NBC commentator said:

> Every time someone requests a poll they can't find Sam Rayburn . . . . He has other things on his mind. [Rayburn had walked off the platform moments before and returned immediately after this commentator's remark.]

Some attention was also given to Farley, a veteran Democratic "boss," "talking and arguing to beat the band" about an unidentified subject matter.

When, after the Illinois switch, NBC began to talk of pressures and persuasions, the fact that the Illinois chairman, Jacob Arvey, was known to be a leading Stevenson proponent implied an unholy alliance between his group and the southern old guard. Any huddles caught by the camera were repeatedly taken as a sign that something was afoot, something that was not quite cricket, a meaning that was indeed absorbed by the NBC monitors.

Another crucial factor in the emergence of divergent definitions was the timing of certain interpretations. Thus, on NBC the idea of a Stevenson-South deal went unrefuted for some hours after the Illinois switch. On CBS, news of the Stevenson disavowal of complicity in the switch was reported while balloting was still in progress. It therefore helped shaped partisan definitions of the switch. Both ABC and NBC announced the Stevenson disavowal only some time after the balloting had ended and the issue was resolved—at least temporarily. Moreover, during the next episode ABC followed the news of the Stevenson disavowal with a report of how Arvey, "the boss of Chicago," had made a deal "on behalf of Governor Stevenson to keep the South in, and they, in turn, are supposed to vote for Stevenson later in this convention." The impact of the ABC and NBC reports of the Stevenson disavowal was lost, and the Illinois switch left the impression of an engineered attempt to force through a unity candidate.

(4) (9:55-11:45 p.m.) *Nominations roll call resumed.* The nominations roll call and the routine demonstrations for favorite-son candidates were resumed after this interruption of some three hours, during which the convention successfully appealed the chair's ruling not to seat Virginia. All three channels used this resumption of the nominating roll call to analyze previous incidents and to bring the viewer up to date on plans for an adjournment move, which each network anticipated about an hour before it occurred.

Networks. There were no apparent differences in the information offered by the networks. Nonetheless, the preconceptions on which each network based its own coverage are clear.

ABC may have failed to analyze the maneuvering and switching of votes during the Virginia roll call, but it explicitly related all this to a deal within a half-hour after the result in favor of seating the noncompliant delegates had been announced. The commentary coupled delegates' resentment at a "so-called Arvey-Byrd" deal with resentment at Rayburn because he had "not counted votes fairly but gaveled through certain proposals." ABC's first anticipation of the move to adjourn (10:45-10:49) was fitted into this context. Resentful Harriman-Kefauver forces were said to be trying for adjournment on this premise.

They claim there is so much confusion. It is only fair to give them a chance to talk things over. I predict Rayburn will overrule it [the motion to adjourn] and the session will go on all night.

Later, ABC reported a strategy conference called by a group of self-styled liberals and addressed by Hubert Humphrey of Minnesota; these "Liberal-Kefauver forces" (as Humphrey referred to them) were going to call for an adjournment until twelve noon because they needed time to rally their forces. "Watch," said the commentator, "for the strategy to develop on your screen." Directly following this report, ABC interviewed McKinney, chairman of the Democratic National Committee, on the plans for the rest of the evening. Said McKinney:

A move on foot to recess. . . is to the interest of a particular candidate, not to the interest of the convention. [We're not] going to recess.

The NBC treatment of the interim period was quite similar, except that the continuous talk about "hidden pressures" did not disclose their nature and origin; these continued to be left to the viewer's imagination. Two hours after the vote change, the viewer was told only that ill will had been engendered by the "*mysterious* shift of the Illinois delegation." This "ill will" was borne by "liberals" and directed against "Dixiecrats" and "bossism" (rather than being related to a North-South fight or Kefauver-Harriman strategy, as on ABC). NBC quoted several delegates to the effect that Rayburn's ruling on Louisiana was part of bossism and a deal with the Dixiecrats. Of the background strategy meeting, NBC first told its listeners:

[The] effort to get a recess. . . of short duration for caucuses. . . [is] to burst the Stevenson balloon. . . and also to burst this control that the liberals are claiming that the bossism people have taken over here at the convention.

Later, Humphrey, in a televised interview, was asked, "Why are you planning this adjournment move?"

We need the adjournment. . .has been emotion and tension. . .terribly wrong to drive through any kind of final vote on our nominee tonight. . .We'll use a roll call because I want the delegates in this convention to run the convention. I love the galleries and all the fine people who are working on the floor of the convention, but. . .on a voice vote you have people joining in just because they like to shout.

Meanwhile, CBS continued to emphasize the political strategy involved. It reported that the "leadership" expected to go ahead with the balloting after nominations had been completed. Mike Mansfield of Montana, presiding at the time (11:28), was reported to have said that the convention would go through two ballots. Senator Blair Moody of Michigan, an acknowledged leader in the move to stop the seating of Virginia, had remarked "grimly" to a CBS reporter "that it looks as if they will continue balloting tonight."

The strategy meeting of what it referred to as the "so-called liberal coalition" was placed by CBS within this same context of candidates' chances. Its leaders were said to be determined to keep the convention from going ahead to a ballot. Humphrey had said, "We need time to regroup our forces. . .will use this as a *test vote of strength*." The significance of such a move was clearly noted by a CBS commentator upon hearing this intention:

> If it becomes part of the tactics of the Stevenson and liberal bloc forces to take different sides, it might well be a simple *test vote of strength* to adjourn. That might be one for the books.

Summarizing the contrast in commentary: ABC now explicitly saw the move to adjourn in terms of Kefauver's *political* fortunes and the need to rally forces, rather than as a North-South contest. It was predicted that Rayburn, a southerner from Texas, whose "fairness" had already become a major issue for ABC monitors, would simply rule the move to adjourn out of order. The viewer was invited to watch the drama unfold. NBC, in line with its policy of supplying a minimum of interpretation, relied largely on Humphrey to clarify the intended move and, through him, thus further paid tribute to "pressures." On CBS the contest was clearly between the convention leadership who opposed adjournment at this time and the ''so-called liberal coalition'' determined to use, if necessary, a roll call for adjournment as a test vote of its (and, by implication, its opponents') strength.

(5) (11:45 p.m.-1:07 a.m.) *The adjournment issue*. As the chairman recognized Governor Battle of Virginia just 15 minutes before midnight, Senator Douglas could be seen waving a banner and shouting with the support of others, ''Mr. Chairman!'' Douglas, in an aside, could be heard to remark, ''I seem to be having some difficulty although they're looking me straight in the face.'' Douglas led his associates in continued shouting, disrupting the other business, and repeatedly asked whether the chair would recognize his motion to adjourn. Rayburn, calling a motion to table, did after some ado grant a request from Senator Lehman of New York for a roll call on the tabling of the motion to adjourn. The roll call itself was drawn out by repeated polls of large delegations designed to stall the proceedings, by attempts to challenge the legality of Rayburn's rulings, and by a number of minor wrangles. At the end of the vote, it was evident that the strategy of the Kefauver-Harriman group to force an adjournment and so prevent the convention from going on that night to a ballot for the nomination had failed.

Networks. Each network commented in its own characteristic way on the angry outburst of Douglas to get recognition from the chair. Having anticipated the adjournment move, ABC gave no further explanation of the strategy involved. Pointing to Douglas trying to get Rayburn's attention, the commentator said, ''*You know why*. They want to ask for a recess. . . . Since you folks at home know what is going on *behind the scenes*, you know the conflict now is between Senator Douglas and the chairman.'' Twice thereafter ABC reminded its audience that the recess had been asked for by the ''Kefauver-Harriman forces'' who needed time for some ''fence-mending.'' In line with its emphasis on exclusives and its search for the inside dope about the convention, ABC also made three references, while the voting was in progress, to some ''big deal.'' After a vote change by Kentucky on the motion to table, the viewer was told, ''When something happens that we don't see or hear about. . .you can count on it that something must have happened.'' Later this was elaborated as the probability that a deal between the South and Stevenson backers might be shaping up. At the beginning of the vote the opponents of the adjournment had not been identified, but later it was made clear that they were mostly from the South or Stevenson backers.

On NBC the emphasis was on the liberal backers of Douglas. The context had previously been supplied: the Douglas-Liberal group needed time to fight certain pressures working to advance the Stevenson candidacy. After midnight the NBC viewer received no guidance as to the purpose of the move. The issue was presented simply as one between those who wanted ''to go home'' and those who wanted ''to stay and get more accomplished.'' As before, the commentator pronounced himself overwhelmed by the confusion. He continued to read ''human emotions'' and motives into facial expressions of key figures, but beyond the human drama, no significance was imputed to the progressing roll call.

CBS emphasized the Kefauver-Harriman tactics throughout, most often designating the group as the ''Kefauver-Harriman-Liberal coalition,'' for which Douglas happened to be the spokesman. The commentary on this network had a simple theme: ''A vote to adjourn is a vote for Harriman-Kefauver; a vote against is for Stevenson.'' It described the complexion of the political coalitions and their motives much as did the other networks, but the idea of a *test vote of strength* among the leading candidates was unique to CBS. It limited itself to factual fill-ins. After Douglas had shouted to protest, CBS explained that ''the chair has refused to recognize Senator Douglas.'' During the vote, the ''yes'' people (in favor of tabling the motion to adjourn) were pointed out as generally for Russell or Stevenson, but such information was not interpreted for the viewer. Nor were there any references to a deal. Yet the idea of a test vote of strength de--emphasized political and moral issues and focused attention on the tactics employed by each side and their chances for success.

Monitors. CBS monitors, in a final evaluation of the adjournment move, called it a tactical maneuver by the Northern liberals who had behaved very badly and forced Rayburn to act as he did. The NBC monitors were furious at Rayburn and felt that they ''had never seen anything like that.'' In part, they echoed the commentary, although they had repeatedly discounted it as ''stupid.'' Some examples of their on-the-spot interpretations:

> Is this a Rayburn move to keep the party all sewed up tight?
>
> Is Rayburn in cahoots with someone...?
>
> Here it seems impossible to tell how many were for and against. When asked about vote on roll call, says there were not one-fifth of delegates, but it looked like many more.

This emphasis led pro-Stevenson monitors on NBC to favor the adjournment move as a justified ''protest'' against Rayburn's actions.

ABC monitors, like those on NBC, also focused on Rayburn. One summarized the epilogue during which Louisiana and South Carolina were seated:

> The Byrnes-Stevenson coalition is satisfied since Byrnes will support Stevenson, a moderate civil-righter. So ''unity'' wins out! The candidate will satisfy the majority of this coalition party.

The North-South axis of the struggle and the hint of inside dope on ABC led this pro-Stevenson monitor to condemn that candidate—temporarily.

The Inferential Structure

Some of our monitors were most critical, to the point of annoyance, at the commentary. Nevertheless, they tended to accept interpretations that were not in line with what they would have wished to believe. Such a finding has an obvious bearing on any evaluation of the role of television in forming political opinion. It caused us even greater consternation when we found, from systematic content analysis, that essentially, the *same range of meanings* and the *same factual information* had been available to viewers on each of the networks. The only theme exclusive to one channel was the CBS view of the adjournment move as a deliberate ''test vote of strength'' and its refraining from alluding to deals. The overwhelming similarity of manifest content led us to look for more subtle ways in which commentary could generate a conception of the convention that permeated its entire coverage. The coverage, judged by usual indicators, was not biased. Still, when the same elements were combined into different configurations, viewers on the different networks drew different inferences, even if this was not in any way the intent of the network. We have labeled this configuration the *inferential structure* of the telecast.

The seating dispute and the subsequent move to adjourn the convention illustrate how such inferential structuring can unwillingly introduce rather striking biases into the information conveyed over television and influence how an event comes to be defined, even though the realistic weaving together of many visual elements into focus *while* it is happening remains one of the main goals of TV reportage. Most TV news staff are convinced that they can do this better than other media, because television adds to the spoken or written word the element of actuality as the unique characteristic of its visual dimension.

In the case of the Democrats' seating fight the structuring resulted from newsmen's assumptions about what information was salient at any moment and through their choice of themes to depict the mood of the convention. Although such assumptions have much to do with the journalists' own definition of the event, they are not impervious to judgments about what will appeal to audiences. The precise strategy by which to implement a general standard of objectivity (neutrality) is closely linked to these definitions, and each network developed a policy of what to show (floor proceedings or background and personalities), what background and interpretation to provide, when to provide it, and how to link together the diverse aspects of the complex convention story.

One approach aims at objectivity and neutrality by exploiting television's potential for the "instant reply," by giving anyone involved or directly affected a chance to confirm, refute, or elaborate on other reports. An alternative is to take literally the notion that the picture speaks for itself. This allows an anchor or reporter to take a back seat, making the most of the actuality and filling in only when it appears absolutely necessary. What may be called ''focus in depth'' is a third alternative. It, too, makes use of actuality, except that the news staff frames the event by providing what it deems the indispensable context for understanding what is being shown. Each of these has its potential pitfalls.

What follows are thumbnail sketches of three definitions of objectivity and how they affected interpretations viewers obtained from having watched different networks. The characterizations, based on how the networks functioned during the 1952 conventions, are mostly matters of emphasis. They should not be taken as absolute or as statements of how they function today.

The instant reply. Live coverage can elicit immediate reactions from relevant participants as long as there are arrangements for direct transmission from the chief points of interest where news is likely to break. The mobility of resources can be exploited to give participants an opportunity for input. During coverage of a convention, contenders and their managers can refute rumors, dispute uncontested claims, or evaluate one another's strategies. This certainly adds to the drama. It also lets viewers follow developments from a number of angles and, where there is doubt or difference, puts them in a position to judge.

> We thought of sideshows more often than the others. We were always looking for new angles that hadn't been thought of before.
>
> We thought many times that floor-time—straight coverage of the convention floor—was wasted time and we could do better by going behind the scenes. But we did things behind the scenes only if they were newsworthy.
>
> You were always supposed to be looking for a story. Through our five or six reporters, we could cover any point at which a story developed. We worked as a news service. We tried to cover all angles of the convention wherever there was the greatest news interest.

The main point was to get the jump on the other networks. ABC, at the time limited by its smaller staff and unable to compete with the other networks in terms of gadgetry, tried to win audience attention by emphasizing action, wherever it might occur. Thus it supplied a paucity of information during high points, relying on the picture and sounds of floor activity to hold the viewer's interest. But when the convention proceedings appeared to bog down, ABC tried to maintain the drama by shifting to stories and special features dug up by its news staff. They "tried to make more of a show out of the convention, instead of simply allowing it to run its course."

Thus, the decision to make a play for the sideshows was deliberate, but ABC did not have many alternatives. It was competing against more established networks, and all its network affiliates were in multichannel communities. Consequently, it had to try to draw its audiences away from other stations. Whenever the floor proceedings were dull, it reasoned, or whenever there was a commercial, viewers would flick the dial to another channel to see what it was showing. Ultimately they would stick with the network that brought them the best show. Thus, ABC styled its coverage, not vis-à-vis the newspaper that could serve as ally, but largely in terms of the networks with which it had to compete.[6]

ABC also gave its commentators considerable prominence. "Our staff of commentators was the best advertised, both with regard to quality and quantity. . .and we had all sides, all shades of opinion represented. Big names among your commentators are important. We had them. We could, for example, present a commentary by _____ then balance it with an interpretation from _____ ." ABC also would balance a specialist on the human side of the news with a specialist on the science of politics, each giving his own slant. Balance and objectivity were maintained by giving equal exposure to all sides.

These frequent shifts of focus may have increased the suspense felt by the audience, but this was often at the cost of an integrated interpretation. Thus, unexplained picture material that did not lend itself to a ready interpretation only compounded any confusion viewers may have experienced. These shifts made them more disposed, as during the coverage of the seating fight, to accept explanations of mystifying turns in terms of behind-the-scenes and kingmaking activities.

To the extent that ABC emphasized the action of the convention, the central figure during the action on Thursday night was Chairman Sam Rayburn. Whatever and whoever was shown on the screen, he was a constant landmark. Given no guidance by the commentator during the early part of the evening, monitors centered their attention on Rayburn and ignored some of the other key figures. As the picture of the floor communicated to the viewer was one of confusion, Rayburn's rulings began to appear as personal arbitrariness, and by the time background and interpretations were supplied, the viewer had been so completely oriented by references to the "unavoidable North-South conflict," the "puzzling Illinois switch," and "backroom strategy" that they fitted into a picture of sinister forces at work outside the range of the TV camera.

The picture worth a thousand words. If one compares the television coverage of a political event to that of the printed media, the prime contribution of the camera is immediacy, not contextual coverage. Accordingly, television tells the story as it happens, without any editing and with comment on the picture limited to what is absolutely required. Interpretation and context will be provided by the newspaper (or news magazine). Editorials and columnists offer comments and opinion, while news articles provide interested readers with analysis in depth.

Here is how one network NBC executive justified their policy of minimal interpretation:

> We are forcing the newspapers more and more into a position where they *have* to give interpretation. . . . .For example, during the Nixon speech [the famous Checkers speech of the 1952 campaign], we brought it as it happened while the newspapers satisfied the want for interpretation—what it meant, its significance, and other evaluations. People want newspapers to fill in. . . . .We tell the running story, whereas the press ties up the story.

Following this practice, commentary by NBC was deliberately held to a minimum to let events at the Republican and Democratic conventions tell as much of the story as possible. Commentators were cautioned against doing too much "explaining of the picture." One informant recalled that, on at least one occasion, ‘‘We told the announcers to keep quiet to let the picture speak.’’

This network tried as much as possible to simplify the story of the conventions. It wanted, in particular, ‘‘to show the audience that these politicians were just people.’’ This goal was implemented by assigning the anchor man a rather limited function. The network put him in the control room, where he could look at the monitor, and laid down the

> policy that, as a TV commentator, he should not talk about things that are not seen. . . . Our feeling about [this man] was that he really knew politics and the people in it. In our view, the role of a commentator is that of a friendly but knowledgeable man.[7] He is to be the same as a person sitting next to you, watching the set with you. To be sure, he has more knowledge and experience and he supplements the picture, even if it is merely identifying the figures on the screen.

Along the same line, cutaways for interviews or special commentaries were to be offered only when they would not disturb the continuity of the event and so interfere with the viewers’ efforts to think things through for themselves. Interpretations in depth were generally relegated to on-air time before the sessions or, in the case of an episode that clearly acquired amplification, *after* the action had more or less terminated.

> This notion that ‘‘the job of TV [was] . . . to stay with the convention as much as possible . . . emerged in the course of covering the first [Republican] convention’’ without any explicit discussion or final decision. [We, the authors, asked whether this policy had been based on any indicators of audience reaction, such as phone calls from viewers.] Complaints (as well as praise) of all kinds were received, but policy was ‘‘first to let the audience know that the floor was dull before we cut away for something else.’’

In line with this policy, the principal NBC commentator steered clear of lengthy political analysis. He referred to himself as ‘‘sitting in a 20-foot cubicle, watching the same picture as you are,’’ repeatedly expressing bewilderment at what was going on, marveling at

Rayburn's "quick decisions" and his "ability to count" the number of voice votes and standees. This personalization of politics through the use of human-interest angles tended to transform tactical maneuvers among the contending factions into issues of faith and distrust of the leading personalities, in this case of Sam Rayburn. Yet Rayburn's actions were not entirely comprehensible to the uninitiated. Seen in personal terms, Rayburn's heavy-handed denial of a request for adjournment appeared to viewers as arbitrary.

Hence, Rayburn's personal motives came gradually to be interpreted in the light of the commentator's repeated references to unseen pressures—whose nature was never specified—and accumulating ill will. Like monitors on ABC, our NBC monitors were suspicious of and puzzled by maneuvering beyond their comprehension. However, NBC monitors had the assurance that the network commentator shared with them both their image and their confusion.

Focus in depth. Neither a near-simultaneous juxtaposition of divergent viewpoints nor maximum exposure with minimal guidance will assure that a correct political meaning will be read into a televised event by its audience. To present a picture of complicated events in some depth requires a well-organized reporting system. To paraphrase, things are not just what is seen. Only on the basis of available reports can directors decide where to send their cameras and how best to fill in the pertinent facts for the viewer. The idea that TV is just the picture was emphatically rejected by a number of newsmen we interviewed as an "untrue shibboleth"—the transmission of actuality requires "proper presentation and interpretation." In fact, one CBS producer said, "You can be no better in your televising than the reporting to the top."

The CBS coverage in 1952 was aimed explicitly at what one of their top producers called

a reasonably adequate picture of the whole complex of the convention.

We wanted a political coverage of the conventions. . . . We reported seriously and concentrated on the political meanings. We refrained from interviews with purely human-interest appeal—humor and so forth. . . .It's not up to us to make it a good show. It's not a show but a convention. Our job was to let people know and help them to understand what was going on at the convention.

CBS used its commentary to supply the necessary context, though it did not ignore special interviews or live shots of events off the floor. Studied objectivity is required in factual and interpretive commentaries, and the right kind of pictorial material must be available.

CBS sought to cover the convention as a news service would. Information was channeled through a central point where various reports were collated and, if used, their source was identified for the viewer. Throughout the long evening, CBS never let its viewers forget the political implications of the many moves on the floor. It attempted to identify each maneuver and with an occasional fill-in tried to make some sense of what was being shown. In this way it disseminated the idea that every development had some explanation. As a consequence, viewers saw more and were better able to exercise their own judgments. The incidents appeared to monitors to occur in a much more rational—albeit political—atmosphere, and they interpreted what they saw accordingly, namely as a showdown among several factions with Rayburn trying to mediate.

Conclusion

Even when journalists largely abrogate to the camera the responsibility for reportorial accuracy, picture selection and commentary can affect audience understanding of complicated and ambiguous incidents. Our study demonstrated that this can occur without any deliberate intent on the part of the commentator to put across a specific interpretation. Rather, the specific slant each network gave to the proceedings at the nominating conventions hinged on assumptions each made about its audience.

How different assumptions can lead to different interpretations has been documented in the instance of the Democratic seating fight. There a quasi-experimental situation allowed us to link the differences in styles of network reporting to differences in meanings conveyed.

From the perspective of history, these differences in meanings may appear trivial and politically insignificant. Nevertheless, viewer interpretations have a special authenticity, for viewers—especially in the live coverage of events—believe they have "seen for themselves"— they are unaware they have been influenced by the style of coverage. Back in 1952 viewer perceptions of sinister forces (the "hidden hand of Truman and Democratic bosses") behind the Stevenson nomination did not help the Stevenson candidacy and surely contributed to his devastating electoral defeat in November. In explaining what happened during the course of the convention, 64 percent of a sample we interviewed after the convention spontaneously cited the then-unpopular Truman as the principle kingmaker. Actually, Stevenson's nomination is generally regarded as the result of a genuine draft.

Finally, an ironic note on the effect of television coverage on the national nominating convention as a political institution. We have quoted the CBS producer insisting that the convention was not a show but a convention, that it was not the job of the networks to make it a good show. Yet, over the years, the political parties have more and more staged and produced their meetings to make them good shows for television. Speeches have been pared to the bone; polling of delegations takes place off camera; special films touting the party and the candidates are ostensibly shown for the benefit of the delegates but crafted for transmission (at the network's expense) to the millions watching; keynote and acceptance speeches are prescheduled for prime time. Where there is no contest for the nomination (as in 1972 when Richard Nixon was renominated) the entire production can be scripted in advance, with all major business scheduled for prime time. In that case, the networks are, in fact, transmitting not a convention whose main purpose is to choose a candidate but a political show designed to serve as the first major event in the electoral campaign.

With the focus of the presidential nominating process transferred, especially since 1972, to the state primaries and the likely party nominee all but a foregone conclusion by convention time, the television industry has become ever more reluctant to invest huge amounts of time and effort into transmitting what is less a genuine political event than a staged political show. For the first time, in 1984, there were no plans to let the public see for themselves in their entirety the final rituals of the nominating process.

NOTES

1. David G. Williams, "Choosing Presidential Candidates," *Political Quarterly*, 23 (October-December 1952): 368.

2. For a more detailed historical account of the Republican and Democratic conventions of 1952, the reader is referred to Paul T. David, Malcom Moos, and Ralph M. Goldman, *Presidential Nominating Politics in 1952* (Washington, DC: Brookings Institution, 1954).

3. Herbert Hyman and Paul B. Sheatsley, "The Political Appeal of President Eisenhower," *Public Opinion Quarterly*, 17 (Winter 1953-54): 443-60.

4. Williams, "Choosing Presidential Candidates," 371.

5. "Letter from Chicago," *New Yorker* (August 2, 1952): 50.

6. Sixteen years later ABC broke with tradition and announced it would not attempt full coverage of the 1968 nominating conventions.

7. In these days—and for years to come—there were only anchor*men*.

4

Ordeal Before Television

THE KENNEDY-NIXON DEBATES

In 1960, Richard M. Nixon and John F. Kennedy were the first presidential candidates to appear together before the television cameras. Four times—altogether four hours—within a span of four weeks they answered questions put to them by a panel of four newsmen. These "debates"—broadcast live—were major campaign events. In their first encounter, on September 26 in Chicago, and on October 7 in Washington, D.C., and October 21 in New York, the two men spoke from the same studio. On October 13, when Nixon was in Los Angeles and Kennedy in New York, they met each other at a distance—through the split-screen technique.

Judged by the audience they reached, the broadcasts were a huge success. Between 65 and 70 million watched any one telecast; somewhere between 85 and 120 million were estimated to have witnessed at least one of the four.

Reminiscent of the famous Lincoln-Douglas debates a century before, these four programs were everywhere referred to as the Great Debates. Still, to label them "debates" is not entirely accurate. The programs conformed only superficially to the format of a debate. For one thing, the two candidates neither challenged nor addressed one another directly. Instead, reporters took turns asking questions that, according to the rules, had to be directed alternately at each of the two candidates. There were strict time limitations. Two and a half minutes were allowed for a direct reply, at the end of which the other "debater" had one and a half minutes for rebuttal. The enforcement of these rules was left to a newsman who served as moderator and also introduced and closed the program.

The first and last programs were restricted to specific topics: domestic policy and foreign affairs, respectively. In these two debates, but not in the others, each candidate received eight minutes for an opening statement defining his position. Reporters then pursued these same topics with their questions, whereas in the other debates they were free to range over any topics they wished.

The television appearances of Kennedy and Nixon were certainly a major innovation, but the idea was not nearly as new. In 1956, President Eisenhower, running for re-election, had refused a challenge from his opponent, Governor Adlai Stevenson, to debate on television before a national audience. Soon after, support for such a face-to-face confrontation during the next campaign began to build up. A main stumbling block, however, was a clause in the Federal Communications Act of 1934. Section 315 of that act required any broadcaster who offered free time to a political candidate to offer "free and equal time" to every other candidate for the same office. The Federal Communications Commission had interpreted this clause literally. The requirement could not be met simply by an offer of equal time to the *major* candidates; the offer had to include, in fact, every candidate. But consider what this meant: In 1960, there were sixteen officially declared candidates seeking the presidency. They included such perennial contenders as the nominees of the Socialist Labor party, the Prohibition party, and the American Vegetarian party, as well as some new hopefuls such as the nominees of the American Beat Consensus, the Tax Cut party, and the Afro-American Unity party. Obviously, only a very small circle of the electorate could even have identified these candidates, yet all could have pressed for free and equal time.

Despite their eagerness to carry the televised debates, the networks clearly did not wish to assume the costs of granting similar time to the whole gamut of legally qualified candidates. Hence, during the winter and spring of 1960, they sought, unsuccessfully, the abolition of Section 315. They did succeed, however, in extracting from Congress, just before it recessed in August, a temporary suspension of the equal time rule.

Once the legal obstacle was removed, further progress depended on the ability of the interested parties to agree on the time, number, and format of the debates. Viewpoints on the purpose of the debates diverged considerably, and the final resolution was a compromise. The major interest of the networks was in a show that would effectively dramatize the capabilities of television. Nixon's managers wanted a single debate with cross-questioning between the two candidates in classic debate tradition. Kennedy's representatives asked for five debates, hoping to give their lesser-known candidate the maximum possible exposure.

At the beginning of the campaign, Kennedy had clearly been the underdog. In contrast to Nixon, who had won the Republican nomination with almost no serious challenge, Kennedy had been forced to wage a preconvention campaign against Senator Hubert Humphrey of Minnesota and then stave off a last-minute, emotion-packed try by Stevenson backers to secure a third nomination for their man. Kennedy, therefore, had considerable fence-mending to do. Many Democrats felt that he had bought rather than earned the nomination. They were not yet ready to give him their full support.

Nixon had been spared all this. Besides, he could, as a member of the outgoing administration, cash in on the experience gained during a number of missions abroad. His prestige, assumedly, went beyond party lines. And it must be noted that though Nixon was just about four years older than Kennedy, neither youth nor lack of experience was ever cited—as in the case of Kennedy—to show Nixon's unsuitability for the presidency. The issues mentioned here were not of course, the only ones, but they were the ones most relevant in assessing the impact of the televised debates.

Immediately after Kennedy's narrow election victory, observers began to suggest that television had been the undoing of Richard Nixon. On the Monday following the election, Kennedy himself was reported to have said, "It was TV more than anything else that turned the tide."[1]

A Panel Study of Viewer Reactions

Our study of the televised debates made no attempt to pass judgment on the accuracy of this diagnosis. This is because an electoral campaign consists of many events and involves many overlapping issues. To disentangle the influence of any single factor (event or issue) on the outcome of an election is always difficult. To do so with the 1960 campaign begins to border on logical absurdity. The closeness of the Kennedy victory—he won by fewer than 20,000 votes—showed that to win he needed every single one of the breaks he got. His victory was attributable only to a concatenation of all the factors working in his favor. He needed the votes of southern blacks and got them, apparently through his intervention for Martin Luther King when King was sentenced by a Georgia court (on a technicality) to four months of hard labor. The support of New York's liberal Democrats—equally important—was obtained through the efforts of Eleanor Roosevelt, Governor Herbert Lehman, and others in the party's reform wing there. Labor's enthusiastic help everywhere supplied a crucial balance, and the rise of unemployment that fall undoubtedly helped make Kennedy's campaign rhetoric about "moving ahead" more persuasive than it could otherwise have been. There is no way of showing that the TV debates, rather than some other event (or factor), supplied the decisive margin of victory.

The issue of the impact of televised debates must, moreover, be posed against a background of what has been fairly well established about the impact of mass communications during electoral campaigns. The mass political fare generally has two effects: (1) it increases the relevancy of political identifications people use to make up their minds, and (2) it promotes consistency between voting preferences and the images of candidates, opinions on issues, and so forth, through which individual voters support these preferences.[2] Campaign events can have a clear influence on the outcome if they somehow crystallize the votes of one side more strongly than those of the other, or if they bring about mass switches—the latter is much less likely.

The potential for change during the span of a presidential campaign is severely limited by the fact that most voters have closed minds even before the postnomination campaign begins. Many persons simply direct their attention so as to bolster a preference already held. Generally speaking, there is little inclination to seek out deliberately and to weigh carefully and dispassionately the viewpoints and arguments presented by both sides. Hence, televised debates differ from the usual campaign communications in several respects:

First, "double exposure" is inherent in their very format; there is no practical way for viewers to expose themselves to the personality of one candidate without the other, or to listen to the arguments presented by him (or her) without surmising at the same time how well they stood up on the rebuttal.

Second, it stands to reason that debates, which emphasize the give-and-take between two candidates, will have their main impact on images of their personalities.

Third, advance publicity, viewing habits, and perhaps the unique suitability of television for the debate format combine to attract audiences considerably larger than those usually exposed to campaign telecasts. In 1960 the novel debates overshadowed most other campaign events.

Ours was a small-scale panel study of 95 New York viewers. In this kind of study, the same persons (i.e., the members of a panel) who are interviewed the first time are later reinterviewed. We aimed at interviewing every one of our respondents at some length three different times: late in September just before the first debate, then immediately after that debate, and again after the fourth and last encounter.[3] These interviews enabled us to detail how vivid, new perceptions of the candidates arose in response to this double exposure. They also indicated how these sometimes disturbing perceptions were handled by viewers and related to—or isolated from—their vote decisions. Although changes in voting intention unquestionably constitute the clearest measure of impact (and interviews did give us information about this), the study focused on how the debates influenced the images and comparisons of the two candidates by viewers.

On purely statistical grounds, this sample warrants no inferences about the same effects in a larger population, national or local. Of the interviews, 24 were self-interviews by college seniors enrolled in a mass communications course at a nonresident New York City campus. The other 71 were obtained by these same students from voters outside the college community. Selection procedures were designed to give us a fairly even distribution of potential Kennedy and Nixon supporters and as wide a range as possible on a number of other characteristics.[4]

The observations illustrate the processes underlying communication effects as they occur in individuals. Among this panel there was an immediate and dramatic improvement in the Kennedy image after the first debate. The impression he made was considerably better than that made by Nixon. Both the absolute advantage Kennedy enjoyed and the gains he scored were particularly great among those who, before the debates, had not as yet decided how to vote and among those who identified themselves as independent voters.[5] These dramatic changes in imagery were, however, *not* accompanied by shifts in voting intentions of anywhere near comparable proportions. These are, to a degree, independent. Consequently, we will take up first the impact of the debates on voting intentions, which reflect decisions made, and second, the manner in which new perceptions entered into candidate images and were then related to electoral choices.

Changes in Voting Intentions

Among the shifts in voting intentions, one can distinguish three types: *Crystallization* represents a movement from being undecided or even ready not to vote at all toward a clear-cut preference for one of the two candidates. *Switching* is a movement from one candidate to the other; but a switch that is temporary or a weakening of a commitment without an actual change to the other candidate constitutes *wavering*. Table 4.1 summarizes the aggregate change within the panel over the period in which the debates took place. No evidence was collected on how or whether respondents actually did vote in November.

As shown in Table 4.1, the largest gain for Kennedy came from the crystallization of intent. It illustrates his success in rallying to his side a larger number of the uncommitted than Nixon. After the fourth debate, the preference of 23 persons initially uncommitted were

Table 4.1 Voting Intentions*

	Before Debates		After 1st Debate		After 4th Debate	
Decided for Kennedy	37 ⎱		47 ⎱		52 ⎱	
		39		53		56
Leaning toward Kennedy	2 ⎰		6 ⎰		4 ⎰	
Undecided		23		12		7
Leaning toward Nixon	2 ⎱		2 ⎱		1 ⎱	
		33		30		32
Decided for Nixon	31 ⎰		28 ⎰		31 ⎰	
		95		95		95

*Based on respondents with whom three interviews were completed.

thus distributed: 15 either for Kennedy or clearly leaning his way: 3 for Nixon, 5 still undecided or determined not to vote. The decisive shift to Kennedy came right after the first debate, when 8 decided for Kennedy and 4 more indicated a definite leaning toward him.

There were only four switchers. Three of them went from Nixon to Kennedy and one from Kennedy to Nixon. The Kennedy switchers defected (or at least began to lean) to Kennedy right after the first debate; all three said they had been impressed with the performance. The pro-Nixon switch recorded by the end of the debate series was not evident in any way after the initial television encounter.

Six persons initially for Nixon wavered. One of these moved into the undecided group after the first debate, and one after the series was over. The other four weakened in their preference but did not end up as undecided: They either continued to lean toward Nixon or returned to Nixon after the last debate. Only one Kennedy supporter wavered in that he grew less certain of his preference after the first debate but continued to lean toward Kennedy.

All told, then, there were 22 changes within our panel—18 crystallizers plus 4 switchers. Over 80 percent of these changes (18 out of 22, to be exact) benefited Kennedy. Apparently he was able to tap a traditionally Democratic potential of persons who, for a variety of reasons, had deferred their decision. His added strength came largely from weak Democratic party identifiers, that is, persons who considered themselves independent but acknowledged a general preference for Democrats. Among 11 weak Democratic identifiers who changed to Kennedy, 9 had been too young to vote in 1956 and 2 had defected to vote for Eisenhower in 1956. Five others who changed to Kennedy were self-styled Democrats; their switch in the course of the debate was a return to that allegiance. Only 2 of the votes gained by Kennedy can be said to have come from across party lines: one of these was a Republican, the other a self-styled Independent; both had voted for Eisenhower in 1956.

Nixon, on the other hand, won two votes from persons who favored Stevenson in 1956: one from a Democrat who had previously voted Republican, and another from a new voter who thought of himself as Independent.

When viewed against the voter's party identification and voting history, very few of the intra-campaign switches contradict the voter's political past. The majority of switchers were merely responding to inclinations that had clearly been present earlier and might have been activated even without the debates. Nixon failed to consolidate sufficiently the inroads Eisenhower had made into the large Democratic potential, the heritage of the New Deal era—inroads that any Republican had to maintain or expand if he were to win. As the campaign progressed, among this panel of voters Kennedy gained votes at a 4 to 1 ratio. The debates, being the major and perhaps the most dramatic campaign event, hastened the polarization of the electorate but not, as far as our evidence goes, along lines contrary to tradition.

The evidence from this study, as well as from others,[6] shows that the first debate accelerated the movement toward Kennedy and strengthened pro-Democratic commitments. Nevertheless, one cannot definitively conclude that these changes would not have occurred without the debates. Kennedy had already been making headway among voters, and it is possible that these votes would have crystallized as they did simply as a function of time. One thing is clear, however: The debates provided new arguments for supporting Kennedy and, therefore, strengthened convictions. The public, in particular, thought the debates the most important element that led to Kennedy's victory. Perhaps the same amount of enthusiastic support for his campaign would not have been forthcoming without this dramatic confrontation between the two candidates. No one will ever be able to tell.

Pre-Debate Images

Voting preference is usually linked in various degrees with party identification, orientation to political issues, and images of the candidates. Each of these variables exerts some independent influence on the vote, and when all three are consistent—as when traditional party identification goes with a preference for that party's candidate and there is agreement with his or her stand on issues—one can predict with a high degree of reliability how a person will vote.[7] Issue orientation and candidate preferences are clearly more variable and volatile than party identifications. They usually account for cross-overs between elections. And since it can be said with some assurance that the debates highlighted the competitive performance of the two candidates, one can also confidently say that any changes in voting preferences resulting from the debates were mediated primarily through changes in the images of the candidates.

Nixon had used his association as Vice-President with Eisenhower, but he had also been working hard to build up his image as a statesman in his own right. He had already demonstrated his skill as a debater by the apparent cool confidence with which he delivered his famous Checkers speech (see Chapter 1). More recently, he had received much publicity from his Kitchen Debate with Premier Khrushchev. Television newsreels and press photographs had prominently featured an episode from the Vice President's trip to Russia, showing him with his finger pointed at the Premier, apparently scoring a point. Nixon himself reported that Vice-Premier Mikoyan had taken him aside afterward in order to compliment him: "I reported to Mr. Khrushchev. . .that you were very skillful in debate, and you proved it again today."[8]

Kennedy had also been in the public eye. He had emerged from World War II as a war hero and then served in Congress for some 14 years, first in the House and then in the Senate. His book, *Profiles in Courage,* had been a bestseller, his marriage to Jacqueline Bouvier a major social event.

The image viewers had of Nixon *before the debates* was, not unexpectedly, much sharper and clearer than the one they had of Kennedy. Nixon had held *national* elective office and, as a result, was far better known. Of our panel, 70 percent said they were "more familiar" with Nixon; 18 percent said they were equally familiar (or unfamiliar) with both; only 12 percent thought they knew Kennedy better. Yet, certain well-defined images of each candidate were widely shared by the panel.

The image of Nixon. First, the impression that the vice presidency entailed more responsibility and afforded better preparation for the presidency than serving in the Senate was accepted, at least tacitly, even by most Democrats. Second, Nixon was remembered as a roving political ambassador who, while vice-president, had dealt with angry mobs in South America and debated with Khrushchev in Russia, though viewers assessed these accomplishments differently. Third, Nixon's formidability as a TV personality and debater was acknowledged by both those for and against his candidacy. Finally, respondents saw in Nixon an experienced and skilled politician; even opponents who heartily disliked him doubted that he would ever again resort to tactics which had been successful against past political opponents, tactics which they distrusted and which made them distrust Nixon.

The image of Kennedy. The Kennedy image was simpler but also somewhat more personal; it was less closely tied to his past political efforts, and so Kennedy, unlike Nixon, emerged more as a man than as a political man. The dominant image of the senator, even among many who intended to vote against him, was of a "fine young man" with some potential. He was most often viewed as competent and cool, an ambitious young fellow who knew how to build a political organization, as evidenced by his nomination. Both those for and against him widely referred to Kennedy as "vigorous" or "vital." Doubts were voiced, however, about his convictions; many considered him "snobbish" and were highly suspicious of the political influence of his family and of his Catholicism. As an aside, it may be mentioned that the most unfriendly image of Kennedy was shared largely by the Catholic Republicans interviewed, of whom two were among the most outspoken in their opposition to a Catholic, especially a Catholic such as Kennedy, in the White House.

Table 4.2   Expectations and Actual Performance in First Debate*

Political Before 1st Debate	Nixon Better	About the Same	Kennedy Better	Don't Know, No Answer
	Expectations of Performance			
Nixon (30)	21	6	3	0
Undecided (22)	9	8	4	1
Kennedy (39)	11	12	13	3
Total	41	26	20	4
Percentage	45	29	22	4
	Actual Performance			
Nixon (30)	8	10	12	0
Undecided (22)	0	2	20	0
Kennedy (39)	2	9	28	0
Total	10	21	60	0
Percentage	11	23	66	

*Of 97 respondents with whom pre-debate interviews were completed, 6 said they had not watched the first debate. The comparison remains essentially unaffected by whether or not the 6 nonviewers are included.

Expectations Before the Debate

People looked forward to the debates as a match of the candidates' forensic skills—their ability as it was so often expressed, to "put their views across." The partisan hoped to see his candidate perform effectively and thereby improve his chance of winning. Most of those interviewed thought the debates might affect the voting decisions of others but doubted that they would have any effect on their own thinking.

There was, however, a significant difference between the expectations of Nixon partisans and Kennedy partisans (Table 4.2). Two-thirds of Nixons's 30 partisans felt confident of their candidate's superior debating skills; only 3 thought Kennedy would do better. Even among Kennedy partisans, Nixon was considered a formidable opponent. A reading of the interviews reveals that only a few Kennedy supporters had real confidence that their man would be a match for Nixon. In the way they evaded a flat prediction, many implied that they were worried by Nixon's reputation as a political infighter.

Those who thought they "might be influenced" by the debates put a special stress on the image the candidates would project. A number intended to look specifically for "the way a candidate answered," apart from what he might say. "I want to see," said one, "whether they hem and haw before they answer, whether they mean what they say, and whether they are sincere." Others said they would look for signs of knowledgeability and an ability to stand up "courageously."

Finally, many who were undecided and a number of party faithfuls lukewarm to the candidate said they would seek information on how the candidates stood on important issues. They expected that the debate format, because it offered a unique opportunity for the "instantaneous reply," would force the candidates into clear-cut statements of policy and expose past records.

The First Debate

The first historic encounter took place in a Chicago TV studio on September 26, 1960, at 9:30 p.m. (EST). Veteran newsman Howard K. Smith, in his capacity as moderator, introduced the program and the four reporters on the panel. Kennedy had drawn the first position, and, consequently, led off with his opening statement. Paraphrasing Lincoln, he asked whether the world could exist half-slave and half-free. All he said, more or less, led up to what would become his familiar slogan: "I think it's time America started moving again."

Nixon answered his opponent by agreeing with the general goals Kennedy had set forth. To stay ahead, he said, the nation would have to continue moving ahead. The point he disputed was that America, under Eisenhower, had been standing still.

Subsequent comments on the first debate indicate that—to paraphase Lincoln once more—the nation did not long remember what they said there, but it did remember how they looked when they said it. People wondered, in particular, why Nixon's performance had not lived up to expectations. Had the room been too hot? Was he still ailing from the infected knee for which he had undergone treatment in July?

Controversy centered on how certain production details might have affected the ability of the candidates to project themselves.[9] Extreme care had been taken with the production. A new set had been built with special attention to background color and lighting. There had been requests from the managers of both candidates, especially with Nixon's, about the placement of lights and what shots *not* to take. Some of these remained subject to discussion for years.

After the first debate, a newspaper story charged that a makeup man had deliberately sabotaged Nixon's appearance. It now seems firmly established that Nixon himself vetoed the recommendation that he wear any makeup beyond some powder to cover his "five-o'clock shadow." If Nixon looked hot and uncomfortable, this was at least partly due to his own production advisers. Their demands for additional lights overrode the objections of CBS's senior lighting director. They also requested that left profile shots of Nixon be avoided and that no reaction shots be taken while the candidate was wiping perspiration from his face. Yet, one reaction shot caught him sweating and apparently glaring at the camera. Kennedy looked youthful, healthy, and suntanned by comparison.

Nixon's own comment on these events of the first debate was that he had made a "basic mistake." He had concentrated "too much on substance and not enough on appearance." While he denied what some supporters contended—that he was not feeling up to par physically—he indicated that he had, in fact, been quite rundown but didn't know it at the time. The camera, like a microscope, had revealed his true physical condition to the audience even before he himself had become aware of it.[10] Before the second debate, Nixon put on five pounds.

Impact of the First Debate

The impact of the first debate was quite dramatic. Of our panel who watched or heard the first debate, 89 percent thought Kennedy had bested Nixon or at least had fought him to a draw (Table 4.2). This seems also to have been the predominant reaction throughout the country. A national sample of approximately 1000 viewers interviewed by the Gallup organization between September 24 and October 4, 1960, found that about twice as many thought Kennedy did better than thought Nixon did better. The single most important result of

Table 4.3 Change in Candidates' Image After First Debate (Percentages)*

	Better	Unchanged	Worse	No Answer
Kennedy personal image	45	45	5	4
Nixon personal image	20	47	29	4
Kennedy informedness	41	53	3	3
Nixon informedness	14	67	11	8

*Based on 91 respondents. Rounded to nearest whole number.

the debate lay in its destruction of the image, so widely held, of Richard Nixon as champion debater and television politician par excellence. This re-evaluation of the comparative ability of the two men as performers is what helped crystallize the vote of undecideds and caused partisans to revise their images of the men as persons and as presidential timber.

Changes in the images of candidates as *persons* mainly reflected viewers' political preferences. But, as Table 4.3 shows, Kennedy scored net gains, creating a more favorable personal image of himself. His unexpectedly able performance dissolved many doubts about his maturity and experience, even among Nixon supporters. By contrast, Nixon's personal image deteriorated dramatically among Democrats and the undecided; moreover, 5 out of 30 Nixon supporters had a less favorable view of Nixon the person. Still, while some Kennedy supporters found Nixon less well informed than they had supposed, the Nixon supporters, who had thought their candidate very well informed before the debate, afterward found him even better informed. Thus, among the viewers as a whole (as shown in Table 4.3), the personal image of Nixon deteriorated, but the judgement of Nixon's informedness remained pretty much as before.

A judgment of overall attitude toward the two candidates was made from answers to questions about what viewers had discovered about each man—how able he was, what he stood for, how he had voted, how he performed, and so forth. Table 4.4 uses the categories "Improvement" and "Deterioration" with regard to this *overall* image. The categories "Favorable (Unfavorable) Image Validated" were added to indicate persons whose overall judgment changed but only insofar as they became more certain in their judgement than they had been. The potential for improvement was limited by the fact that each candidate entered the debates with a fund of good will among his supporters; the potential for deterioration was limited by the hostility each already encountered among the opposition.

As expected, many respondents merely validated a favorable image of their own candidate and an unfavorable image of his opponent. What interested us was, first, a general improvement in the overall impression of Kennedy, an improvement that was very marked among Kennedy partisans, and extended even to supporters of Nixon. Again, what was true of our viewers was true of viewers throughout the nation. Among a test audience recruited by the Gallup organization in the Trenton, New Jersey area, the proportion who held a "very" favorable image of Kennedy increased 16 percent following the debate compared with an increase of 4 percent for Nixon. The Survey Research Center (University of Michigan) found that among Independents, favorable responses to Kennedy after the debates were twice as frequent as favorable responses to Nixon.[11] The second interesting result was that, because most Nixon supporters merely validated an initially favorable image while five indicated less favorable impressions, the image of Nixon held by the panel as a whole deteriorated. Third, gains made by Nixon among Kennedy supporters are noteworthy even though they were not large enough to offset the trend, that is, they occurred among a group whose image to begin with had been strongly negative.

Cumulative Impact

Reactions to the first encounter set the tone. The images of the candidates, once firmed up in response to that initial debate, changed very little thereafter, even though many of these impressions were clearly not in line with voting intentions. Thus, both candidates had scored some gains among persons supporting their opponent. One might have expected these viewers, whose intentions were not reinforced, but even undermined, by the first debate, to gear their subsequent communication behavior so as to bring candidate preference and image in line.[12] There are several ways to do this besides changing one's preference: by refusing to watch further debates, by turning to sources of information more favorable to one's candidate, and by continuing to look in subsequent debates for clues reaffirming one's original convictions.

Because of alternative ways of reducing dissonance (other than avoiding the debates), among our panel there was no evidence that dissonance introduced by the first debate led either to more or less viewing of the debates that followed. The number of debates watched was unrelated to (1) initial candidate preference, (2) judgement of who had won the first debate, (3) amount of change in image, or (4) education of the viewer.

But responses after the last debate showed rather clearly how much people had come to rely on interpretations they had read in newspapers and news magazines, usually publications reflecting their own views. Viewers' later observations showed considerable stereotypy and lacked the originality that had characterized responses after the first debate. From this it appears that journalistic interpretations and personal conversations supplied a frame of reference permitting the assimilation of information from subsequent debates without stirring new doubt or conflict.

Another way of reducing strain between image and voting preference involved a reassessment of the various elements that made up a candidate's political personality and of their relevance to electoral choice. The televised debates dramatized competitive performance. A viewer whose image of Nixon's prowess as a debater had suffered a serious blow could, from there on, deny that this was any reflection on Nixon's qualifications for the office. On the contrary, he might even be drawn more strongly to Nixon by sympathy and react negatively to a candidate too quick with his tongue.

To stress the importance of the candidate image here is not to ignore the stability introduced by party identification and by the network of associations that activate the electorate at election time. In the rhythmic pattern of politics, party images often become blurred between national elections. The political personality chosen by each party to head the ticket and speak for party policy plays a crucial role in the electoral campaign, which is aimed at moving party identifications back into the foreground of attention and refurbishing the party image. The party, temporarily united behind the candidate, appeals through him or her to the electorate. But the strain toward consistency among voters' images of personal self-interest, national interest, party policies, and so forth, includes the image of the party candidate.

The image of a political personality projected by television[13] depends upon evaluations of three component elements: the individual's television *performance*, here as a debater; the fitness for the *political role* in which he or she is cast, here that of candidate aspiring to the presidency; and the *personal image*—what kind of human being is this? what is he or she like as a real person? The appeal of a political personality is a function of the way the individual on the screen projects along each of these dimensions and whether these are related or isolated in the viewer's cognition. The relationship among these elements, as well as the relationship between these elements and political decisions, is similar in certain respects to the relationship between information and attitudes on which the information supposedly bears. New or negative information does not necessitate a reassessment of pertinent attitudes. Neither does a changed perception of political performance necessarily carry over to perception of the individual performing, and so forth. The rest of this chapter takes up this question of how new cognitive elements introduced so vividly in the first debate were dealt with by viewers. The essential question is why dramatic changes in evaluations were followed by less dramatic changes in voting intentions.

Performance, Personal Image, Political Role

Even though partisans wanted their man to win so that they could reassure themselves and convince others, few viewers, whether partisan or uncommitted, would have seriously proposed before the first debate that a candidate's ability to score points under the rules agreed on for that debate was a test of fitness for office. Yet, it was his unexpected performance that helped Kennedy project among his potential supporters a personal image congruent with the political role he was playing.

Kennedy supporters. The image of Kennedy was transformed from that of an eager, affable, young, and ambitious political aspirant into one that emphasized the competent, dynamic, and quick-thinking candidate.

"His debating techniques showed a quick mind."
"He was alert and interested at all times."
"He seemed to know all the time where to refute Nixon."
"He never fumbled."
"He presented himself as a doer, a leader, a positive thinker."

These are only illustrations of how Kennedy, by his performance, established among potential supporters his character as well as his right to the candidacy. Lukewarm supporters became enthusiastic because, as several put it, "People could *see* he was qualified." Said one: "I've switched from an anti-Nixon Democrat to a pro-Kennedy Democrat."

Most of these potential Democrats had expected Kennedy to be beaten and, because of this, were prepared to isolate competitive television performance from their consideration of his qualifications for the presidency. At the same time, Nixon's much heralded competence as a performer was a focus for many negative perceptions about his political role. But Nixon's failure to live up to expectations as a performer did not destroy this negative image. The focus on performance also meant that the personal image projected through TV was not likely to gain him trust or to inspire confidence in his qualifications among Democrats. On the contrary, some respondents who had explicitly discounted performance in this regard now went so far as to draw from his poor performance conclusions about his fitness. One interpreted "the way he fumbled, ingratiated himself, appeared nervous and not quite rational" to mean that Nixon was "psychologically too upset to be entrusted with the leadership of the country." Observed another, "The poor facial expressions and nervous tension lead me to go as far as to say he looked frightened." The relevance assigned to performance as a measure of the man and the candidate changed among many Democrats.

A poor performance, expected or not, need not result in deterioration of the personal image if it is not linked to political role. Thus six Kennedy supporters, though judging Nixon the poorer performer,

Table 4.4   Changes in Overall Valuation of Candidates After Debate

Political Preference Before 1st Debate	Improve- ment	Favorable Image Validated	No Change	Unfavorable Image Validated	Deteri- oration
		Kennedy Evaluations			
Nixon (30)	10	1	7	12	0
Undecided (22)	11	0	9	2	0
Kennedy (39)	19	15	4	1	
Total	40	16	20	14	1
Percentage*	45	18	22	15	1
		Nixon Evaluations			
Nixon (30)	1	16	7	0	6
Undecided (22)	2	0	9	3	8
Kennedy (39)	6	0	13	14	6
Total	9	16	29	17	20
Percentage*	10	18	32	19	22

*Rounded to nearest whole number.

emerged with a more positive overall image of Nixon (Table 4.4). Reading the explanations they offered for this more charitable view, one discerns a gnawing distrust of Kennedy that led them to question the spontaneity of his performance and to personalize its content. Yet in extending sympathy to his apparent victim, their electoral choice was not affected, nor did they think less of Kennedy. For example, one housewife (one of the few to anticipate Kennedy's superior performance) had explained: "He is a magnetic person, with much polish and a great deal of sex appeal. He'll make a good appearance and will greatly appeal to the younger female voters." Her praise before the debates was thus given grudgingly. She emerged from the first debate unimpressed with "Kennedy's ability to quote figures... [since] Kennedy was paying others to get the facts," and she went on to describe how pleased she was that "Nixon gave him a run for his money and didn't take a back seat." She was a regular Democrat, and her vote was not swayed by the increased attraction she felt for Nixon.

Again, one student (a new voter) found Nixon's performance "almost pathetic" and suffered for him. To him Nixon appeared "sometimes pleading, avoiding questions, shocked when attacked, nervous, and anxious, [and] at times I felt very sorry for him.'' For the first time, the young man said, he had recognized Nixon as a ''human being, a complicated personality'' rather than a political symbol. This student was one of the few who called the first debate ''not quite fair''; he thought newsmen had been ''kinder'' to Kennedy. But the pro-Republican press, he noted, must have helped ''to heal Nixon's wounds'' by calling the debate a draw—in the respondent's view Kennedy had clearly won. Performance ultimately moved him from undecided to Kennedy, but after the first debate he described himself as ''less in favor of Kennedy than before,'' even though his overall impression of Kennedy had clearly improved.

Nixon supporters. The Nixon political personality, as already pointed out, was dominated by his perceived political role. Statements by his supporters about the kind of person Nixon was were usually formulated in terms of qualifications for office and his ability to perform. An inventory of terms most frequently used before the first debate to describe Nixon's personal image included experienced, competent, better informed than Kennedy, a hard worker, a good American, forceful, honest, sincere, calm, strong, and such phrases as ''he can face up to the Russians'' and ''he can handle Khrushchev.'' An occasional respondent noted that he was a good family man or had a pleasing personality, and a few attributed the distrust he was known to evoke in others to his ''reserve'' or ''efficiency.''

Nixon's performance in the first debate undermined the image of the superior debater most of his supporters had held. The keen disappointment many of them felt was translated into votes for Kennedy only among those few whose choice was founded on rather weak party identification. Most countered Nixon's shaky performance by one or more of three techniques: *isolation, selective perception,* and *personalization.*

Isolation (in the sense of denying the relevance of information to behavioral commitment) has already been noted in the predebate responses of Kennedy backers who minimized debating skill as a test of political competence. Now it was the pro-Nixon group who, despite the fact that they had supported evaluations of their candidate by referring to his debating skills, no longer emphasized such skills when his performance proved disappointing.

Selective perception is illustrated by claims that both candidates had been "primed beforehand," an observation often documented by "Kennedy's ability to rattle off figures." Nixon's claim to the presidency was most often justified after the debate by his long advocacy of "sound policies." The candidate's performance was ignored, while the policies he advocated came in for extra attention. By focusing on the political content of Nixon's statements, his supporters, who, presumably, were in agreement with what he believed in, could still define him as the winner, and there was understandably a larger proportion who thought that he had done better or at least as well as Kennedy. Said one, "I think Nixon did better, but of course I'm prejudiced." Others thought that reporters were favoring Kennedy, feeding him easier questions. Kennedy was also accused of having broken the rules by his note-taking and, after the third debate, by reading from notes.[14] Different evaluations of performance thus are a function of elements singled out for attention and of the context in which they are interpreted.

The technique of *personalization* is perhaps a special variant of selective perception. It involves molding essentially ambiguous attributes into an unfavorably personal image of the opposition, and vice versa. For example, one of his supporters remarked on Nixon's "not smiling at all, being ill at ease, and on the defensive," but then went on to interpret this as being "more careful, more subtle, and thinking over a problem." Another woman admitted that "Kennedy came over nicely, if you like his type. He was snide and impolite to make notes while Nixon was speaking." In her final interview, the same woman explained at length that the better the Kennedy performance, the more she came personally to dislike him, while her confidence in Nixon increased: she felt, as she put it, "a real personal contact" with him. Nixon, it was said by another, though a target of Kennedy's "brashness," "never likes to offend anybody." His being "too polite" thus became an explanation of why he failed to live up to expectations.

Personal traits used to explain the performance were also related to political role. To many, Nixon's hesitations indicated "thoughtfulness" and "cautious modesty," both congruent with the political role a President is expected to play, and thus a favorable contrast to Kennedy's "boasting." As one Nixon supporter put it: "Kennedy always began his statements, '*I* will do this' and *I* will do that.' Whenever Nixon started to say '*I*,' he checked hmself by saying 'the *Republican party* will.' " In another reference Kennedy was seen as "quick-acting, but if he's to talk to Khrushchev, he'd say something he later would regret." Moreover, Nixon, according to some, was not at his best in the first debate because he had recently been hospitalized for an infected knee. He had, however, shown great fortitude: "Nixon could stand up to Kennedy [said one person after the fourth debate]. That shows he could stand up to the Russians."

While Kennedy did improve his overall image among one-third of the Nixon partisans, he improved it largely in terms of "informedness." Of 30 Nixon supporters who saw the first debate, 13 admitted that Kennedy was better informed than they had thought. But only 5 out of the same 30 got a more favorable personal image. Many Republicans could only react with hostility on seeing that he was a formidable adversary. It is hardly surprising, therefore, especially in view of the short period covered by the debates, that political preferences should on the whole have remained stable, even though the debates had a definite impact on imagery. What our research most clearly documented was the variety of ways in which perceptions can be brought into line with electoral choice.

Summary and Implications

Exposure to the televised debates resulted in some rather dramatic changes in candidate image. Voting intentions changed much less, for images were interpreted to serve preference.

On balance, the impact of these debates on the persons studied appears to have favored Kennedy more than Nixon. But when viewed against the backgrounds of voters, the majority of whom had identified themselves with or voted for the Democratic party in the past, Kennedy's gain does not appear to have entailed a large-scale crossing of party lines. Most of the undecided were Democrats-in-conflict, who were won over because Kennedy succeeded in identifying himself with the tradition of the Democratic party.

As the lesser known of the candidates, Kennedy stood a greater chance of being helped by these joint appearances as well as by the campaign generally, an anticipation borne out by this and other research. Still, some of the very elements in the Kennedy performance that worked in his favor among an urban group of viewers such as ours may have produced different responses in other surroundings. For example, note the personal hostility Kennedy's smooth performance aroused among some Nixon voters—in communities where attitudes prevail that were rarely encountered among our sample (such as anti-"big city" or fundamentalist sentiment), the responses may have differed greatly.

Though evidence from our study of the Kennedy-Nixon encounters did not suggest that dramatic and immediate changes in votes could be expected from such TV spectacles in the middle of a campaign, there were, nevertheless, important sleeper effects that could not be observed by the methods we used. The reactions to the debates were influenced by what viewers remembered about the two performers from past telecasts or (especially in the case of Nixon) as they remembered it from what they read about those telecasts afterward. Efforts to use the debates were revealed in interviews with campaign workers. Among Democrats, the Kennedy performance sparked the organization of viewing groups, generated enthusiasm, and apparently led to greater campaign efforts, all of which together may have influenced the final vote gains as much as the debates as such.

All things considered, the debates marked an important turning point in the campaign. Thus it was that future contestants became leery about risking their reputations in open debate with lesser-known challengers. There would be no presidential debates in 1964 when incumbent Lyndon Johnson was far ahead in the polls. Nor did Richard Nixon, once known as the Great Debater, risk debating his opponents in 1968 and 1972. Still, the readiness of any nominee, or would-be nominee, to debate the issues before the television audience has increasingly become an issue in its own right. The press and the public draw what conclusions they wish from the unwillingness of any candidate to meet an opponent face-to-face.

As for the most important effect of the 1960 debates, we tend to agree with pollster Sam Lubell, who believed they made it "easier for the electorate to accept the election results."[15] Kennedy's hairbreadth margin of victory could have been the cause of much bitterness. So might the fear of a Catholic president have undermined the legitimacy of his presidency. Yet, by the time of Kennedy's inauguration, most Nixon backers seemed sufficiently persuaded to give him the benefit of the doubt. Perhaps this would have happened in any event, even without the television performance. Be this as it may, it would seem that the image projected over TV stood Kennedy in good stead as president. By the time he was assassinated just three years later, the positive image he had projected during the debates had been reinforced and converted, in many cases, into potential support for a second term that never came.

NOTES

1. Theodore H. White, *The Making of the President 1960* (New York: Pocket Books, 1962) 353.

2. Classic summaries of this impact are to be found in Bernard R. Berelson, Paul F. Lazarsfeld, and W.N. McPhee, *Voting* (Chicago: University of Chicago Press, 1954) appendix; and Eugene Burdick and A. J. Brodbeck, ed., *American Voting Behavior* (Glencoe, Ill: Free Press, 1959) chapters 12 and 13. More recent campaign studies have introduced only minor modifications into these propositions about mass media impact. See Jay G. Blumler and Denis McQuail, *Television in Politics; Its Uses and Influence* (Chicago: University of Chicago Press, 1969); Harold Mendelsohn and Garret J. O'Keefe, *The People Choose a President; Influences on Voter Decisions* (New York: Praeger, 1976); and Thomas E. Patterson, *The Mass Media Election; How Americans Choose Their President* (New York: Praeger, 1980).

3. Altogether, 104 persons were interviewed before or after the debates; 97 were interviewed before the first debate, but 2 of them could not be reinterviewed. Seven others were interviewed only after the first debate. Statistics were based only on those 95 persons interviewed three times.

4. Of 97 interviewed before the first debate, 13 were under 21 and too young to vote; 23 were between 21 and 24 and thus were first voters; 19 were between 25 and 34; 33 were between 35 and 54; and 7 were 55 and over. The sample contained 50 persons of Jewish origin, 26 Protestants, 18 Catholics, and 3 who gave no religion; 7 persons added on the second wave were Catholic. The socioeconomic level of the sample was somewhat above average and contained, as noted, a large number of students. Persons gainfully employed divided rather evenly among three groups; professional, managerial, and white-collar employees; sales person-

nel and small businessmen; and blue-collar workers. Of those who voted in 1956 and responded to a question about how they voted, 44 percent had voted Republican and 56 percent Democratic. Asked which party they belonged to or identified with, 59 percent responded "Democratic," 21 percent "Republican," with the others declaring themselves Independent or unaffiliated, or refusing to answer. In traditionally Democratic New York City, most of the independents revealed themselves to be, by voting record, attitudes, and so forth, inclined toward the Republicans.

5. For similar results, see Elihu Katz and Jacob J. Feldman, "The Debates in the Light of Research: A Survey of Surveys," in S. Kraus, ed., *The Great Debates* (Bloomington: University of Indiana Press, 1962) 173-223.

6. Katz and Feldman, "The Debates in the Light of Research."

7. See Angus Campbell, Gerald Gurin, and Warren E. Miller, *The Voter Decides* (New York: Harper, 1954); and Angus Campbell, *et al.*, *The American Voter* (New York: Wiley, 1960).

8. Richard M. Nixon, *Six Crises* (Garden City, NY: Doubleday, 1962), 258.

9. A careful and objective inside account of the production is that by Herbert A. Seltz and Richard D. Yoakum, "Production Diary of the Debates," in Kraus, *The Great Debates,* 73-126.

10. Nixon, *Six Crises*, 341.

11. Press releases by the two organizations.

12. The theoretical argument for this expectation was first laid out in L. Festinger, *A Theory of Cognitive Dissonance* (Evanston, IL: Row, Peterson, 1957).

13. This conceptualization of the television personality is discussed in more detail in K. and G. E. Lang, "The Television Personality in Politics," *Public Opinion Quarterly*, Spring 1956, pp. 107-116.

14. Accusations by some Nixon supporters that they had seen Kennedy cheat indicate the influence of press reports on what is seen. After the third debate, Nixon and his spokesmen charged Kennedy with violating an agreement that no notes be used. Kennedy aides denied knowledge of such an agreement and claimed that the controversy concerned only Kennedy's reference to a quotation. In any event, the cheating that some viewers had seen could only have been read in the newspaper. There had been no previous public mention of this rule.

15. "Personalities vs. Issues," in Kraus, *The Great Debates,* ch. 9.

5

Late Voters and Early Returns

The television and radio coverage of the 1964 national election made communication history. For the first time there was a definite chance that conclusive returns, including convincing projections of the final outcome, would be available to many voters before they themselves had voted.[1] While, as early as 1952, the networks had used computers to pick winners, such machines, however novel and fascinating, had not been taken very seriously. Regarded as toys, they were part of a game in which amused reporters periodically checked to see if their computerized predictions were coming at all close to the mark.

By 1964, when Senator Barry Goldwater was challenging President Lyndon Johnson, computer applications in this area had reached a new stage of sophistication. At the same time, the networks and press associations had finally pooled resources to provide the public with the fastest possible tally of results. Given this combination of improved and collaborative effort, it seemed likely that within minutes—and certainly within the hour—after many polls closed in the East at 6:30 p.m., the networks could be pointing to significant trends. In the West, it would be just 3:30 p.m. local time. In California, most populous state of the Union, most polling places would remain open till 8:00 p.m.

These possibilities, which have by now become routine, were raising exciting but somehow perturbing prospects. Throughout the country, but especially in California, citizens were being warned of dire political effects in the event the networks announced a probable winner early on election night. Newspaper editors and columnists, radio and TV commentators, political candidates and their managers voiced their concerns. Some raised the spectre of vote shifts as returns indicated a clear winner. There were allusions to last-minute bandwagon effects benefitting the man shown to be ahead along with talk of a large sympathy vote for the apparent underdog. These possibilities were not, however, the chief cause for worry. Anxieties focused particularly on the probability of a large drop in voter turnout in the West if—as just about everyone expected—the early returns were to show Johnson with a commanding lead in the East. What most concerned people then was that the broadcast of early returns would produce a "late election-day slack."

Candidates and their managers naturally tried to anticipate how such slack might affect their chances for election. For example, the day before the election, Senator Pierre Salinger, a California Democrat seeking election to the seat he held by appointment, took up the issue in a press conference. He was sharply critical of the networks' alleged plans to declare a winner as early as 6:30 p.m. California time. The thousands who might be dissuaded from voting, Salinger argued, would include more Democrats than Republicans and thereby jeopardize his prospects in what was being billed as a very close race. In the same vein, Dean Burch, of the Republican National Committee, appealed to the networks on election day to refrain from early and unwarranted interpretations until after polls everywhere had closed.

Were these fears warranted? Some Californians may have remembered what had happened in the Republican primary the previous June. With New York's Governor Nelson Rockefeller pitted against Goldwater for the Republican nomination, CBS had, at 7:24 p.m., flatly declared Goldwater the winner on the basis of incomplete returns from the southern counties. Rockefeller was still leading in the tabulated returns and polls were still open in the populous San Francisco Bay area, a center of Rockefeller strength. As it happened, the CBS prediction proved correct—Goldwater did win but by the narrowest of margins. Afterward, there were charges, widely reported by the news media, that persons lined up at northern

California polling places, upon hearing the CBS projection, concluded that the election was over, that their vote no longer mattered, and left without voting. To be sure, these claims remained unconfirmed, but they gave rise to suspicions that the media coverage of the returns had been the cause of Rockefeller's defeat.

The issue—the effects of broadcasting returns before all polls are closed—was very new in 1964 but it is still with us and the focus of periodic controversy. On election day 1964, we set out to investigate what effects, if any, the broadcast of early returns might have had on persons who learned about the probable outcome before they voted or, in the case of nonvoters, before polls closed and they still could have voted. Our focus was on the whole range of their reactions: How did what they heard and saw about how the election was going affect their votes? As a result, did some people switch from one candidate to another? Did some who had not yet made up their mind whether to vote make up their mind to do so? Were some persons about to vote dissuaded by the returns from voting? We also wanted to know how people felt about voting when they already knew the outcome and how they felt about the broadcasters' practice of making predictions from an incomplete tally of votes.

Obviously, the research could do no more than document the effects of such broadcasts in *one* election, but we tried to design the study so as to throw some light on what was likely to hapen in *future* elections with different odds, different candidates, and different circumstances. Put another way, we wanted to understand what factors would help explain any effects observed in this election, to understand what might be expected to happen under different conditions and, in the light of these observations, consider the long-range implications of such broadcasts for the political process. Presumably, for instance, people over the years would grow more sophisticated about the fast count and early predictions. How would they adapt and what would such adaptation mean with regard to their attitudes toward voting or their belief in the legitimacy of the electoral process?

Another question that concerned us was the significance of election night as a unifying experience. Traditionally, the nation, assembled together to await the outcome, holds its breath, then accepts the decision and buries the partisan hatchet. Would election night coverage now breed new controversies centering on the returns—about how they might have influenced the election or how such returns might be manipulated in the future? Would voting practices in different time zones have to be altered to take account of the phenomenal speed in assembling and conveying information?

For our purpose—since we were not measuring the net effect on the election outcome but exploring the full ramifications of early returns—intensive interviews with a limited but carefully chosen sample of eligible voters seem preferable to brief questions asked of a larger number of people presumed to be representative of all voters. Accordingly, face-to-face interviews were conducted with 364 registered voters in the East Bay area of California who had not yet gone to the polls by 4 p.m. EST[2], the time the election broadcasts were scheduled to start. For purposes of comparison, 116 interviews were also held with registered voters in greater Cleveland who, likewise, had not voted by 4 p.m. local time. Since polls in Ohio closed at 6:30 p.m., before the beginning of the election coverage, none of these late voters and nonvoters could have been exposed to early returns.[3]

The method for selecting respondents from precinct lists was the same in California and Ohio. At 4:00 local time, we went to voting places, previously selected, with rosters of their registered voters. We then crossed off the names of persons who had already voted and systematically drew names from the remaining list. This yielded a sample of persons who had to be either late voters or nonvoters. Interviewing began the day after the election and was completed within 11 days.

What People Knew Before Voting

Events clearly corroborated the expectation that an early winner would be declared from very incomplete returns. Explicit projections of a Johnson victory by the three major networks came at 3:48 p.m., at 4:43 p.m., and at 4:50 p.m. PST, while voting in California and other neighboring states was still in progress. In the California polling precincts we studied, three out of five registered voters who had not yet gone to the polls by 4 p.m. local time had, by the time they voted, heard something about how the race for President was going or, if they were nonvoters, before polls closed (see Table

Table 5.1 Election News and Conclusion Drawn in Percentages

	California *(N = 364)*	*Ohio* *(N = 116)*
Had heard something	61	14
Had heard nothing	37	85
No answer	2	1
	100	100

Table 5.2

Conclusion from this Election News *by those who had heard something*	*(N = 220)*	*(N = 16)*
Johnson had won; certain to win	56	56
Johnson ahead; will probably win	16	25
No conclusion, too early	25	19
Goldwater ahead or doing well	3	0
	100	100

5.1. The news available to many of these people was quite definitive. Over half of those who, before voting, were exposed to some election news (which means one out of three persons interviewed), concluded from what they had heard that a Johnson victory was certain and that the race for President was, for all practical purposes, already decided. Only six persons (less than 2 percent of the 364 people interviewed) were left with the impression by the election news that Goldwater was making a comparatively strong showing (see Table 5.2). There was little ambiguity about the overall impact on perceptions of whatever returns were heard.

The two broadcast media were plainly the chief sources of early election news; radio and TV were mentioned as the primary source of information by 81 percent of those who had heard something by the time they voted. More people mentioned radio than television, probably because Californians, who are wedded to their cars, tuned in as they drove home from work or to the polls. Yet television, despite its smaller audience, was clearly the more effective of the two in giving people a clear idea of the likely outcome. This effectiveness was not so much an attribute of the medium as of the way people made use of it. People were more likely to be listening to radio when there were only scattered returns; they turned to television only after work, when the returns coming in were more definitive and viewers could give them their undivided attention. It appears that the network coverage provided a clear omen of an impending Johnson victory from the minute it went on the air. Of those who started to follow these returns from 4 p.m. PST, 71 percent said that, as soon as they turned on their set, they knew "right away" that the race was more or less decided. This proportion increased to near 90 percent among viewers who first tuned in at a later hour. The 15 percent who received whatever prevoting information they had from "other people" were only hearing secondhand what had originally come over radio or television.

It must nevertheless be emphasized that not all the information with which California late voters went to the polls, and which was available also to nonvoters while they still had a chance to vote, came from the network election coverage that began at 4 p.m. Even in Ohio, where polls had closed before these broadcasts could be heard, one out of seven persons interviewed claimed to have had some outcome news while still free to make a decision, and a few even said that, before voting, they had become certain of an impending Johnson landslide. There had been news bulletins on radio and television and scattered bits of returns from early-voting hamlets in New England in the Cleveland afternoon paper. These same reports had been heard even earlier in their day by Californians but were soon overshadowed by reports on voting trends in all sections of the country.

Nor did viewers or listeners in California who had become certain the election was decided necessarily reach this conclusion after hearing computer-based predictions. The person who had heard such a prediction was more likely to be certain about the outcome than others who had not, but by far the largest number of those "certain" about the results before they voted said the trend was evident from the tally of the popular vote.

Comparing the conclusions reached by three groups of voters helped to pin down this impact of the early network coverage. Among California late voters who had

— followed network returns before voting, 56 percent became "certain" that Johnson had won;

— not followed network returns before voting, 20 percent became "certain."

— Of all Ohio late voters, 14 percent became "certain."

The last group, surely, could have had only the scantiest information on election trends. If they reached a "certain" conclusion, it was because, as some put it, the news only confirmed what they had known all along.

These observations show that conclusions drawn from available news did not depend solely on news content but also on what people had expected beforehand. Thus, it obviously took more convincing information to invalidate an expectation that Goldwater would win than to confirm one about a Johnson victory. Those who had anticipated a landslide became certain of the outcome, before voting, about twice as often (42 percent) as those who had given Goldwater a near-even or better than even chance to win (22 percent). Political preference, by contrast, made little difference: Goldwater supporters were as likely as Johnson supporters to accept the (for them) unpleasant fact of a Johnson victory.

The Broadcasts and Voter Turnout

How much late election day slack could be traced to the network election coverage? Interviews with the 364 Californians, all registered voters, yielded just one case of late election-day slack traceable to having heard broadcasts: An angry Goldwater enthusiast had become so dismayed at the news of the lopsided Johnson margin that he simply gave up and did not vote, even though he claimed that he had never given Goldwater much of a chance in the first place.

A single case hardly provides a sound basis for quantitative generalization. Still, one of the most startling and unexpected findings of our study was the low rate of nonvoting among registered voters.[4] We simply could not find many nonvoters, despite the fact that our California sample was so drawn that it should have yielded one interview with a nonvoter for every three with late voters. Yet the total yield of nonvoters was only twelve! In Ohio, also, few nonvoters were located.

This dearth of nonvoters seemed explicable in one or both of two ways: Either (1) our techniques were at fault in that nonvoters were somehow evading our interviewers or were falsely stating that they had voted when they had not, or (2) the registration lists on which we had relied for our sample were in some way inaccurate so that they exaggerated the actual amount of nonvoting. We accordingly made a special effort to check on suspected nonvoters. The California precinct rosters that voters had to sign before they could cast a ballot were compared with our registration lists. This produced 351 names of persons officially registered in these precincts who, according to this record, had not shown up at the polls.[5] Selected interviewers were then instructed to make a special effort to contact these nonvoters and determine whether they had in fact not voted or, if they were unable to reach them, to ascertain the reason why they were so hard to reach.

The mystery of the missing nonvoter was resolved when it became apparent that a considerable number of our official nonvoters were in fact spurious nonvoters—71 percent of the California nonvoters and 59 percent of the Ohio nonvoters, it turned out, had either moved out of the precinct or died. For people in this group, the "nonvoter" label was a mere artifact of their names still appearing on the lists of precincts where they no longer resided.

On the basis of official records, the nonvoting rate among registered Californians would have been 14 percent; in Ohio it would have been 16 percent. We tried to correct for this inflation in the number of nonvoters by subtracting from the group of supposed nonvoters those who, according to family or neighbors, had died or moved out of the precinct. We continued to count as nonvoters those about whom no information could be obtained (15 percent of the alleged nonvoters in California, and 19 percent in Ohio). Still, even when so cautiously corrected, the proportion of bona fide nonvoters in California dropped to 4 percent and that in Ohio to 7 percent. Thus, relative to Ohio, nonvoting in California, where returns were heard, appeared even lower than it did before. The 4 percent nonvoting in California accordingly represents the maximum number within which broadcast-induced late election-day slack could have occurred. That is to say, if *every* registrant who did not vote had heard network returns before polls closed and thereby decided not to vote, a maximum of 4 percent of the electorate could have been so affected.

Moreover, much of the verified nonvoting in the West, as in the East, turned out to be due either to illness or to unavoidable and unanticipated absence (being out of town on election day). Hence, this logical—but obviously improbable—upper limit to broadcast effects must be further reduced by at least the number who were physically unable to vote. Among those remaining—perhaps 2.5 percent of all registered voters—lack of political interest was clearly the most important reason for failure to appear at the polls.

Was nonvoting more frequent among Republican or Democratic registrants? According to official registration records, Democrats made up the majority of those who stayed at home. But, based on our corrected lists, there was a slight excess of Republican nonvoters. Given the importance of factors, other than exposure to returns, that can account for nonvoting, there was no reason to suspect that this slight excess was a response to the broadcasts.

When we focused directly on the impact of network broadcasts, their subordinate importance as a cause of slack became still clearer. Nonvoters, compared to late voters, had less interest in and were less involved in the election campaign. Fewer of them had followed returns before polls closed. The same characteristics that accounted for their lower rate of broadcast exposure also helped to explain their failure to vote. Also, we found nobody among our respondents who had deliberately delayed voting until they could determine how the election was going.

Vote Decisions: Crystallizations and Switches

Now to some other possibilities—that the election broadcasts had encouraged vote switching or helped crystallize the votes of persons who otherwise might not have voted. With these possibilities in mind, we had asked every voter to tell us about any political decisions made on election day. We asked about this before the questioning turned to the effect of the broadcasts.

Both in California and Ohio, most election-day decisions that were mentioned had to do with voting on candidates for lower offices or on some propositions put before the voters. An identical 2 percent of late voters in each state reported a decision affecting their choice for President. All of these involved a vote crystallization, rather than a switch, by a person who, after some prior doubts, had finally come to a firm decision. But these decisions were not evenly distributed between the two candidates. Of the seven crystallizations in California, five resulted in Goldwater votes, one in a vote for Johnson, while the seventh refused to tell how he had cast his ballot for President. Of two crystallizations in Ohio, one was for Goldwater, the other for Johnson.

The natural question is whether the apparent preponderance of these last-minute shifts toward Goldwater reflected the influence of early returns or whether these votes would have crystallized in any event. The evidence suggests that the majority of these last-minute decisions were made by anti-Goldwater Republicans, moderates under cross-pressure who, until the last minute, could not make up their minds to vote for so conservative a candidate. Such crystallizations in Ohio, obviously, could not be attributed to the election broadcasts. But even in California, no cause-effect relationship could be established. In fact, the seven last-minute crystallizers, on going to the polls, had been rather less "certain" of the outcome than other late voters.

When we look at the process of vote crystallization, it becomes quite evident that the mere approach of a moment for decision forces the voter to make a choice. Thus, nearly one out of five late voters in California—compared with one out of six in Ohio—reported having "seriously considered" at some time during the campaign either not voting at all or voting but not voting for President or Senator. All but a few had resolved these doubts before election day. Three late voters in California and two in Ohio actually cast ballots without voting for President. The number who voted but passed up the opportunity to vote for U.S. senator was larger. Obviously, the presidential contest plays a central role in getting out the vote, and anyone inclined to cast a ballot cannot, without some unease, refrain from voting for the highest office.

Attitudinal Reactions

If the election broadcasts in 1964 had little influence on vote decisions, did they cause people to feel differently about voting? The large majority of late voters and nonvoters—72 percent who had heard some returns—said, when asked about this, that the information had made them neither more nor less eager to vote. Where it did make a difference, "being more eager" outnumbered "being less eager" by a 3 to 2 ratio.

Why should anyone upon hearing that the outcome of an election can not possibly be overturned by votes yet to be cast become *more* eager to vote? Why would those who feel *less* like voting because of what they have heard go ahead and vote anyway? Even though these reactions are rarely translated into changes in overt behavior, they help explain the prevalence of stability over change and also point to the kinds of circumstances under which such covert tendencies may pass the threshold of action. In examining these attitudinal responses, we have a twofold purpose: to specify the role played by broadcast returns in the 1964 election and to understand what has happened in elections since.

To begin with, whether a person experienced any change in attitude toward voting in the Johnson-Goldwater race depended on the conclusion drawn from whatever news had been heard. The more certain a person was of the conclusion, the more likely that this would translate into some kind of reaction related to the futility of voting.

Second, voters who had concluded that the election was not going as they expected reacted even more strongly. To be sure, the polls had all along been predicting a clear-cut Johnson victory, and those still entertaining thoughts of a Goldwater victory were clearly a small minority, but when these people, however few, saw the Johnson landslide materialize before their very eyes, they tended to become "less eager" rather than "more eager" to vote.

Finally, underdog perceptions (Goldwater supporters seeing their candidate losing) elicited more reactions one way or the other than bandwagon perceptions (Johnson supporters finding that Johnson was winning or about to win), and bandwagon perceptions, in turn, elicited more reactions than perceptions that the race was still very much in doubt.

In contrast to the rather conclusive presidential returns, the very scattered and partial returns from the California Senate race, available to a few who voted very late in the day, showed the outcome of that race to be still very much in doubt. The report that Salinger was actually trailing in the vote count had a galvanizing "underdog" effect on supporters who had expected him to win, making them "more eager" to vote.

Also, some late voters, explaining their reactions to presidential returns, spontaneously mentioned the Senate race: Several had heeded Salinger's warning not to be dissuaded from voting should early returns show a Johnson landslide. Moreover, the news that Johnson had won was likely to make persons anticipating an "extremely close" Senate race more eager to vote, regardless of whether they were for or against Johnson. In any case, the uncertainty of the senatorial outcome helped forestall any slack that might have followed once those who had not yet voted heard that the presidential contest was all but over. We have here an example of a *reverse coat-tail* effect, whereby concern for the candidate in the lesser race rebounds to the benefit to the head of the ticket.

The Law of Minimal Consequences

Why was the overall effect of the broadcast returns on the behavior of voters so minimal? In explanation, we point to factors and conditions, some general and some specific to the 1964 election, that make it difficult for election broadcasts to change vote intentions. However, we emphasize that the failure to observe significant changes in the short span of time between hearing returns and casting a vote (or choosing not to cast one) does not preclude the existence of significant effects either in other elections or over the long run.

The minimal impact of broadcast returns is attributable to three specific conditions:

(1) the small size of the group potentially open to influence,
(2) the neutralization of any impetus toward change by countervailing influences, and
(3) the stability of certain attitudes that support the habit of voting.

The susceptible group. To be susceptible to influence on election day, a person has first of all to have registered, then defer voting until significant returns begin coming in, tune in on the election coverage or at least talk with someone who has tuned in, and, finally, find the expectation on which one's vote intention had been predicated invalidated by broadcast returns. A confirmation that what one has expected to happen has, indeed, happened will not deter a person from voting as intended.

According to estimates, some two-thirds of all California citizens of voting age had registered for the 1964 election. By 4 p.m. on election day between 25 and 30 percent of those on our polling lists had not yet voted. Of those interviewed, 40 percent had been following election returns prior to voting and others had heard something about how the race was going. Among those who went to the polls in the hour before closing time, nearly everyone had heard something or other. Yet despite the large number who knew something about the likely outcome of the race before they voted or still could have voted, only 12 percent received information that invalidated their expectations. After all, most had anticipated a Johnson victory.

In addition, studies of media behavior during an electoral campaign show that it is those least interested and least involved who are most open to influence. Those who never register are, for that reason, quite obviously beyond the range of possible influence from election-day returns. Among those registered and thus potentially open to influence in 1964, it was—as could have been anticipated—the less interested, less involved, and less politically sophisticated who, on election day, believed unrealistically that Goldwater had a good chance of winning. For the same reasons, these were the persons least likely to have heard something about the outcome before they went to the polls. Hence, most of the relatively few persons whose expectations were subject to invalidation were not subject to influence from the broadcast returns. As for the rest, the election results did not contradict what they had expected. That the returns should have surprised so few people indicates that any bandwagon or underdog psychology at work would already have worked its effects before election day.

What voters had heard by the time they went to the polls was largely a function of when they voted. The question is: Might some people have waited to vote until they had heard how the race was going on? Our study provided no evidence to substantiate this possibility. When we compared those who voted during the last 90 minutes before the polls closed with other late voters, there were no indications that this group was any more volatile in its preferences than the rest. Nor, lulled into complacency by returns, had they been lured to the polls and persuaded to vote in a last-minute electioneering effort. On the contrary, the "late late" voters included a rather large number of the better-educated and political sophisticated independents, particularly Republicans in conflict over Goldwater, who had gone to the polling place after work. A number of them reported that, during the campaign, they had changed their minds several times about whether to vote for Goldwater, defect to Johnson, or not to push the lever for President. They were nevertheless disinclined to sit out the election because of their concern, shared by many others, about contests for other than the top office. Going to vote still made sense to them, even though the presidential race seemed irrevocably decided by the votes already cast and counted.

Countervailing influences. Reports reaching voters on election day were interpreted within the context of what they already knew and of other competing messages. Among a flood of election-day messages were those urging Goldwaterites to vote early and so avoid demoralization should Johnson pile up a big lead in the East. There was also Salinger's reminder to his supporters that he still needed their votes despite the apparent Democratic tide. Also, the nonpartisan saturation campaign to get out the vote—to be sure to cast a ballot, regardless for whom—continued right through election day. Appeals from the mass media, from election workers, and even from friends and associates inundated people from all sides.

Many respondents reported that they themselves, on election day, had urged others to be sure to go to the polls or that they had themselves been so urged by others. Reports of last-minute attempts to win votes by partisan argument were far fewer in number. Only 12 persons, out of the 364, indicated that they had been the target of a suggestion (or had overheard a chance remark) that it no longer made much difference whether or not they voted, or that they had voiced this feeling to others.

The motivation to vote. Casting a ballot means different things to different voters. Thus the way voters responded to returns broadcast before they voted depended a good deal on what the act of voting meant to them. We could distinguish three different orientations that moved people to vote.

There were those primarily motivated by the *utility* they perceived in their action. The widespread expectation that news of a Johnson landslide would produce slack rested on an image of most voters being so motivated, with their participation dependent on their perception of their own vote as able to influence the outcome. Once an election appears decided, as this one did, voting assumedly loses all utility; it no longer makes any difference whether or not one votes. Those so motivated would be most easily dissuaded from going to the polls by the one-sided returns.

A second kind of orientation to voting, *partisan involvement*, however, contributes to the stability of reactions even where the vote would appear to have no utility. The vote, from this perspective, serves above all as an ideological expression, as a declaration of solidarity and, to that extent, is independent of any immediate practical consideration. The act itself becomes a way to bear witness to one's ideological preference. Voters with such partisan orientations find reasons to vote even where it may appear to make no difference in the outcome. They assess the implications of the margin of victory in terms of the victor's mandate and what it means for the future of the party. Republicans, in California, knowing that the race for the presidency was foredoomed nevertheless voted to help avoid a spill-over effect on other races. Democrats, with a partisan orientation, voted as an act of faith even though Johnson no longer needed their help. Party loyalists, in particular, are likely to assess the implications of broadcast returns for the outcome of other races—for example, as we have seen, the possible effect of news about the presidential race on the outcome of the California senate election. Other partisans, no doubt, voted because they wanted to hold down the Johnson margin; some, to repudiate the Goldwater brand of Republicanism so unambigously that it would cease to be a political force.

A third orientation related neither to perceived utility or a partisan outlook supports stability in electoral participation. Many people—even in an age of political cynicism—regard voting as an *obligation of citizenship* or, as one Californian expressed it, "a God-given right" that must be exercised. From this perspective, casting a ballot is an expressive gesture, a form of testimony to one's commitment to the democratic process. Even where there is no real contest, one votes from a sense of duty. Those whom our study showed to become "more eager" to vote after hearing broadcasts were persons who saw the vote as the only way to influence government officials, who had a good deal of confidence in their own political know-how, and who were primarily voting for (rather than against) a candidate. Whether or not they believed their vote could still make a difference, they voted because it was their obligation as citizens to do so.

To understand, then, why there was so little slack and why, on the contrary, so many voters continued to flock to the polls when it no longer seemed to make any sense, one must recognize that people vote not just to have a say in the outcome but to express their partisan loyalties and their affective commitment to the political system.

How Typical Was 1964?

It is apparent that, to begin with, those late voters susceptible to influence by news of the Johnson landslide were few in number. Moreover, what returns they heard were interpreted within a framework of prior expectations and meanings that they attached to their vote. Factors of this sort have usually limited the short-run conversion potential of media messages in natural settings. Thus the entire set of relationships between election night broadcasts and their effect on late voters has to be seen as subject to what has been called the "law of minimal consequences."[6] In line with this, our findings on the 1964 election show that short-term effects of broadcast returns were certainly limited, if not downright minuscule. Yet insofar as this "law" is nothing more than a probability statement, we must ask whether the specific conditions that explained the limited impact in 1964 have prevailed, and will invariably prevail, in every election. We must also emphasize that this so-called law applies only to immediate and short-run effects. It says nothing about the more subtle and often more enduring effects of network election broadcast practices that had not yet made themselves evident.

Impact in other elections. In one sense, the situation on election day 1964 differed from all other presidential election days that would follow: The fast count and the early declaration of a winner were still novelties. Novelty would increase the likelihood for impact. Yet this was the type of election least likely to produce broadcast effects. It was characterized by (1) the altogether unambiguous way in which early returns foretold the final result and (2) by the high proportion of late voters for whom this information merely confirmed exactly what they had expected. These two factors work in opposite directions. On the one hand, the near certainty of information makes it

Table 5.3   Circumstances Characterizing Elections

Indication	Pre-Election Forecasts	
of the Outcome in Early Returns	One-Sided Race	Close Race
Conclusive: Outcome Decided	1. Confirmation 2. Upset	3. Resolution of Doubts
Ambiguous: Outcome Still in Doubt	4. Selective Interpretation	5. Confirmation of Doubts

difficult for voters to retain contrary beliefs or to withhold judgment by focusing selectively on some items of information while ignoring the apparent trend. On the other hand, most forecasts before the election had been so one-sided in their indication of an easy Johnson victory that very few people experienced the election news as any kind of surprise.

In 1964, pre-election forecasts indicated that the race would be one-sided; early broadcast returns, declaring the outcome decided, confirmed the prediction. This represents but one combination of circumstances involving pre-election forecasts and network projections based on early returns that may characterize a particular election. Table 5.3 shows schematically a limited number of possibilities. The key word in each box characterizes the type of viewer response one would logically expect in each combination of circumstances.

Type 1, of course, represents the 1964 situation. It also represents what happened on election night 1972 when the incumbent Richard Nixon defeated George McGovern. Early returns, for most late voters, simply confirmed their expectations of a sure victory for the incumbent. CBS gave the election to Nixon at 8:30 p.m. EST (5:30 p.m. PST). Figures compiled by the U.S. Bureau of the Census showed that nearly 15 percent of voters on the West Coast cast their ballots after 6:00 p.m. when, assumedly, the contest was over. Yet, as in 1964, with early returns only confirming what most expected, any impetus toward election-day slack on the part of disoriented voters was minimized. Since Nixon's landslide did not translate into significant Republican gains in the Congress, the early network projections did not give rise to prolonged debate after the election.

Like Type 1, Type 5 also identifies a situation in which early returns mainly confirm what has been expected. However, in the latter circumstance, the forecast of a close race is confirmed as early returns show that the outcome is still in doubt. This confirmation of expectations can have a quite different effect from that in Type 1—mobilizing those who have not yet voted. The longer the early returns project a see-saw battle, the stronger the impetus in the direction of voting.

This type 5 effect turned up in our 1964 study, as illustrated by the concurrent California Senate election between George Murphy, a Hollywood actor, and Pierre Salinger, who had been press secretary to President Kennedy. Pre-election forecasts had indicated that this would be a very close race and the first scattered returns, available before all polls closed, showed the outcome to be still very much in doubt. These results, as indicated earlier in the chapter, had a positive mobilizing influence on late voters.

The ambiguity in early returns is present in two types of elections. Type 5 represents one kind of ambiguity in that the race appears to be so close that it may not be decided until returns from most states are in. The ambiguity in a Type 4 situation is of another sort: With only a small number of districts reporting, the tally of the popular vote may contradict the explicit projection of a network or contradictory interpretations by commentators on the same network or by different networks may leave the viewer bewildered. This kind of ambiguity is unlikely to produce change, positively or negatively, in the motivation to vote. Viewers are prone to interpret such discrepancies selectively in accordance with what they have been led to expect.

The potential for slack is greatest as a result of the invalidations that occur in the Type 2 and Type 3 situations. Here the returns inspire a clear redefinition of the outcome. Expectations have been upset and it appears that there is nothing that a disappointed voter can do to change the outcome. In the Type 2 invalidation, the expected winner turns out to be the loser; in the Type 3 election, what was expected to be a close race turns into a comfortable (or even a landslide) victory for one of the candidates. Harry Truman's victory over Thomas Dewey in 1948 was a Type 2 election but this predated the problem of early returns and late voters.

1980, however, provided a classic case of a Type 3 invalidation. Pollsters had been predicting a close race between President Carter and his Republican challenger, Ronald Reagan. It turned out to be anything but that. Not only did the broadcasters—now relying on exit polls (interviews with voters leaving the polls)—call the race long before polls everywhere had closed but President Carter's concession speech was televised at 9:50 p.m. EST, an hour before the polls on the Pacific Coast closed and while it was still mid-day in Hawaii. Both the NBC projection, which came at 2:15 p.m. PST, and the Carter concession may have had a measurable effect on turnout. When news of the NBC statement reached the lines waiting outside the polls to vote, according to news reports, many voters simply went home.

Several West Coast congressmen—Democrats—blamed NBC for their defeat, though, as far as we know, reports of any large-scale defection from the polls have never been authoritatively confirmed. In a California poll of registered nonvoters, conducted in mid-January, 10 percent said they did not vote specifically because of the projections; another 6 percent said it was because of Carter's early concession on television. The two months since the election may have influenced these "recollections," or they could be taken as justifications of an evident lapse in meeting an obligation of citizenship. Also in January, the Survey Research Center of the University of Michigan recontacted its national sample by telephone to ascertain the time they had voted and the time they had heard election news coverage. From an elaborate analysis of voter turnout among those who had not heard returns, including a check of local election records to ascertain if respondents were eligible and had indeed voted, John Jackson inferred that voting among those in the East exposed to early returns was about 12 percent below that expected had they not heard these returns. Yet Laurily Epstein and Gerald Strom argue from these same data that the election coverage could at best have discouraged only about .02 percent of those registered from casting a vote.[7]

Philip Dubois, who used aggregate data to compare turnout in a number of states over a number of years, however, confirms the suggestion of a "late election day slack" in 1980. His results, he wrote, were

> consistent with the assumption that the unusual circumstances of the 1980 election (i.e., the failure of public opinion polls to predict the landslide outcome and the relatively large number of undecided or weakly committed voters) were conducive to having late day voters in the West discouraged by the projections of a large Reagan win.[8]

This issue is hardly closed.

Under what conditions do broadcast returns become either self-fulfilling or self-defeating? To answer this question, one must take a number of factors into account. First, there is the infrequency with which voters change their minds, especially on election day. Yet in a closely contested election even a minuscule percentage of the total vote, if concentrated in the right places, can overturn the result. However, a second factor works against this possibility: in a close contest, early returns are unlikely to bring unhedged projections of the outcome, networks being more than reluctant to go too far out on a limb on election night. A third factor is the credibility of any early prediction. The earlier a network is willing to predict the outcome and the more such predictions find public acceptance, the greater their potential impact on voting behavior.

All things considered, there is a likelihood that Type 2 elections, in which expectations are widely invalidated, will become rarer. Improvements in polling techniques and continuous polling, even up to election day, reduce the likelihood that results will be far out of line with predictions. More important, the proliferation of published polls and their wide dissemination leads to greater uniformity in pre-election expectations; everyone draws on the same sources of information. The self-appointed expert with his ear close to the ground has virtually disappeared, and the projective element in popular estimates—whereby supporters overestimate their candidate's chances—is likewise on the wane. Still, upsets attributable to last-minute shifts, such as apparently affected the outcome of the 1980 election, are within the realm of the possible. Such instability is apt to be greatest in nomination primaries, in particular those that come early in the campaign, for instance, the 1984 Democratic primary in New Hampshire, where voters confounded both the politicians' and the pollsters' predictions by choosing Gary Hart over Walter Mondale.

If Type 2 invalidations are apt to be less common, Type 3 invalidations may occur more frequently. With polling now big business, reputations count for more, making political pollsters more apt to shy away from flat predictions. Increasingly, they have qualified their estimates in every conceivable way to avoid the kind of fiasco that occurred in 1948 (when most polls signaled that Truman was about to lose). In 1980, some public opinion researchers, though aware of a last-minute drift towards Reagan, were cautious to the end in predicting a close race. Thus, the close race that turns out to be not so close is always a possibility.

Many late voters, in 1964, felt that pre-election polls had influenced the outcome of the election. How so? Because ''nobody wants to vote for a loser.'' Yet it would have been hard, even had we tried, to document the charge that Goldwater or any other big loser— McGovern, in 1972, for instance—lost votes because pre-election polls showed they were losing. A vote decision is not a simple act but subject to many and often conflicting considerations. Yet our study did show that the candidates' standing in the polls exerted an *indirect* influence on voters, insofar as these indirectly affected their responses to the early election returns. Forecasts of an altogether one-sided race had eliminated the element of surprise, thereby immunizing most late voters and rendering them nonsusceptible to influence. It would take a polling fiasco, comparable to that in 1948, to upset the expectations of a significant part of the electorate.

Nevertheless, there will always be voters whose expectations deviate from those disseminated by polls and mass media pundits. Mavericks, whose expectations are invalidated by broadcast returns, are bound to turn up in every election. To the extent that these voters respond by acting contrary to what they had intended, network projections will always remain a source of potential instability. Still, as noted, this potential for instability is reduced inasmuch as those likely to hold such deviant expectations are also less likely to pay attention to the early returns and also to react less politically.

The impact of confirmation or invalidation also depends on whether voters' interest in an election centers on a single race (or referendum) or on a whole range of contests. We have shown that interest in other races inhibited slack in the Johnson-Goldwater election and there is no reason to believe that it has been otherwise in other presidential years. Logically, all other things being equal, the danger of slack from broadcast returns would be greatest in areas of one-party dominance, with voters remaining unconcerned about the effect of low turnout on the outcomes of local races. It would be equally great in party primaries with a contest limited to a single office and in a referendum on a single issue. Here a close race could indeed be decided by early returns that dissuade voters.

Primaries and referenda are additionally vulnerable because of their lower rates of electoral participation. To the extent that a large number of those registered to vote are only marginally committed to voting, they are also likely to be more responsive to any last-minute effort to bring out the vote or to broadcast returns that tell them their voting no longer matters. By contrast, the electorate in presidential elections seems far less volatile. Among California voters in 1964, those voting for President exhibited a clear committment toward voting, for whatever reason. Once registered, most people vote. Where they fail to vote, it can be traced to illness or other impediments that make it difficult to show up at the polls on election day. Any practice, however well-intentioned, that swells the number of marginally committed voters eligible to vote in a national election—whether the easing of registration requirements or the adoption of procedures for automatic registration—also contributes to the likelihood that the broadcast of early returns will have an effect on voting.

Long-Range and Ancillary Effects

Any innovation in political communication—whether the admission of the press to legislative debates, the broadcasting of political party conventions, the televising of presidential press conferences, and so forth—invariably invokes alarm. Based on an oversimplified notion of individual reactions and the ramifications of these reactions for political institutions, fears as well as visions of supposed benefits are usually exaggerated. The subtleties with which things generally work themselves out are recognized neither by the alarmists nor enthusiasts. Indeed, this high-pitched sense of alarm may itself serve as one of the firmest guarantors against sudden change.

Our finding that the early projection of a winner by the networks had practically no effect on the outcome of the 1964 presidential race has been replicated since for other elections.[9] Yet the issue remains alive and increasingly vexing. The televised concession of Jimmy Carter, made while voting in the West and Hawaii was still in progress, has in fact given it a new relevancy. Most people, like many of the late voters we interviewed two decades ago, remain convinced that both pre-election polls and early returns on election day do influence how people will vote—themselves excepted!

Nothing that has been determined about the impact of broadcast returns, either in our or other studies, demonstrates that these have no effects. Even those late voters who do not change their intention to vote (or not to vote) may believe that casting a vote, while knowing that the race for President has already been decided, amounts to a partial disenfranchisement. They cannot help feeling that their ballot somehow counts for less. Only their partisan commitments or their sense of a civic obligation to vote moves them toward the polls.

That the outcry against the early returns continues to center on the disenfranchisement of the late voters out West is natural enough. But from another viewpoint, sometimes articulated, western voters can be seen to enjoy an unfair advantage over their compatriots in the East. Are they not in a better position to weigh the consequence of their ballot and to capitalize on this knowledge? They can deliberately decide to vote late and then base their decisions on political trends. It was altogether possible, we suggested after our analysis in 1964, that voters in areas where early returns are available long before polls close would learn to consider carefully the utility of their vote before casting it. Imagine a very close election, in which the early broadcast returns indicate that California—or California in combination with Oregon, or Alaska, or Hawaii—has the electoral votes necessary for victory. With the electoral votes of other states already accounted for, attention would turn to the vote in the West. Especially where the contest was expected to be close and where many people had considered voting for a third-party candidate, would not some be tempted to delay their vote until they knew how the election was going? That so few voters should have consciously postponed voting in 1964 did not mean that others might not do so in other elections.

There are circumstances under which the early broadcast of returns could alter the general aversion against voting for a third-party in American presidential elections. Under a two-party system, the necessity for electoral coalitions has long been a formidable barrier in the way of such protest. People who see themselves voting for the lesser of two evils are disinclined to defect to a minor party for fear of bringing the greater evil to power. Early returns improve their knowledge of the odds, especially as the predictions gain credibility. The performance of the networks, when computerized projections were initially introduced, had been pretty mixed. For example, in 1960, one network first called the election for Richard Nixon but then quickly modified this prediction in favor of Kennedy as sizable returns came in. No such blunder has since haunted the broadcasters in national elections, but the calling of state and local contests has proved more hazardous.

Past mistakes have evidently made broadcasters more cautious even as they have refined the technology for making predictions. They have gone out of their way to explain to their viewers how predictions are made and to hedge these with semantic qualifications: "probable winners," "indicated winners," "declared winners," and so on. When some early predictions of individual races had to be reversed, there was little public outcry inasmuch as the broadcasters had allowed for just such possibilities from the start of their coverage.

Long-term adaptation to the fast tabulation of votes and to computerized predictions based on exit polling—an established practice since 1968—involves learning how to live with them. For the individual voter, this means understanding the meaning of an apparent trend as well as the difference between an early projection from scanty evidence, a definitive trend in the electoral vote, and a clear indication of defeat. Even as early as 1964 the more experienced viewers among the election night audience, we found, were not only more knowledgeable about how predictions are made but had more faith in the accuracy of these predictions. As more voters come to understand the distinction between a tally of the vote and a projection of trends from sample districts and exit polls, more will also recognize that broadcasters are simply applying a new technology to improve their coverage of returns. The real departure from past practice lies in the new practice of actually declaring a winner before the votes have ever been cast.

Given the controversy over returns, voters in western states no less than party managers have become acutely aware that they may be subject to influence. They are gradually adapting to the speed-up in disseminating returns. One can deliberately vote early before significant returns become available; one can shut one's ears to any election news; one can persuade oneself in advance that what really counts is the margin of victory; or one can focus on the state and local races still to be decided. The growing awareness of pre-election polls and what they predict limits the effect of last-minute broadcast predictions. To repeat: Whatever bandwagon or underdog psychology may be at work in electoral decisions will have worked its influence on voters before election day.

All this adds up to a strong argument for treating American election broadcasts as the conclusion of the media campaign coverage with its constant tracking of the race and concern over who's ahead. Nowadays most people learn where candidates (or would-be candidates) stand in the polls even before they have had much chance to learn about them or to develop a firm preference. Insofar as voters consciously orient themselves to what the pundits predict, voting becomes as much a tactical decision as a statement of preference. In and of itself, tactical voting is hardly a new phenomenon created by the polls. Anyone who has ever considered voting for a third-party candidate in a two-party race knows the dilemma: Should one waste a vote on a sure loser or support the less undesirable of the other candidates? Credible polls supply the kinds of information that make tactical voting more scientific. They also can be used to substantiate or discredit the charge that third-party challengers are nothing but spoilers. In 1980, for instance, the League of Women Voters made John Anderson's right to participate in the televised presidential debates as an independent candidate without party endorsement contingent on his achieving a 15 percent showing in at least two national preference polls.

Motivations for voting appear to have been shifting. This is attested to by the increase in ticket-splitting and the incresing volatility in voting behavior. Party loyalty may still be the one best predictor of the average person's vote, as determined by the classic election studies of the 1940s and 1950s, but parties are less and less able to count on traditional allegiances. An increasing number of tactical voters, intent on registering a protest or on having some influence on the nominating process, are oriented to the polls in casting their votes. A British Gallup survey found three percent of British voters in 1979 admitting that they were influenced by what the polls had been saying "when [they] finally decided which way to vote." In the June 1983 national election, this percentage was up to five. While there was little difference between Conservative and Labour voters on this score (2 versus 3 percent), 9 percent of the independent voters said they took the polls into account. This suggests a significant amount of tactical voting. Thus the polls have, to an extent, preempted the potential effect of election night broadcasts.

The ubiquity of political polling cannot in itself account for the new voter volatility, either in the United States or Britain. In 1983 a number of other circumstances contributed to the swell in tactical voting: The election was conceded to the Conservatives; policy issues remained submerged in a lackluster campaign; and it was no longer essentially a two-party contest. The Alliance (a coalition of the new Social Democrats and the Liberals) constantly invoked the published polls to persuade voters that it offered a viable political alternative. If dissatisfied Labour party supporters would only recognize this, they argued, the Alliance could overtake Labour in the national vote total and replace it as the main opposition party. Winning roughly 25 percent of the popular vote, the Alliance ended a close third, about three points behind Labour and close to what most public polls had predicted. But unlike Labour, the Alliance had no regional base. Its strength was so distributed that it won seats in only 23 (out of 650) districts, compared with 209 taken by Labour Party candidates. The polls, having nationalized the election, helped bring this disparity in representation into sharp focus and, for a brief time, until other policy questions once again moved into the forefront, it became a natural issue for the Alliance.

Technological innovations, by their nature, call for new rules to cope with their consequences. Certainly, the wide use of exit polls, the development of electronic data banks, rapid data processing, computerized graphics, and so on, make it possible to have reliable forecasts ever faster and even before the election is over in any state. In 1984 network public opinion analysts, based on exit polls in primary states, often knew the outcome by early afternoon. There is no reason to believe that it is not also practically possible to project the winner of a national contest before polls have closed in any one state. There is no denying that voters have a keen interest in learning the outcome as soon as this information becomes available. Therefore, there is fierce and expensive competition among networks to be the first to call the race. But does the public have a right to know as soon as it is technologically possible to know? Even if it does not, voluntary restraint by the networks is difficult to enforce. At the same time, legal restraints to forbid exit polls or the broadcast of early returns pose hard First Amendment questions that are not readily answerable.

We still believe that the proposal for a uniform polling day, first publicly suggested by Dr. Frank Stanton of CBS in 1964, may be the best solution to the still troublesome question of broadcast effects. Balloting all over the country ending at the same hour would permit the fullest exploitation of the new technology. Results from all parts of the country would be available at about the same time, so that suspicions about the possible effect of early returns would be ruled out. Indeed, there would be no early returns. While exit polling would, no doubt, continue, this would serve the purpose which it was originally meant to serve. In announcing the results, the journalists could use the information gained therefrom to give an interpretation in depth to the results—what groups and sections voted which way and what all this indicated.

With all polls closing simultaneously, the outcome would most likely be announced soon thereafter, and there would be no long night of waiting for the returns to come in. To be sure, the long election-night vigil has played a not unimportant part in the political life of the voters. Especially since the advent of radio, it has served as one of those unifying occasions during which the nation comes together to demonstrate that what unites us is more important than what divides us (Chapter 6). To stay up on election night to learn who will be the new President has become one of our cherished rituals. Yet, with the fast count and early broadcast projections, the nature of the ritual has already changed. As early as 1964, a near-majority of Californians, asked whether the fun had gone out of election night, agreed that the experience was no longer the same.

Election night has become less a contest between candidates than a contest between network pollsters to see who can come up with the right answer soonest. With a uniform ballotting day, it could become an evening in which we all learn together what has happened but, in addition, learn a good deal about how it has happened and why. The losing candidate could once again graciously wait to concede until the whole nation had voted. The victor, now that all the people had spoken, could move to close ranks and lead the country. As for the people, they would no longer have to wonder if projecting the winner of the election before the polls were closed might somehow have changed the course of history.

N O T E S

1. Interested readers will find a fuller description of this study in the authors' *Voting and Nonvoting* (Boston: Blaisdell, 1968).

2. The sample was chosen to include voters with a wide variety of characteristics deemed relevant to understanding their reactions to the broadcasts. Thus, we selected precincts in Alameda and Contra Costs counties with sharply contrasting socioeconomic characteristics.

3. The early poll-closing time in Ohio turned out to be an advantage. Regular network news programs heard at 6:30 p.m. Eastern time reported significant news of election trends, even though they were not formally part of the election coverage.

4. Two studies, one by H. Mendelsohn, 212-225, and the other by D. Fuchs, 226-236, report similar observations. See their articles in the *Public Opinion Quarterly*, 30 (Summer, 1966).

5. Of these, 234 had been drawn into our original sample.

6. For a full statement, see Joseph T. Klapper, *The Effects of Mass Communication*. (Glencoe, IL: Free Press, 1960).

7. The California Poll finding is cited in *Congressional Quarterly*, August 8, 1981, p. 1438; Jackson and his colleagues have written a number of articles on their study. See his "Election Night Reporting and Voter Turnout," *American Journal of Political Science, 27* (November 1983), pp. 615-635; Laurily Epstein and Gerald Strom, "Survey Research and Election Night Projections," *Public Opinion* (February-March 1984), 48-50.

8. Philip Dubois, "Election Night Projections and Voter Turnout in the West," *American Political Quarterly*, 11 (July 1983), pp. 360f.

9. In addition to previously cited studies by Mendelsohn and by Fuchs of the 1964 election, see S. Tuchman and T. E. Coffin, *Public Opinion Quarterly* (Fall 1971), 315-326, on the 1968 election; L. K. Epstein and G. Strom, *American Politics Quarterly* (July 1981) on the 1980 election.

6

Watergate

TELEVISION AS A UNIFYING FORCE

A good deal of attention has been paid to the part played by the media, and especially television, in stirring up political conflict and helping to keep it stirred up. Within the past decades the American networks have been charged with fostering political division by seeking out controversy and emphasizing confrontation. In the 1950s they were accused of exacerbating racial conflict and creating national division by their coverage of school integration protests in the South. In the 1960s the ubiquitous presence of television was said to have helped foster and spread rioting in the urban ghettoes. Still later in the 1960s the networks, by readying their cameras for protestors everywhere—on the campus, marching in the streets, storming the Pentagon—were held responsible for escalating internal conflict over the war in Vietnam.

Drawing mostly on materials from our study of the press and public opinion during Watergate—that is, the long controversy that led to the first resignation of an American president[1]—we want to suggest that the case can just as readily be made that television, through its live coverage of major political events, even those that are most potentially divisive, more typically serves as a unifying than as a divisive force.

That television should act as a unifying force on certain ritualistic occasions where the whole world is watching is not surprising. Where the events being televised are highly symbolic occasions that serve to reaffirm common purposes and express individual loyalties—as in the swearing-in of a President or a State of the Union address to Congress or the wedding of a Prince—TV enlarges the audience and, ever more, turns what would otherwise be a small ceremony into a spectacle for the whole nation and, even, the world.

However, there are other televised political events that involve highly partisan and potentially divisive controversies where the elements of contest and conflict are explicitly recognized. Yet by opening these controversial, or potentially controversial, political negotiations to the public view, TV tends to downplay and mute the image of dissent. That television, in covering these events, transmits a picture different than reality is an observation that can, by now, be taken for granted (Chapter 2). The further suggestion here is that the televising of the controversy changes its reality.

In this chapter we focus on three blockbuster media events that were part of the Watergate controversy. All were covered live and in full by the television networks, drew record audiences, and attracted international attention. All were bona fide episodes in the unfolding controversy and, as part of the controversy, intrinsically controversial. Yet all of them were transformed by their televising into occasions that, for different reasons, served as much, or more, to unite the nation than to divide it.

Media Events

First, what kind of events and what kind of coverage are we talking about? Researchers venture into muddy water when they write of the "manufacture" or "construction" of reality by television.

Those who refer to the social construction of reality usually do so on the assumption that media reports about the world are somehow unreal—distorted either by the deliberate slanting of the news by the media to suit editors' views of events or the actual creation of factitious happening by news-hungry reporters.[2] That there is indeed always some discrepancy between image and reality, between what we apprehend and what is out there, seems undeniable but hardly a peculiarity of news reports. Here we will be speaking about how the interposition of the media, particularly television, between an event and its audience creates a new rhetorical situation.

A good start is the apparently simple and clear division between two kinds of events to which the media may respond. Thus, Boorstin has differentiated between what he calls spontaneous events, which do happen and would happen even without the media reporting them, and other pseudo-events, which are artificial in that they are planned, or planted, in order to be reported, even though no outright deception is involved.[3] Much effort goes into manipulating the media to cover the right events. According to Boorstin, it is this absence of spontaneity, the fact that an event is specifically planned for the convenience of the news media, that makes it a pseudo-event. Yet much of politics is nothing but communication, and publicity is always a potential resource. The revelation that a supposedly spontaneous event has actually been stage-managed can be as much a pseudo-event as the initial fakery. Interpreted in this literal fashion, the category of pseudo-events becomes so all-embracing as to make it include nearly all communication by elites to the public. However evocative, the distinction between these and real events strikes us as not analytically very useful.

A more useful distinction is that between events that remain privileged and those that are public. What the availability of mass media—and especially the electronic media—has done is to shift the boundary between the two spheres. Much of the real give-and-take of political bargaining continues to take place off-stage, but political actors are now forced into a posture of openness, into putting on their best possible face, and into an effort to manage their image, all by way of legitimating themselves and their reactions to their constituents. This imperative is hardly new; it precedes the advent of the modern media. Yet the ubiquitous presence of television cameras at parliamentary debates, in the court room, and other once sanctified retreats has added a new dimension. The opening of esoteric decision making to a wider public tends to blur the line between the privileged and the public and to change the symbolic significance of once privileged events.

Such is the pressure to open privileged negotiations to public view that the practical distinction, in considering media effects, is that between transactions that, while ongoing, remain privileged and those that are publicized, with a wider audience looking on as they unfold. The reality of privileged events is a product of what those involved in the transactions choose to reveal, how they present the facts, how they interpret for public consumption what has happened, what the media organizations find out, and what they select out for reporting. In privileged events, whether those involved are plotting a common strategy or in dispute over tactics or goal to pursue, they speak to and for each other, however aware they may be that the results of their negotiations will, in some manner, be publicized. Many of the most important political negotiations remain privileged—as in the case of many court and legislative and executive transactions at the highest levels of government. But more and more pressure is being brought to open all kinds of privileged negotiations to coverage by the media. With the spread of cable and the availability of almost unlimited channels for transmission, the pressure is bound to grow.

The Rhetoric of Events

Television has the power to transform the substance of privileged events by giving them wide publicity, but not much attention has been given to how this comes about. We propose to examine the process by looking at some televised Watergate events—the Senate hearings in the summer of 1973, the impeachment debate in July 1974, and Nixon's resignation that August—as rhetoric. We begin with the assumption that the language in which events are reported affects both the event there to be experienced and the way in which it is experienced. Leaving out such unanticipated crises as assassinations, riots, or demonstrations run amok, one can classify major televised political events as either *unifying occasions*, where the rhetoric stresses commonalities and the need to ignore differences in pursuit of the common good or as *controversies*, in which the elements of contest and conflict are explicitly recognized and people are expected to take sides. Many events fall between these two extremes, but the distinction is nevertheless fundamental.

An equally basic distinction concerns the audience to whom the rhetoric is mainly addressed. Inasmuch as any political event, if televised, becomes a public event, it always has two audiences. One consists of political insiders who, whether or not they are on stage, are participants. The second consists of bystanders and onlookers, of people who read newspapers and watch television. Both audiences are important to the political actors, but each type of event differs depending on whether the action (or rhetoric) is directed primarily toward other insiders (an exclusive audience) or at the mass public (a nonexclusive audience) who are only peripherally involved.

We begin with these two simple dichotomies—whether the dominant rhetoric is unifying or controversial and whether the audience to whom the rhetoric is primarily addressed is exclusive, that is, limited to political insiders, or nonexclusive, that is directed toward a larger audience, including the public at large. Following this schema, any televised political event theoretically fits one of four types:[4]

Ceremony . . . . Unifying/exclusive audience
Spectacle . . . . Unifying/nonexclusive audience
Deliberation . . . . Controversial/exclusive audience
Debate . . . . Controversial/nonexclusive audience

Unifying events. Though the ceremony and spectacle are both meant to be unifying occasions, they are geared toward different audiences. The ceremony, with or without media coverage, would exist as a ceremony. Ceremonies, when staged expressly for the media audience, are spectacles.

The unifying ceremony is defined, above all, by participation in a common symbolic order. The category includes a broad range of political events routinely covered by television, such as the inauguration of a new President, the official reception given a visiting head of state, and such human interest items as negotiators shown shaking hands or initialing an agreement after a grueling session of bargaining. Theirs is a symbolic gesture by which the parties signal that the agreement reached means more than the issues that once divided them.

A President taking the oath of office is making a symbolic commitment of a similar nature. The third parties are there to be witness, as they are in a wedding ceremony, but they only reinforce a commitment that would have been made even without television cameras to record it.

Where time-honored ceremonies are televised, there are, of course, adaptations. Television has the power to transform a ceremony to resemble a spectacle by giving it wide publicity. Awareness of the larger audience can introduce pageantry into what was intended as a solemn or holy occasion, so that the line between ceremony and spectacle becomes blurred. Pageantry has always surrounded most of these ceremonies, but now is attuned to the presence of the cameras and commentators. Yet they remain ceremonies and not spectacles because the participants involved act as they would even without the presence of the larger audience. When Lyndon Johnson, without fanfare, took the oath of presidential office in 1963, on the plane carrying John Kennedy's body back to Washington, this was a ceremony. When in January 1965, elected President, he took the oath of office in full view of the nation and with the usual pageantry surrounding the event, it was still a ceremony. Nor does the intrinsic nature of the royal wedding as a ceremony change, however spectacular the coverage, however large the audience. Television may change the nature of audience participation in these events but it does not change the intrinsic nature of the occasion.

In a ceremony transformed into a spectacle, the participants no longer necessarily express what they feel. Publicity makes what they feel less important than what they *appear* to feel. The primary audience is the larger audience and what counts is that the whole world is watching. Participants become performers acting on behalf of everyone within an integrated structure of motives. Televised political events in this category include the homecoming of heroes— like that of General Douglas MacArthur in 1951 (Chapter 2), of the American prisoners-of-war from Vietnam in 1973, or of the American embassy hostages released by Iran in 1981. Also included would be the official mourning following the assassination of President John F. Kennedy in 1963. The symbols employed in these events reaffirmed the historic unity of America at times when this seemed to be badly in need of reaffirmation. Similarly, presidential trips, such as Nixon's state visit to China in 1971 that ended more than two decades of diplomatic separation, can serve as spectacles. And certainly the 1977 Jerusalem meeting between Begin of Israel and Sadat of Egypt, which dramatically ended years of hostility between two Mideastern powers, was more a spectacle than a simple ceremony. Both communicators and their audiences recognize these as occasions in which it is mandatory that the rhetoric play the unity theme and common purpose and that any hint of divisiveness be, so far as possible, avoided. If unavoidable, it is usually played down. Empty seats in a stadium, sparse crowds along a parade route, the presence of counter-demonstrators, or protest signs can be selectively disregarded either by cameras or by editors. The rhetoric is usually demonstrative with much self-praise and with vilification reserved for those outside the circle of common identity.

At times the element of spectacle is deliberately injected into events that are partisan in both origin and intent. What is controversial can be packaged in the unifying disguise of pageantry, as in presidential state-of-the-union addresses to Congress, in press conferences, and even in the state visits just mentioned. This format is part and parcel of many campaign events, especially where the campaigner occupies the office he or she seeks to retain, and especially when campaigning involves the delivery of major addresses to well chosen audiences. The Nixon re-election campaign in 1972 was replete with such events and so were the Watergate years. News organizations sometimes pierce this veil of deception by treating what appears to be a non-controversial occasion as controversial. They can inject some balance by scheduling their own analyses right after these events or by giving time to opponents to present their dissenting views.

Controversies. Typically, the media have become the focus for extended political controversy. Here we have distinguished between two forms it may take: *deliberations*, where some policy or political decision is thrashed out before an audience observing from a front-row video seat; and *debates*, in which competing parties or candidates or advocates make use of the media to appeal to that larger audience.

In any deliberation, each side seeks to persuade members of the other camp by appealing to common interest both sides share and to win converts with whom to form a dominant coalition. This differs from the debate, where the two sides are not really addressing one another but vying for the approval of a public that serves as jury, referee, or arbiter. Whether deliberation or debate, participants, communicators and audiences understand and expect the proceedings to be partisan and controversial.

The coverage of deliberations should give the public some insight into how policy questions are thrashed out. The most familiar events in this category are national nominating conventions, whose business it is to formulate a party platform and to nominate the standard bearer of a winning coalition (Chapter 3). Also, most congressional hearings—including some, like the Army-McCarthy and Kefauver hearings which we have mentioned—fit this mode. Like conventions, they are bona fide episodes in the political process. Yet publicity changes the proceedings insofar as participants cannot be oblivious to the probable viewer response. In theory, the television audience has no part to play in the ongoing deliberations, and news organizations covering these events are supposed to act only as clarifiers, to supply a context to what is shown on the screen. Yet they feel compelled to keep viewers interested and even entertained. Interviews, offsite or behind-the-scenes coverage, and other media-generated activity that lend life to the proceedings become as much a part of the event viewers witness as the official proceedings. Consequently, an event known through television affords an experience different from direct participation. How far television, by its coverage, should or can intrude on what it covers becomes a matter of news judgment and often itself a subject of political controversy.

The debate is different. The two sides are not really addressing each other but vying for the approval of a public that serves as jury, referee, or judge. It acts as a third party toward whom the adversaries mainly direct their remarks. Its presence is an essential part of the event. As in the televised debates between candidates for the same office, which have become an institution on the American political scene, each performance is openly partisan, though within a framework of rules carefully crafted to give neither contestant unfair advantage. In this sense the proceeding is genuinely bipartisan. Audience members cannot judge which contestant is superior in forensic skill or more qualified for office without exposing themselves to the opposing viewpoint. Television provides the transmission facilities but otherwise is not expected to intrude.

The Watergate Blockbusters

In the rest of this chapter, we want to focus in on three blockbuster media events during Watergate but, first, a brief background for those who need to refresh their recollections of the Watergate saga and those who have no recollections at all.

On November 7, 1972, Richard Nixon was reelected President by a landslide, losing only Massachusetts and the District of Columbia. The vote was a clear reflection of public opinion. Yet, less than two years later, following a long controversy over the events and cover-up collectively known as "Watergate," Nixon took the unprecedented step of quitting the presidency. There was no public outcry; most Americans approved. According to every poll estimate, no more than two of every ten Americans, and possibly as few as one in ten, were unhappy with the outcome of the controversy that had obsessed the nation for so many months.

This almost universal approval of such an extraordinary turn of events was extraordinary. The legitimacy of the presidential succession could itself have been open to serious challenge. For Nixon's successor was Gerald Ford, a man picked by Nixon himself to be his vice-president after the elected vice-president, Spiro Agnew, had been forced to resign in disgrace. Yet the legitimacy of the changeover was hardly questioned.

Television contributed to the noncontroversial resolution of a crisis that threatened to tear the nation apart through the extensive and full coverage it gave to certain critical events. The visibility of the controversy helped more than anything to legitimate the process by which Nixon was ousted. What if elite events had remained privileged, as they so often are? What if the hearings of the Senate Watergate Committee had not been covered in full during the summer of 1973? What if the House Judiciary Committee had not held its impeachment debate in public for all the world to see? What if the ceremonies of transition from Nixon to Ford had remained a private affair? Chances are that the Watergate controversy might have ended as it did but it would not have ended on so uncontroversial a note.

As part of the ongoing controversy, all three events were inherently controversial. Yet, to repeat our contention, they were all transformed by their televising into occasions that, for different reasons, served as much, or more, to unite the nation than to divide it.

The Watergate Hearings: May 17-August 7, 1973

The hearings of the Senate Select Committee on Presidential Campaign Activities represented a familiar political format for politicians, broadcasters, and the audience alike. Congressional hearings, in the early days of nationwide television, had been one of the first big drawing cards, especially the Army-McCarthy hearings in 1954. Over the years, other hearings had been televised and highlights recorded by news teams for later airing on news shows had made their coverage a stock part of the journalist's trade. Yet, no other deliberations had attracted as much attention as the Army-McCarthy confrontation until the Senate Watergate hearings came along 20 years later.

Watergate had begun as a narrowly political issue. It first surfaced with a bungled break-in on June 17, 1972 to the headquarters of the Democratic National Committee at the Watergate complex in Washington, D.C. During the election campaign that summer and fall, certain facts surfaced tying the burglary to persons employed by the Committee to Reelect the President. The Watergate story moved closer and closer to the White House as it came to include such related matters as the deliberate circumvention of campaign finance laws, "dirty tricks" perpetrated by persons in the employ of the reelection committee, and the illegal use of federal agencies against Nixon's enemies.

During the campaign Watergate was largely dismissed as the usual politics; it did not emerge as a major issue. While there were doubts about the Republican version of the break-in, hardly anyone connected the incident with the President himself. Though the basic facts that later became such a familiar part of the Watergate saga had been publicized and were in the public domain, most people did not find the Watergate affair important in making up their minds how to vote. Nixon's Democratic challenger, Senator George McGovern of South Dakota, was soundly trounced in November.

A half year after Nixon's landslide victory, however, Watergate had become the center of a full-blown political controversy. Nearly everybody was aware of it—96 percent by mid-May 1973, just before the Watergate Committee's hearings were to begin. There was also growing public concern. Even before the hearings, Watergate had made its way, for the first time, onto the Gallup list of "most important problems facing the country today." Beginning in March, persons close to the Oval Office began to be implicated in the scandal, and suspicion that the President himself might have been actively involved was gradually growing. By early April, more than four of every ten persons interviewed in a nationwide survey now believed that Nixon knew about "the Watergate situation in advance." Most people still regarded the President as "a man of high integrity" whom they held in high repute but ratings of his performance in office were beginning to decline.

One by one Nixon's aides came to be implicated in the scandal. On April 30, the White House announced the resignations of John Ehrlichman and H. R. Haldeman, his two closest assistants, along with those of his attorney general and White House counsel John Dean. Nixon now conceded that "there had been an effort to conceal the facts" but denied any complicity either in the break-in or any attempt to cover up. He praised Ehrlichman and Haldeman ("whose zeal" might have "exceeded their judgment") while trying to cast Dean, whose lawyers were seeking immunity from prosecution in exchange for his testimony, in an unfavorable light.

From mid-April to mid-May, 56 percent of the evening newscasts (on 23 weekdays) led off with a Watergate story. Part of the story was a developing controversy between Senator Sam Ervin, chairman of the Senate committee, and the President over the testimony of Nixon's aides. It was in this charged atmosphere—with the nation very much aware of Watergate and curious about what Dean, Haldeman, Ehrlichman, and others would have to tell—that the Ervin Committee hearings went on television.

Given the highly partisan nature of the proceedings, their televising could have sharpened the polarization over Watergate that existed as they began. Though the committee had been set up by the Senate as a whole to include four Democrats and three Republicans, neither all its Republican members nor even all the Democrats had been keen on letting the cameras in. The networks were no more enthusiastic given the loss of advertising revenue they expected while Nixon stalwarts charged that they could impugn the reputation of government officials and indirectly do serious damage to the institutions of the government. Since the public, they argued, was ready to believe the worst about all politicians, any adverse publicity from the hearings could put all elected officials under some sort of a shadow.

The hearings were investigatory in intent, meant to serve the Senate in deciding whether and what legislation was needed to curb abuses during the 1972 campaign that had come to light since. But the Democratic leadership of the committee, backed by its chief counsel, wanted to seize on this opportunity to hold hearings before television as the best way to educate the public, to alert them to the inherent dangers to the political system if the illegalities engaged in by Nixon's campaign arm, the Committee to Reelect the President, were tolerated. The extent of their success in achieving this goal is difficult to assess in the light of the many other events previous to and concurrent with these hearings. Of one effect of the television publicity we can be sure, however. Had the hearings not been televised, they would have been less structured and the senators less subject to strict procedural rules. Nor would they have been conducted with so little venom. In this case, what might have been a bitter controversy but with a limited audience had to be more carefully staged. With the whole world watching, senators had to be on their guard. The critics of Nixon and his loyal supporters engaged one another in a spirited but altogether civil debate. What united the two sides in political opposition was that the committee appear serious. This common interest sometimes seemed greater than what divided them.

There have been a number of rhetorical analyses of these hearings, which need not be repeated here. Nor do we mean to imply that the hearings served as a unifying force. We mean only to point out that television converted them into something less than the divisive force they might have been. Nixon's media strategy was to depict the hearings as a political vendetta, with Senator Ervin and the Democrats "out to get the President." Yet public opinion polls tell us that most people thought the hearings were fair and approved their televising; those most inclined to believe the hearings were unfair and to blame the media were those who were not following them.

Ervin and his chief counsel, Samuel Dash, mapped the hearings as an educational endeavor, following a building-block strategy of presentation. In the first scene-setting phase, witnesses detailed the circumstances of the break-in to the Watergate headquarters and the apprehension of the burglars. Then the accusatory phase began with the appearance of ex-Nixon aides, with John Dean as the star witness, telling his story of White House complicity that led up to the bungled burglary. Finally, Nixon loyalists—Mitchell, Haldeman, and Ehrlichman—took their turns to refute the testimony of Dean and others and give their side of the story. Thus the hearings, from the beginning, were designed to give the public a chance to decide for themselves, by watching the witnesses and the give-and-take between witnesses and senators, who was telling the truth and what the truth was. As the hearings went on, and especially after the revelation of the existence of the White House tapes, the problem before the committee and before the public was less and less "which of the President's aides were lying" than a matter of how to get at the truth that was there to be revealed in the tapes.

Though any sharp confrontation between committeemen or between committeeman and witness made the nightly news, the front pages of newspapers, and good pictures for weekly news magazines, there were, in fact, fewer such confrontations than might have been anticipated. Of the Republicans, Howard Baker, of Tennessee, who had presidential ambitions, took the high road on TV, emphasizing the quest for the truth. Facing the witness, he persistently sought to determine: "What did the President know and when did he know it? To have asked in more straightforward fashion whether the President, and not Dean, was lying was unthinkable. Senators no less than most Americans regard that office with almost sacred awe. Senator Edward Gurney, of Florida, Nixon's personal defender on the Committee, provoked the first open partisan clash of the hearings by chastising the venerable Ervin's questioning of Nixon's chief fundraiser. "I, for one," he declared (June 13), in an obvious appeal to the television audience, "have not appreciated the harrassment of witnesses by the chairman." The audience in the room, heedless of prior warnings, burst into applause as Ervin, the Senate's leading constitutional scholar, described himself in his folksiest North Carolina manner as "just an old country lawyer," saying, "I don't know of the finer ways to do it. I just have to do it my way." After a few more tries, in which Gurney was also bested by Dean in the most dramatic confrontation of the hearings, he did not overplay his hand.

Most witnesses were contrite, mainly noncombative. The networks let the witnesses speak for themselves—they did not overuse reaction shots of the audience in the room. Republican Lowell Weicker, Ervin, and others invoked all the sacred symbols. As a result, the majority of the public, including many Republicans who continued to believe the Republicans had done nothing worse than other politicians, approved the mission of the committee—which was getting at the truth. Television changed the nature of the proceedings. Without its presence they would have been more confrontational. It muted the confrontational and whatever the 37 days of televised hearings were seen as—an entertaining show, overdramatized, or a circus— the hearings were not widely regarded as a political vendetta. The strength of the sentiment approving the committee's quest for the truth only became evident a few months later in the outpouring of outrage when Nixon fired Special Watergate Prosecutor Archibald

Cox, who had refused—in Nixon's words—"to cease and desist from his Watergate fishing expedition." Referring to the unprecedented half million telegrams delivered to congressional offices the weekend of the Cox firing, Chief Counsel Dash wrote:

> In large part this public reaction resulted from the keen interest millions of Americans had developed in the Watergate facts during our committee's televised public hearings that summer. Ironically, Cox had tried to stop the hearings. Now he had reasons to be glad he had failed.[5]

The Impeachment Hearings (July 24-July 30, 1974)

The impeachment debate did not involve a hearing but a meeting in which a standing committee of the House of Representatives was expected to reach a decision, that is, to vote on whether or not to recommend articles of impeachment against the President to the full House for its consideration. No decision-making process of this kind had hitherto been televised; its televising was made possible only by a special vote of the assembled House and transformed what was meant to be an esoteric deliberation behind closed doors into a debate with the whole world watching. The audience was expanded to include the nation at large, with both sides sharing equal access to the viewing audience under rules intended to assure the judicial character of the debate. Speakers addressed the onlookers as much as they did their colleagues.

Since this was an unprecedented event, there was considerable ambiguity in the rhetorical situation with which committee members and news personnel alike had to cope. The debate itself became a debate as much about whether or not there was a legitimate basis for impeachment as over the specific charges and articles to be proposed. Yet at certain points the debaters, by evoking symbols of national unity—the Constitution, the office of President, and the sacred nature of the duty thrust upon them—endowed the proceedings with the solemnity of a unifying ceremony. This was especially true of their opening remarks and the formal vote on the first impeachment amendment. Television, merely by its presence, introduced some element of spectacle but the low profile both camera and commentary maintained kept this to a minimum.

Chairman of the committee Peter Rodino had long warned that it would be a national disaster if the committee's inquiry were to degenerate into a partisan confrontation. Although it would have been unrealistic to expect a total absence of partisanship, he had, throughout the deliberations of the committee, worked to keep the usual kind of political invective at the lowest possible level. It was not only important that the committee, in its deliberations, be fair but that it appear fair. Systematic analysis of the televised content of the final debate shows that both the language employed by committee members and the language employed by hearings emphasized the nonpartisan and legal-judicial nature of the proceedings. What committee members had to say about themselves, about the committee as a group, and about the process in which they were engaged helped convey this impression. Television focused on the actual proceedings and kept comment to a minimum.

Committee members depicted themselves as a body of lawyers, working on the constitutional and legal issues related to impeachment in a nonpartisan and objective fashion. The tone of the debate was set during the opening sessions which lasted through Wednesday evening, July 24, and the morning, afternoon, and evening of the next day. All members were recognized for 15 minutes apiece for "purposes of debate only," signaling that they were not to use their time for political rhetoric. Most did not, generally using the time to discuss seriously the background, rationale, and evidence relating to the articles. But members also used the allotted time to address their constituents or to appeal to the public at large. Some remarks also appeared to be directed at colleagues in the House, who would make the ultimate decision on whether Nixon should stand trial in the Senate. As in the case of the earlier Senate hearings, sacred symbols were constantly invoked. Few would forget Barbara Jordan, a black congresswoman from Texas, speaking slowly, in a strong clear voice, as she declared that her faith in the Constitution was "whole, complete and total" and that she was not going to be an "idle spectator to the diminution, the subversion, the destruction of the Constitution."

Almost without exception, speakers did not demean the work of the committe or question publicly the integrity of its staff. Rather, those opposed to impeachment concentrated on the conclusiveness of the evidence. The occasions on which the debate took on a political coloration that threatened its reputation for fairness were rare. Partisan infighting erupted on the day when the first vote on an article of impeachment was expected; true to form, on the nightly news that followed, it was described as a "bitter fight." Then again on the last day of the debate, with three articles already passed, dissension arose over the purpose of passing further articles. Republicans who had already voted for impeachment now saw this as "pushing too hard" or "political overkill." The order in which the last two articles were debated was interpreted as pure politicking—and it was. Loathe to inject the still-lingering bitterness over the Vietnam War into the debate, Rodino and his chief lieutenants were relieved to have had the Cambodian bombing (the charge that the President had "illegally waged war") taken up in the afternoon, when fewer people would be watching. But they had no objection to debating the tax article (charging "willful income tax evasion and the illegal use of government funds to improve Nixon's home") in prime evening time, even though the Democratic leadership had no intention of pushing for adoption of either measure. If the Democrats chose to make the order of debate a political decision, the Republicans were not prepared to let them get away unscathed. Charles Sandman, of New Jersey, told the committee but mainly the assembled audience, "This bunch of baloney was supposed to be taken up this afternoon and not tonight, but there is a bigger audience on TV tonight than there was this afternoon."

Despite these partisan incursions, content analysis shows that both what was said during the debate and what commentators had to say about it conveyed an image of fairness. Television focused on the actual proceedings and kept comment to a minimum. It helped convey an image fairness and thereby advanced the committee's purpose just by being available. In this sense, to use McLuhan's enigmatic phrase, the medium was the message. However inherently political was the impeachment process, both the participants and the communicators were aware of the solemn nature of the occasion and, as so many put it, their "awesome responsiblity." The language of politics, for the most part, gave way to the language of the law and the need to proceed according to the dictates of the Constitution.

In short, in making what usually would have been a privileged deliberation a public event, television transformed it. With the whole world watching, the rhetoric of the debate was muted, with appeals and arguments couched in language that was universalistic and transcended the morality of ordinary political behavior. In this sense, television coverage of these extraordinary and potentially divisive deliberations served as a unifying rather than a divisive force.

Resignation Night: August 8, 1974

Finally, we turn for our third illustration to the memorable Thursday night on August 8, 1974, when Richard Nixon, in a 16-minute address, announced to the nation that he would resign next day.

Even before the speech, which began at 9 p.m. EST, there was little doubt that he was about to step down. The only remaining uncertainty was over what he might say and how he would say it. Would he, as some feared, attack the media and the liberals for having engineered his downfall? Or would he confess and acknowledge some guilt in connection with Watergate?

In the 57 sentences of his televised address, the resigning President dealt with four themes: the resignation and the reasons for it; the need for a smooth transition; the extent of his guilt; and a defense of himself and of his administration. A sentence-by-sentence analysis shows that the first three themes were touched on only in the first half of the speech. The President's rationale for resigning was dealt with in 11 of the first 25 sentences. He did not claim that he was driven from office. He did state that he was leaving reluctantly, against his own personal preferences and instincts ("I have never been a quitter") and contrary to the urgings of his "entire family." The compelling reason was that he no longer had "a strong enough political base to justify continuing'' the effort to complete the term of office to which he had been elected. He was putting the ''interests of the nation'' before ''personal considerations.'' Nixon repeated this ''personal sacrifice'' theme six times, stressing that the country needed a full-time President and a full-time Congress.

Some of this explanation was coupled with pleas that people be understanding and patient and cooperate with the new President. This need for a tranquil transition was the second main theme of the speech. Ten sentences assured the public that with Ford the leadership of America would be in good hands. The first essential was ''to begin healing the wounds of the nation, to put the bitterness and divisions of the bitter past behind us'' The imagery—''healing the nation''— seems to have been borrowed from Johnson's inaugural speech after the assassination of John F. Kennedy. The tone struck was certainly what many had hoped for. Yet he abandoned the theme after the 21st sentence.

Another ten sentences, including the first five, made reference to his "guilt." Nixon admitted no crimes, only "wrong judgments." Apologies? There were none. He gave thanks to those who had supported his cause but disavowed any ''bitterness'' toward others who had opposed him. ''Our judgments might differ,'' he said of these opponents and went on to concede that they, like himself, were concerned with the good of the country, and he, too, Nixon now insisted, had always tried in his decisions ''to do what was best for the country.''

From here on the tone of the speech changed. The second half contained a predominance of statements that can only be called self-serving; they are to be found in 22 of the last 31 sentences, where Richard Nixon spoke of his accomplishments and extolled his own character, citing Theodore Roosevelt's preference for the man ''who at the worst, if he fails, at least fails daring greatly.'' He also defended himself, by indirection, against the charge that he had abused the power of his office. ''When I first took the oath of office as President, five and a half years ago, I made this sacred commitment: 'to consecrate my office, my energies, and all the wisdom I can summon to the cause of peace among nations.' I have done my best in all the days since to be true to that pledge.''

Self-serving statements also occurred in the first part of the speech in conjunction with the three other themes. When all statements relating to self-sacrifice, to Nixon's honorable motives, and to his presidential acts and accomplishments are counted—and we counted only explicit mentions—36 of the 57 sentences (63 percent of the speech) were devoted to self-justification of one sort or another. It was as if the President, having chosen not to go on trial, was now appearing as his own character witness in a television defense before the assembled jury.

The speech lasted just 16 minutes. Yet all three networks thought it necessary to begin live coverage with their early evening newscasts, continuing for two or more hours until the speech began. Their coverage then continued throughout the evening, ABC concluding only at 2 a.m. Given the briefness of Nixon's words, why so much broadcast time devoted to the event? Nothing startling had been expected to happen until Nixon had spoken, and neither the reporters nor the persons they interviewed either before or after his appearance had much to add in the way of new information or interpretation. To the contrary, a media critic, Alexander Cockburn, who reviewed the entire 148-page CBS transcript of its 7 p.m. to midnight broadcast, wrote that ''the news and interesting commentary could. . .be boiled down to Nixon's actual speech and maybe three or four pages besides.''

Though the resignation speech—which contained no admission of guilt but only regret for mistakes—hardly satisfied many in the audience, there was little criticism voiced on television during the evening nor was much dissent voiced about Nixon's decision to depart the office. The public response was strongly downbeat—little protest, little rejoicing. The televising of Nixon's resignation speech, together with the extended before-and-after coverage, helped in two ways to assure the almost unchallenged acceptance of the unprecedented transfer of power: (1) by treating Resignation Night as a ceremonial occasion, deemphasizing partisanship and stressing themes of unity, and (2) by cloaking the unusual in the routines of the usual, thus making the occasion seem familiar and less problematic than it actually was.

So it was that television served as a unifying agent by muting dissent while at the same time discouraging celebration. We would contend that the long broadcast served to frame the main event, with the continuous replays of high points in the speech and the controversy leading to resignation establishing the reality and irreversibility of what had happened. The event was inherently momentous, but would the same short speech, squeezed in between two ABC programs that were cancelled—"Just For Laughs" and "Kung Fu"—have seemed quite the historic occasion that it was?

Without the opportunity the media, and mainly television, provided the public—particularly those not yet reconciled to the need for impeachment—to witness the manner through which Nixon was led to resign, as well as such other blockbuster events as the Senate hearings and the impeachment deliberations, the response to the end of the Nixon presidency might not have been so unemotional. The coverage of the resignation speech was, in some ways, more problematic for the broadcasters than either of the other two events. Passages of power at the top of the government are traditionally handled as ceremonies. But with the hour approaching and public affairs staffs on the air, there was some uncertainty as to whether they could assume that the occasion would prove undivisive. It was the likely tone of the speech that most troubled those interviewed on screen while the nation waited for Nixon to appear. Though resignation with dignity was judged the only sensible way for Nixon to depart, some people, interviewed on screen, thought he might use the occasion for yet another attack on the news media and other enemies. NBC explained that the "tone of the speech" would determine House members' attitudes concerning amnesty and documented this in interviews. ABC and CBS linked Nixon's willingness to "confess" to the likelihood of his immunity from prosecution.

In preparing for the President's speech and his expected resignation, the media evidently had to shift gears. Hitherto they had been a battleground for the various Watergate skirmishes, but now, with the situation about to change, they felt under some compulsion to depict the office of President as one to be revered and its incumbent as worthy of respect. Yet the fact that Nixon had demeaned the office by exploiting its inherent power for clearly partisan purposes introduced some ambiguity into the journalistic role. Their sense of civic responsibility was an inducement to play down anything that could potentially mar the solemnity of the occasion, yet they were also reluctant, as journalists, to transmit only that which political managers believed to be in the public interest. The media event that evolved was a compromise between the two contradictory impulses, but it became the reality to which everyone—political elites, the public, and the press—responded.

Without detailing the content that emerged, as we have done in *The Battle for Public Opinion*,[6] let us point out that the coverage of Nixon's resignation resulted in a novel charge against the networks—that of being too fair, of having bent over backward to be fair, despite Nixon's failure to admit to any guilt and devoting two-thirds of his speech to self-justification of one sort or another. Systematic analysis would appear to absolve the networks of this kind of bias. Rather the networks, not certain of what the outcome of the main event would be, seem to have adopted the model of an election night coverage, where no one seriously expects an upset, but everyone is held in suspense until the outcome is certain. The networks set the tone with their expectations, then with their predictions from early and very incomplete returns, and finally with their interpretations of what the outcome implies. As time passes and the outcome becomes more certain, other issues relating to party unity, the ability of the winner to govern, the political mood of the nation, and the direction in which it is moving become an increasingly important part of the story and take over from the reporting of returns. In other words, the election-night broadcast is more than a vote count; it is also a ritual. Awaiting the verdict, then watching the loser concede and the winner accept the concession helps to convert what began as a highly partisan political campaign into a symbolic affirmation of the democratic process.

In covering the resignation, television followed this ceremonial model of election night. They had preempted all prime-time entertainment programs. They waited for and reported the results, which proved to be satisfactory. If some newspeople and some public figures who were interviewed appeared overgenerous in their praise of the speech, it was partly because their worst fears had not been realized. Many had feared that Nixon might prove a spoiler, that he might throw away his speech and do something irrational as he had once before when he lost a race for the governorship of California. It was then Nixon himself who, by conceding as he did, left the networks free to treat it as part of a unifying ceremony rather than a continuation of a controversy. When Nixon, in the journalists' judgment, acted with a "sense of occasion," it was incumbent upon television to do nothing in their postspeech coverage to detract from that performance. Once it appeared that Nixon would play the gracious loser, the news organizations could respond with the magnanimous gesture of a winner and stress the unity theme, treating the event as part of a ceremony of transition.

Implications

The basic question yet to be answered is under what conditions the publicizing of what could reasonably have remained a privileged event tends to make a unifying occasion out of an intrinsically divisive event. Under most circumstances the very presence of a public, even if only as bystanders, exerts a restraining influence. Though the media may thrive on controversy, the tone they set in its coverage derives from a medley of expectations held by participants and witnesses alike. Where the escalation of controversy may prove unduly disruptive and a threat to the social order, participants are likely to act within a set of self-imposed constraints. The use of overly inflammatory language is simply inadmissable. One has to leave room for compromise by avoiding the kind of heated confrontation that makes ultimate reconciliation overly difficult or impossible. As for journalists they, of course, see themselves as neutral agents or at least as a balancing force.

Television does not always have this influence on the course of events and certainly not when things have got out of hand, as they did, for example, during the Democratic national conventions of 1968 in Chicago, when Hubert Humphrey was nominated. Journalists seemed almost as caught up (and traumatized) by the street fighting between demonstrators and police as the participants. They used their cameras in accordance with their feelings. So intense was the conflict that it became difficult not to take sides. The portrayal of violence on the part of either was bound to cast the perpetrators in an unfavorable light, and journalists with cameras turned on police would often be victimized as if they were demonstrators instead of mere observers.

Yet the potentially restraining influence is still present; it only manifests itself in a different way. Neither police nor demonstrators want to *appear* violent. How tempting it is for the former to use their power to keep away the press or, in extreme cases, even to shatter cameras and make arrests. From the other side one hears the all too frequent complaint that the press and the TV cameras dwell too much on isolated instances of violence, thereby discrediting any demonstration in the eyes of the public and distorting the message it seeks to get across.

Whatever the specific outcome, the presence of the press makes itself felt. The enlargement of the audience beyond the circle of participants creates a third party and, by implication, brings the norms of the larger society to bear on those involved in the conflict. These norms, latent during a confrontation, invite conciliatory gestures, the invitation by itself will not always be enough to reduce conflict.

NOTES

1. Gladys Engel Lang and Kurt Lang, *The Battle for Public Opinion; the President, The Press and the Polls During Watergate* (New York: Columbia University Press, 1983).

2. For examples of the more extreme position, see Stanley Cohen and Jack Young, *The Manufacture of News; Deviance, and Social Problems & the Mass Media* (Beverly Hills, CA: Sage, 1981); or Gaye Tuchman, *Making News: A Study in the Construction of Reality* (New York: Free Press, 1978).

3. Daniel J. Boorstin, *The Image—A Guide to Pseudo-Events in America* (New York: Harper, 1964).

4. In an earlier formulation of this typology, in *The Battle for Public Opinion*, we referred to controversial rhetoric addressed to an exclusive audience as an "esoteric debate" and to controversial rhetoric addressed to an inclusive audience as "adversary proceeding." This change of terminology is to to avoid confusion created by the use of the descriptor "debate." Political debates staged for the television audience were, following this terminology, not esoteric debates but adversary proceedings.

5. Sam Dash, *Chief Counsel: Inside the Ervin Committee—The Untold Story* (New York: Random House, 1976), 43.

6. See note 1, above.

7

Debate and Dilemmas

CARTER VERSUS FORD

At approximately 9:50 p.m. EST on September 23, 1976, the first televised Jimmy Carter-Gerald Ford debate was nearing its end. Then the unthinkable happened: The audio transmission failed. There was a sudden fade out of Carter's voice. People in some 38 million households could see his lips move, as he continued to speak, but he could not be heard. After 20 seconds he lapsed into silence. Sound did not come back on for 27 minutes. Only then was the debate resumed, beginning where it left off in mid-sentence, and brought to a conclusion.

This "audio gap" posed a dilemma for researchers in the midst of studying debate effects. It posed an even more serious problem for broadcasters, politicians, and others involved in the production of the debate. The interruption threatened to expose the semi-fiction under which the encounter was being broadcast as a bona fide news event. The research dilemma was readily resolved and the project salvaged; we discuss our findings in the first part of this chapter. In the second part we look at the way the networks, the politicians and the debate producers coped with their own dilemma largely by ignoring it.

Immediate and Delayed Response

Gerald Ford, in 1974, had become the first unelected president of the United States. Then, in 1976 he became the first to risk his incumbency in a series of televised debates. Though he did lose the election to Jimmy Carter, his loss was not widely attributed to a poor performance in the debates. On the contrary, history now has it that Ford, like Kennedy in 1960, won the first debate, which he had been expected to lose. Yet the answer to "Who won the debate?" is not quite that simple. Our study demonstrates a difference between the immediate and delayed responses of those who watched, that is, between the direct impact of the debate immediately after exposure and the cumulative effects of communication about the debate—press commentary, news reports, polling information, and so on—to which viewers were exposed in the days following the debate.

Researchers have long been aware that there can be delayed or sleeper effects.[1] The exact meanings of a communication are not always evident in the initial encounter with its text. Moreover, a first impression can be modified by supplementary information obtained from significant others or credible mass media sources. Collective definitions take time to evolve.

If the effect of a particular communication item (like a video commercial) can be delayed, this is even more true of a significant communication event (like a televised presidential debate), which invariably elicits a flood of communications—some distinctly partisan and meant to influence reactions, and others, mainly from journalistic circles, intended to provide contextual (and sometimes corrective) information as well as interpretive comment. The latter include the ever-more frantic rush toward a definitive public judgment of the event; the instant analysis, which the Nixon-Agnew administration attacked as a media plot to neutralize the positive impact of the President's appearances on television; and the joining of forces by newspapers, politicians, and pollsters to shorten the time lag between an event and an authoritative measure of the public response to that event.

The issue is both conceptual and methodological. At what point should one take a reading to assess the impact of a major communication event, such as the first televised Carter-Ford debate? One avoids contamination by taking the reading immediately after, but in doing so one screens out the cumulative product of the process by which public opinion forms. On the other hand, the investigator who permits time to elapse cannot easily separate the impact of a specific communication from other demographic, social, and political factors that affect cognitions and behavior. The dilemma is real but did not dissuade us from pursuing the question with what means we had at hand.

The Study Design

The approach we decided on was a cross between a laboratory experiment and a two-wave field survey. Our subjects were students on the State University of New York Stony Brook campus, nearly all undergraduates and first-time voters. We used a before-and-after design. All "before" questionnaires were filled out either the day before or on the day of the first debate.[2] Items in the questionnaire, quite similar to those used 16 years before in the Kennedy-Nixon debates, covered what respondents were looking for, what they thought each candidate stood for, media exposure to past and current political events, interest in the campaign and in voting, and political preference.

One purpose in designing the study had been to assess the influence of the instant network analysis that traditionally follows the telecast of any major political event. We intended to contrast the responses of three groups, of about 100 each, exposed to the same debate but to different network analysis. Due to circumstances beyond our control we could not carry out this mission. To avoid losing our subjects, many of whom quite understandably doubted that the debate would continue, we had to begin distributing our "after" questionnaires during the audio gap, most viewers filling them out before the sound came back on and the debate resumed.

Our major analysis of the debate turned on the comparison of the "before" with the "after" data under two exposure conditions—controlled and contaminated. The students watching in the lecture halls made up the controlled exposure group. While interaction among them could not be altogether prevented, it was held to a minimum. The comparison group had filled out predebate questionnaires in their classrooms but viewed the debate in whatever setting was available—at home, in their college dormitory, or wherever they happened to be. Since these persons had time to discuss the debate and to be exposed to press commentary between the time they watched the debate and the time they completed their "after" questionnaires four to seven days following the debate, their responses may be considered contaminated. Indeed, 92 percent in this group said that they discussed the debates, 82 percent that they had learned what the polls said about who won, and 77 percent that they had read about the debates in the newspaper or news magazines. Over half reported all three.

Impact of the Debate

Was the debate worth seeing? The overwhelming majority said yes. But the affirmative response was smaller in the week following the debate than immediately afterward—77 compared with 93 percent. Of 12 aspects of the debate on which evaluations were solicited, the even-handedness of the moderator received the highest marks; our viewers generally approved the panelists' questions as fair and reasonably difficult. They found the debate more helpful in showing where Ford and Carter stood on the issues than in revealing what they "were really like."

However, the strength of this generally favorable reaction to the debate interested us less than the difference between the immediate response and the response several days after. On every one of the 12 aspects of the debate evaluated, there was a distinct downgrading. The contaminated response was invariably lower than that obtained under controlled conditions immediately after the debate. The erosion of the initially favorable evaluation of the debate followed a pattern:

(1) It was most clearly visible among Carter supporters. Within a week, they had downgraded the worthiness of the debate far more than the supporters of Ford.

(2) When specifically asked what the debate revealed about each candidate, the controlled-exposure group split pretty much along partisan lines; this is to say, each camp rated the debate higher with respect to its own man than his opponent on showing what he was really like, showing where he stood on issues, and the spontaneity with which he answered questions. Among those responding immediately, Carter supporters were more positive that the debate had done something to project their candidate than Ford supporters were about what it had done for Ford. Yet the week after, the Carter advantage had pretty much disappeared!

(3) While Carter supporters, immediately after the debate, believed the debate had helped to reveal differences favoring their candidate, those asked to evaluate the debate after some delay did not believe this. Most downgraded by Carter supporters were, in order of declining frequency: the debate as a help in determining how to vote; in showing the give-and-take between the candidates; as a help in deciding whether to vote; in clarifying Carter's issues stand; in showing what he was really like; and in showing what Ford was really like.

(4) The immediate-delayed differences among persons leaning toward neither candidate, though smaller, by and large paralleled those observed among the Carter following. This, too, suggests that in the days following the debate there was a general shift in perceptions which resulted in its redefinition as more favorable to Ford than it had originally seemed.

On the question of, "Who do you think came out best in the debate?" the same sharp contrast was found between the judgments of those responding immediately and those responding during the week following. The immediately-after group gave the debate to Carter by a better than 2-to-1 margin, and among those who saw no clear winner, twice as many said both had done well as said both had done poorly. The judgments in the contaminated-exposure group were reversed. Here Ford led Carter by roughly the same margin as Carter had previously led Ford, and those who called it a tie were somewhat more critical of both.

The difference between the two exposure conditions persisted when we looked separately at the supporters of each candidate: the percentage of Carter supporters believing, immediately afterward, that he had "done better" was 59 percent compared to a mere 28 percent of those responding the next week. By contrast, the percent of Ford's supporters believing he did better went up from 64 to 70. There was a parallel drop among those with no candidate preference believing Carter had won and an increase in the number who said that both men had performed poorly.

This striking contrast could not be explained by any difference in predebate expectations between the two groups. An almost identical 64 percent in the immediate response group and 62 percent in the delayed response group had expected Carter to win. This expectation was more often confirmed in the controlled-exposure condition, while the expectation of a Ford win tended to be confirmed in the contaminated condition.

There is no apparent need to provide here much further detail on the specific differences we found between the two exposure groups on candidate images and vote intentions. Suffice it to emphasize that, just as there was a general downgrading of the value of the debate and of Carter's performance, so there was some deterioration in Carter's image. Also, with respect to vote preference, the responses suggest that Carter gains that immediately followed the debate may have eroded in the next week. Moreover, whatever losses Ford may have suffered immediately after the debate were recouped.

Changes in perceptions and stated preferences do not always add up to behavioral changes. Moreover, our sample was drawn from a student population, whose lack of long-standing political loyalties and civic commitments makes them more volatile and also more indifferent than the typical electorate. In spite of these caveats, there is an underlying consistency when all data are taken together. They provide evidence of feeling, gradually developing in the week after, that Carter had not scored against Ford the way John Kennedy in his first debate had scored against Nixon. Whatever the immediate personal reaction, the long-term definition was that Ford had improved his chances for election by the debate.

Table 7.1 "Who Did Better" in First Debate by Vote Preference and Exposure (in percentages)

	Immediate				Mediated				Total			
	Ford	Carter	Neither[a]	All	Ford	Carter	Neither[a]	All	Ford	Carter	Neither[a]	All
Ford better	64	8	16	21	70	22	39	39	68	16	27	31
Carter better	4	59	43	45	6	28	15	19	5	42	30	30
Both well	25	21	27	23	18	29	20	24	21	25	24	24
Both poorly	7	12	14	11	5	22	26	17	6	17	20	15
	100	100	100	100	100	100	100	100	100	100	100	100
	(55)	(166)	(73)	(294)	(115)	(205)	(65)	(385)	(170)	(371)	(128)	(679)

[a]Neither includes undecideds and "antis," who split by party affiliation as follows:

	Immediate	Mediated
Dem.	16	19
Rep.	30	31
Ind.	54	50

We have every reason to believe that most respondents were aware that Ford was trailing badly in the polls. Asked before the debate who was the underdog, more respondents had pinned that label on Ford (29 percent) than on Carter (17 percent). Immediately after the debate there was only a slight, insignificant increase in underdog perceptions of Ford. By contrast, among those responding the next week, people had come to think equally often of Carter or Ford as the underdog in relation to the November election. The relation holds with preference controlled, and it holds even more strongly for those with no candidate preference, where the standing of the two candidates as underdog was completely reversed between the two exposure conditions.

Implications

There are several possible explanations for what we found. The question is: Which accords most with our findings?

The first explanation relates to the *nature of the two exposure conditions*. Unless experimental contamination can be ruled out as a cause of variation, no other explanation has any credence.

All persons who filled out questionnaires in the lecture hall during the 27-minute gap had witnessed the debate from its beginning, but what about the others? Only those saying they watched the debate live were included in the sample. Of these, 84 percent, according to their self-reports, had definitely seen the beginning of the debate and 79 percent indicated they had continued to watch during the gap. However, even when responses of those who did not see the entire debate from the beginning through the gap were omitted from the analysis, the contrast in responses between the immediate and mediated groups remains.

Or, can one explain the difference in reaction as a function of viewing in a group versus viewing on one's own? For students in the lecture hall, the debate was a spectacle luring people from their dorms and digs to a public happening; for those watching the debate under other conditions, viewing was a far more routine event. Nevertheless, we have no evidence that the two groups were differently motivated so that there was substantial contrast in what they wanted to see or expected to see. While we cannot completely ignore the possible influence of the viewing situation, we nevertheless discount its significance. Mainly, we were able to minimize interaction among the lecture hall audience, so much so that any group effect was probably weaker than that found among those viewing in the residence halls (where one-third of the later-response group watched) or among those viewing at home, most of whom also viewed in groups.

A second possible explanation focuses on *erosion over time* and is more psychological, drawing on such concepts as selective retention and cognitive imbalance. In simplest terms, the direct effect of the debate (like that of any communication) wears off over time. Once people forget what each candidate said, how he has conducted himself, and so forth, both candidates might be expected to revert to their predebate standing. But this is not what happened in the Carter-Ford encounter. Some of Ford's initial gains, on personal image and performance, were selectively reinforced, but not Carter's. Impressions on these matters are probably less subject to forgetting than perceptions of how the two had differed on some particular issue during the debate.

A third line of explanation draws on *specifically political factors*. Carter's support among college students had been generally diagnosed as ''soft'' and the vote intentions of our own students were no exception. Yet, inasmuch as the proportion of ''certain'' relative to that of ''undecided but leaning toward'' was the same for Carter as for Ford, supporters of both should have been equally open to influence from the debate. But there is a difference between the two exposure groups: More of the delayed response group, being commuters, were likely to have been exposed to the political milieu of heavily Republican Suffolk County. We have no direct evidence to support this conjecture but the possibility does exist that they were more subject to influence from other Republicans than the controlled exposure group, most of whom lived on campus. An initially favorable response to Carter after the debate, if there was one, could in this way have been neutralized in the days that followed. However, such an explanation cannot by itself account for other attitudinal shifts toward downgrading the utility of the debate for arriving at a decision on voting, at least not unless we assume that what these persons saw or learned from the debate was effectively counteracted by communications to which persons were exposed in the week following.

This brings us to the fourth, and last explanation, the one that strikes us as most satisfactory. The delayed-response group must have been influenced by *communications about the debate to which no one in the controlled-exposure group could possibly have been exposed*. The collective definition of the debate—the way it emerged in the public mind—did not depend solely on what each viewer had experienced by himself or herself in intimate communion with the TV set. Rather, it developed over time by way of a process in which each person's impressions were constantly tested against those of others, including the interpretative and analytic commentaries offered by authoritative mass media sources. Impressions gained directly from the debate were accordingly modified and elaborated. Those that diverged too much from the emerging consensus enjoyed little support and, consequently, were likely to fade until they were no longer expressed. By contrast, persons in the immediate-response group had given their evaluations without the benefit of any such give-and-take.

Analysis of media debate coverage supports this explanation. Before the audio had been restored and the first debate officially terminated, network newsmen had already begun to elicit evaluations of the relative performance of the two candidates. Final statements by the two candidates were quickly followed by the evening news and TV reporters' own judgments. Such evaluation came even more quickly on public television, which had no 11 o'clock evening news. Their early appraisals—that neither candidate had gained a clear advantage over his adversary—seem to accord closely with the immediately-after response obtained in our study. The results of two telephone polls (one by the Roper Organization, the other by the Associated Press) broadcast that same evening gave Ford a very slight edge, a numerical divergence from our own findings, which is fully accounted for by the political characteristics of our respondents. Said a *New York Times* headline two days after the event, "Debate Viewed as a Draw by Experts in Both Parties," a view the items supported with findings from various polls. Only thereafter did the weather-vanes of public opinion begin to shift. A Gallup poll published the following week showed Ford the victor by a 13-point margin, and the evaluation by *Newsday* of its own poll on Long Island was that "Ford's" success in the debate seems conclusive." In later recapitulations of the three debates, the first was everywhere scored as a win for Ford.

Whatever one's predilections or political interests lead one to believe, no one so far has been able to provide any really hard evidence that poll reports swing votes.[3] Be this as it may, such information is ignored. Many members of the public are nearly as interested as party strategists in the relative standing of the candidates. Not only are they aware of what a political asset real popularity can be in attracting financial and organizational support but of how it can increase the effectiveness of a president once elected. Similarly, how well a candidate comes across in a debate has some bearing on his or her ability to project as a leader, a wise statesman, and so forth.

Our data contain evidence that many respondents, whatever their own opinion, were beginning to feel that Carter was slipping, that Ford was closing the gap so rapidly that he could no longer be considered the underdog. As yet, no bandwagon for Ford was about to roll but the belief that the debate had improved Ford's chances was gaining ground. At least this was a view that enjoyed great currency in the delayed-response group.

We would not argue that the difference between the responses obtained immediately and after a delay represents a straightforward poll effect. It is more correctly a reflection of the overall image conveyed by the media that Ford had won the first debate. Another significant element in the coverage was the shadow of the Kennedy-Nixon debate. In the days before the debate as well as thereafter, journalists of the electronic and print media invoked the image of Kennedy skillfully using this platform to turn the tide against Nixon. By contrast, Carter had failed dismally. His perceived failure as a debate performer spilled over to other aspects of his image. Negative evaluations dampened enthusiasm not only for the candidate but for the debate as conducted. Unfavorable comparisons to 1960 were common even though the 1976 series had lasted longer, involved more penetrating questioning of the candidates, and forced them to stick more closely to the point than had Kennedy and Nixon.

In addition, the more positive response immediately after the debate and the more negative delayed response suggest that if Carter was judged wanting, this was mostly against the background of high expectations shaped by the relevant past. The press did its part by deploring the lackluster performance of both Carter and Ford, suggesting that how either man handled himself was irrelevant to his ability to meet the requirement of office, and thereby inadvertently helping President Ford exploit the advantage of his incumbency. But which candidate gained more from the debate and why is hardly the point. What matters is that the impact of the 1976 debate—or any of the debates that have followed and will follow—cannot be assessed without taking full cognizance of the context provided by other and less dramatic communications.

The Coverage Gap

The news media, especially television, have repeatedly been charged with sensationalism, with emphasizing the unusual and dramatic at the expense of the normal and routine. Yet in the case of the audio breakdown that interrupted this first Carter-Ford debate, a development with real dramatic potential, some problematic issues arising from the loss of sound were effectively routinized. Throughout the 27-minute gap, when the two candidates intermittently appeared on the screen but could not be heard—if they said anything—all three networks consistently underplayed the unique and dramatic elements in the situation and, in so doing, neglected some real issues raised by the audio gap.

Perhaps the most unreported and potentially most important aspect of the audio failure was the threat it posed to the continuation of the debate series. It was foreseen that there would be two more presidential and one vice-presidential debate. What made these debates problematic were the grounds for the Federal Communication Commission ruling that exempted them from the equal time provision of the law. The exemption rested on a semi-fiction that they were *not* arranged by a broadcaster but were independent events before a live audience in attendance without regard for whether or not the encounter was to be broadcast. The first debate, like those yet to come, was set up by the League of Women Voters Education Fund and, though it was patently designed for television, the network staffs had no control over the arrangements. They had to abide by the fiction that they were reporting a bona fide news event and were not involved in any way in a production staged for a television audience.

The fiction clearly implied that the debate would take place even if television or radio did not cover it. Therefore, the live debate, taking place in Philadelphia's Walnut Street Theater, should have gone on despite the loss of sound for broadcast. The official reason for its interruption was a technical one. The public address system within the hall was tied in with the audio broadcast signal. This was done to prevent feedback and static over the air. Unfortunately, on this occasion, the League had failed to provide its own PA system, in which case the sound could have been amplified in the hall irrespective of what went over the air. Instead, *the live media coverage of the first debate, an event that allegedly would have occurred without it, put a stop to the event it was meant to cover.*

Near the end of the 27-minute interruption, there was a report to the effect that the League might call a halt to the debate. The networks themselves were in no position to do this because it would destroy the semi-fiction that they were only transmitting the debate. Apparently, no network considered cutting its coverage of an event no longer taking place and to whose broadcast they had consented, given the restrictive operating rules, only with the most serious misgivings. But once it had become evident that the interruption was more than momentary, the news organizations had to decide what the event was that they should be covering at this point. Whatever their decision, they had to be mindful of their responsibilities and possible caveats placed on their freedom of action by an event like a presidential debate. Cutting away entirely was precluded by the lack of information on what was happening, by the importance vested in the occasion, and by the fact that the news organizations had geared their resources for instant wrap-up and analysis. They could have kept silent, transmitting the pool picture while waiting for the return of sound but, for rather obvious reasons, chose instead to provide filler material fitting the tone of a presidential debate without intruding on the event in a way that might appear to favor one candidate or possibly affect the outcome.

Anything said during this interim, if the debate resumed, was likely to become mixed in the viewer's mind with the debate itself. This could lay broadcasters open to charges of interference or engaging in instant analysis, not just immediately after the event but while it was ongoing. Prevented by prior agreement from showing audience reactions to the debaters, they also had to be sure not to substitute the assessments of their reporters for those of the audience.

All treated the interruption as temporary but then, as time passed, went over to the kind of commentary and analysis previously prepared for postdebate analysis. (The reader will understand why we thought it necessary to distribute the "after" questionnaires as soon as possible after the audio failed.) Filler material could be presented in three ways: authoritative commentary, usually by the anchor; pooling information between reporters at the same or different locations; and interviews with members of the candidates' staffs. It is easier to maintain control of content and tone in solo commentary through internal balance than in discussion. Newspeople exercise some control over the content of interviews by the persons they select, the questions they ask, and by their ability to terminate the interview. But this is more risky than using an anchor or several reporters talking among themselves. A content analysis showed that CBS relied most heavily on the commentary of its anchor. NBC spent most time in interviews, and on ABC the pooling of information predominated, probably because ABC had direct access to the newspool via its reporter in a glass booth overlooking the theater. One can conclude then that the decision of the media during this gap was to mark time while avoiding interpretations so as not themselves to become the focus of a debate were the broadcast of the scheduled event to continue.

Meanwhile, the candidates, who could be seen but not heard, were also careful to suspend activity until the media event could be resumed. Uncertain whether and when the sound might go on, both Ford and Carter were afraid to be caught unawares. One careless gesture, word, or movement caught and blown up over TV could destroy a carefully contrived image of presidentiality. As Elizabeth Drew, one of the four reporters serving as questioners for this debate, wrote, "The President and the would-be President are like prisoners behind their lecterns."[4]

During the gap the cameras were almost constantly on the candidates, so that they could be seen on one network or another for most of the gap. Yet television did little to emphasize the personal drama in this situation. The pool employed no close-ups and its picture occupied less than full screen. This afforded the audience little opportunity to scrutinize facial expressions or body movements as clues to the two men's responses to the situation. Nor did the picture show what interaction there was between them during this enforced wait.

What news personnel said did little to supplement the picture. They failed to comment either about this personal dilemma or about what was happening on the stage. When CBS reported that "the President and Governor Carter are still at the podium," this just about sums what they told the viewers about the "prisoners' " plight. NBC did little more, twice pointing out that President Ford and Governor Carter were on the rostrum "waiting," which was exactly what the viewers could see for themselves. ABC was in a somewhat better position and could tell the audience a bit more. For instance, they told their listeners that Carter was "sitting with his hands folded, President Ford wiping his brow, and both of them getting a little warm under the lights."

As the camera showed them, Ford and Carter just stood there silently, except for one occasion about 15 minutes into the gap, when the monitor caught Ford looking at Carter. According to a magazine account by Elizabeth Drew, who had a good view of the candidates, they did occasionally steal furtive glances at each other after assuring themselves they were not on camera. A retrospective account by another reporter on the panel, Frank Reynolds, claimed that neither looked at the other. Ford, especially, said Reynolds, stood up there at the rostrum "like a rock—refusing to sit down—trying to project a stronger leader image."[5] Only those in the hall were fully aware of this contest of silence. Commentary after the debate suggested that the audience was intently watching the two candidates for cues about their feelings. Neither picture nor commentary during the gap gave much indication that anything going on the hall might have been worth reporting.

Faint Echoes of Watergate

It is hard now to recall the impact of the sudden fade out of Carter's voice. He was in the middle of commenting on the touchy subject of intelligence agencies and their regulation. Viewers could see his lips move, as he continued to speak, but he could not be heard. Why was what he was saying suddenly and unexpectedly covered by a curtain of silence? Just two years after Richard Nixon's resignation, it was natural for some among the millions in the audience to joke about some kind of conspiracy—the "dirty tricks" of the Watergate years. Carter himself is reported to have quipped, while on stage, "Mr. Kelley [the FBI director] may not have liked what I was saying."[6]

There was drama enough even without speculation about sinister forces at play. The technical failure, and the problems it created, was a bona fide news event to be covered. The ordinary technical failure, which the outage proved to be, was in its own way a real disaster, akin to electricity blackouts. By throwing cold water on the myth of technological invulnerability, it had more journalistic potential than a review of a debate suspended. What was the specific cause? Who was to blame? Was there anything about the specific arrangement under which the debates were broadcast that had increased the risk of such a disruption? The other story there for the telling was the effort to get the debate back on the air. Even with news personnel and cameras banned from the theater, news staffs could have turned their cameras on the ABC control truck outside, if only to say "we don't know what the trouble is."[7] With or without pictures, there must have been a good story in the way ABC engineers tried to locate the trouble, laid plans for bypassing the ABC audio booth, and ultimately connected with a CBS circuit. Yet no authorities were put on the air to tell what they knew of the salvage operation.

To switch to the coverage of an unplanned but bona fide live news event would no doubt have been difficult. The networks had geared their schedules, deployed their resources, and primed their staffs for an immediate postdebate analysis. They were further handicapped by their inability to communicate with the theater in which the debate was being held except through the pool feed. Indeed, the most pervasive theme in the coverage of the gap was the breakdown in internal communication. Yet if the news team found their restrictive working conditions sufficiently irritating to voice their frustrations, they never explained to the viewers the broadcast compromise that was at the root of their troubles.

Nor did anyone with access to the air address the question of why a debate that had been scheduled for the benefit of a live theater audience should not have been able to continue. Nothing was said about the court fight of other presidential candidates to halt the debates, nothing of the problems which continuing the broadcast might create for the networks, nothing of the efforts of the League of Women Voters—most aware of the threat to continued debates—to get back their PA system from the broadcasters. The sound in the theater, it turned out, could have been restored in a matter of seconds and the candidates could have continued even if they could not be heard by the television audience. To have continued under these conditions would have defeated the aims of the political camps in agreeing to the debate—both were primarily concerned that their candidate's carefully honed closing statement be broadcast. Ford's staff especially had put much effort into its wording and delivery to assure a favorable audience response. Parts of the final statement were to be used for short video commercials during the campaign, and it would be part of his election eve appeal. Thus both parties held to the previously agreed-upon arrangements.

Implications

Given the behavior of broadcasters and politicians, what were the implications of this media event? The issue was simply that the debate was no longer exempt from the equal-time requirement. With continued coverage of the silenced debate, the delicate compromise by which the debates had been arranged became vulnerable to new challenges from candidates of minority parties and civil libertarians who, from the beginning, had decried the hypocrisy of the FCC ruling. If this constituted a serious threat, then there was good reason not to alert the critics to the paradox of an event not supposed to have been staged for television being suspended by a technical breakdown in transmission.

We do not know how many of those involved recognized the debate's sudden vulnerability to the broadcast compromise, but two things are clear: Neither the news staffs nor campaign staffs did anything to resolve the evident paradox, nor was anything said about it on the air. Did the issue elude the broadcasters or did they feel as constrained as the campaign managers not to mention it?

Like other industries, television is perhaps more concerned about dramatizing its own public role than exposing and dealing with some of the dilemmas that arise from its presence. To have treated this issue during the gap would have been to give it the widest possible exposure. The issue did subsequently get some airing in the press. Representative Lionel Van Deerlin of California, Chairman of the House Communications Subcommittee, was quoted as saying this "made a mockery" of the FCC interpretation of the debates exemption. FCC Commissioner Abbott Washburn disagreed: Most Americans, he was reported as saying, would agree that the event was a bona fide news event and a "very major one."[8] Still, the fact that this slumbering issue did not grow into a major controversy after the first debate must be partly explained by the failure of the media covering the audio gap to mention it.

A Final Note

Not only did the presidential debates go on in 1976. By 1980—and thereafter—televised debates between candidates contending for their party's nomination became pro forma. During the presidential campaign, then President Carter apparently lost ground when he refused to participate in a three-way debate with Ronald Reagan, nominee of the Republican party, and John Anderson, a viable third-party candidate. Carter and Reagan finally met in a one-time two-man debate before the cameras after the League of Women Voters—again the official sponsor—agreed to exclude Anderson.

Before their debate, on October 28, Carter held, according to the Gallup Poll, a slight edge over Reagan. Reagan's aim was to dispel fears that he was a warmonger; he had to convey an image of reasonableness. Unfortunately, there is no record of the immediate response to the debate. ABC initiated an "instant national viewer poll" in which people, by paying for the call, could phone in to vote on who won the debate. In this brief period, the vote registered was 2 to 1 in Reagan's favor. While scientific survey researchers deplored the Republican bias built into the poll, it got a good deal of press attention. The verdict of *New York Times* columnist, James Reston, was that Reagan had "held his own" against Carter's superior mastery of the facts and thus probably came out of it better than he went in. News comment everywhere contrasted Reagan's relaxed, more genial manner with Carter's focus on detail. Reagan's aides, in public appearance and in print, were quick to proclaim him the victor. By November 3, a New York Times/CBS poll was showing that Reagan was helped by his showing in the TV debate; there had been a sizeable decline in the number of voters fearing he would get the United States into a war. Whatever the immediate response, there can be no doubt that the consensus, as revealed in this delayed response, was that Reagan had won the debate and, in so doing, had thereby quite probably won the election.

NOTES

1. Attention was first called to sleeper effects in Carl I. Hovland, A. A. Lumsdaine, and Fred D. Sheffield, *Experiments in Mass Communication* (Princeton, NJ: Princeton Universi-

ty Press, 1949.) For them, the sleeper effect represented delayed conversion—coming around to the communicator's point of view after a period of time. See also Carl I. Hovland, Irving L. Janis, and H. H. Kelley, *Communication and Persuasion* (New Haven, CT: Yale University Press, 1953), 19-55; and William R. Catton, Jr., "Changing Cognitive Structure as a Basis for the Sleeper Effect," *Social Forces,* 38 (1960): 348-54.

2. Some of these students were enrolled in sociology, political science, and communication classes; most of these courses were at the introductory level and included many who were nonmajors in these subjects. Others had responded to campuswide publicity urging students to attend a public viewing of the debate; these filled out questionnaires right before the debate began.

3. For a summary of the evidence on poll effects see Harold Mendelsohn and Irving Crespi, *Polls, Television, and the New Politics* (Scranton, PA: Chandler, 1970.) See also the entire issue of *Public Opinion* (Winter 1980/81) and *Annals* of the American Academy of Political and Social Science (March 1984).

4. Elizabeth Drew. "A Reporter in Washington, D.C.," *New Yorker* (January 10, 1977), 56.

5. This and other quotes reported here are from videotapes of the debate and network postdebate specials.

6. Drew, *op. cit.*

7. Jim Karayn, TV director for the League, quoted in *Broadcasting* (October 4, 1976).

8. *Ibid.*

8

The Question of "Reality"

"Television as a news medium," wrote media critic David Karp 20 years after its debut, "has acquired a peculiar and powerful status that no other medium has ever held. Marshall McLuhan...has, in fact, classified television's on-the-spot 'actuality' reporting of events as-they-happen as a totally new form of communication [that] has transformed the 'mere' reader into an electronic participant. The viewer is turned on to what is really happening as if he had an electrical umbilicus tied to the tube. In McLuhan's view, the television watcher has finally achieved the status of Aldous Huxley's 'feelie' participant, and damned high time it happened, too."[1]

Such exuberant language may not be atypical, but the message it conveys is disconfirmed by findings from our studies and those of the many other communication researchers. These show that televison, no less than radio or print, always introduces some element of refraction into the image of reality conveyed. The television presentation is only one of the perspectives from which events may be witnessed. Since it incorporates its own special forms of bias, "electronic participation" in McLuhan's global village is clearly a kind different from direct participation in any assembly. If television has acquired a special and dominant status as a news medium, as it obviously has in the United States and much of the world, the reason lies less in the qualities its heralds than in the readiness of reporters, political actors, and the public to believe in the video image. Its critics notwithstanding, many people still believe in its widely touted ability to expose the phony and reveal the truth. Thus, to paraphrase the famous dictum of the sociologist W. I. Thomas: "Since people define certain qualities of television as real, these are real in their consequences for political life."

What is the "reality" of television? How has the medium affected the nature of political participation?

Refraction and the Mass Media

The rapid development of communication technologies that began with the distribution of cheap print and telegraphic news services now allows message content emanating from a single central point to reach even the most distant corners of the earth. As a result, more and more people now have the opportunity to participate in the political, cultural, and intellectual life of far-off places. They live an ever greater part of their lives at a distance, responding to things they can know only through the media of mass communication. This larger world, which once reached them only via the newspaper, now joins them in their homes through the quick flick of a television switch. People everywhere are invited to empathize with strangers in the strangest surroundings. They become sensitized to events, objects, and personalities outside the range of their immediate experience.

The communication revolution, which has so increased the amount and kind of information potentially available to every citizen, is not without paradox. The paradox is generated by the *separation* of experience and participation, two aspects of political life that had heretofore been linked. As the media bring the world closer, the more intimate *acquaintance with* —the product of direct involvement—is replaced by a more superficial *knowledge about* things outside one's purview and beyond the horizon. The new knowledge is *mediated* knowledge; it depends on what the media systems disseminate yet under no circumstance can the picture replicate the world in its full complexity. Despite their ability to compress space and time and to surmount physical barriers to communication, mass media channels still have only a limited capacity. The news system is forced to operate by selection, and the criteria that govern what is selected inevitably introduce an editorial viewpoint that distorts in some way what is presented as reality, even when the editorial purpose is only to clarify.

In contending that distortion is inevitable in every medium, we trust our meaning will not be misunderstood. The bias or distortion that we refer to is not that due to deliberate manipulation. There has been—speaking of the United States—no concerted and sustained conspiracy on the part of the news media to foist a specific imagery about distant events on the public. For one thing, it is most unlikely that every editor would agree to go along. Someone would surely blow the whistle. Furthermore, a case can readily be made that media performance, in avoiding willful distortion, has improved over the years. News staffs are better trained than they were 50 years ago and they have also, it seems, become more skeptical, sharing some of the disillusionment that became fashionable with the passing of the activist 1960s. Compared to earlier generations, they have shown themselves more ready to express their indignation at official attempts to manage the news and less tolerant of their colleagues' clear violations of professional codes. More than ever members of the Fourth Estate espouse a standard of objective reporting that frowns on promotional ballyhoo and attempts by news sources to influence how the news is reported. Gone are the days when a newspaper was so edited that it carried only the news the publisher thought congenial enough to print.

Lapses do occur, and some are serious. Most commonly, an overly eager reporter in pursuit of a good story blows it up out of proportion and gets it by a less than vigilant editor. Occasionally, a big story proves pure fakery; this lapse itself becomes big news. Other lapses have more serious consequences: Everyone knows by now that the news media, overly trustful of what military spokesman were all too ready to reveal, incorrectly assessed the full implications of the American commitment to Vietnam. After that, many reporters, fearful of being entrapped as they were by the official handouts in the early years of Vietnam, overreacted when the Tet Offensive upset their unrealistic perceptions of American strength. Still, the nightmare, conjured up in novels such as George Orwell's *1984* or Eugene Burdick's *Sarkhan*, of a media-created reality, consisting entirely of fictitious wars in far-off lands and deliberately manufactured to mold opinion at home, remains remote as long as there is no political 1984. Competition among the news media provides some assurance against the manufacture of reality by prior agreement.

Nevertheless, the press is an institution, and, like most institutions, it reflects some point of view—or bias. It is, indeed, a natural extension of the social and political Establishment to which it is tied. The financial holdings of the press are considerable; much is at stake and owners, managers, and others with responsible positions have considerable status not only within but outside their own world. To be sure, not every member of the working press shares equally in this prestige. Many are only doing their job, but even most of these find a major reward in their frequent contact with important people whom they routinely cultivate as sources of news. The importance of these informal networks for the flow of news can hardly be exaggerated. The view of the world that emerges focuses on the heads of government or their most powerful challengers. They are the issue makers who, in a tacit collaboration with the press, define the lines of the political debate.

From this establishment perspective, a large part of the world goes unnoticed. Washington is always big news. One can always find something worth reporting between Pennsylvania Avenue, where the White House is, and Capitol Hill, where Congress is. Rioting that takes place ''eight blocks from the White House'' commands attention while other developments, equally threatening but more remote from the centers of power, are not publicized. It takes an unusually dramatic event for them to enter the normal news stream, make their way onto the media agenda and possibly the front page. How else could one have explained the failure of the news media to have adequately publicized certain endemic conditions that became the focus of collective grievances?

We take it as axiomatic that every communication system, no matter how sophisticated its technological base, inevitably injects some bias into the picture of reality it presents. This bias is also evident in the coverage of any specific event. Its image, as mirrored in the press, is a selective reconstruction of that event woven around a theme and a story line that makes it coherent. Some parts of the event will always be out of focus. Reporters and editors can hardly cover everything. They must deploy their limited resources so as to anticipate the big newsbreak, thereby paying more attention to some aspects of a story than they merit while underplaying or totally ignoring others. Under pressure to develop a story, journalists sometimes intrude into the event. Thus, the reporter who asks a question only to provoke a denial can create suspicions that might otherwise go unpublicized. If the denial stirs a controversy, the reporter has created the event that becomes news.

On these occasions reporters are not just playing an adversary role, as they like to believe. Intentionally or not, this kind of reporting can assist the politician looking for an issue or trying to keep alive an issue of little substance. This happened when John Kennedy, as campaigner, blamed the Eisenhower administration for the "missile gap" (between the USA and USSR); the gap disappeared once the 1960 election was decided. While the issue was not a creation of the press, reporters had helped to keep it alive by so frequently making it the object of their questions at press conferences. Likewise, though the Watergate affair did not become a major issue during the 1972 campaign, reporters helped keep the issue going with their questions about the break-in dismissed by the White House as a "third-rate burglary."

The media reality constitutes a symbolic environment. This social construction, superimposed on the natural environment, constitutes at once an enrichment (with new vistas opened) and an impoverishment (since much is left out). Its creation is, to a large extent, a one-way process. Information flows from the professional producers of content to audiences, most of whom can do little more than accept or ignore what is transmitted. Not only do these professional mass communicators talk far more to their audience than they listen but they also listen more to one another than they do to their audience. There is, consequently, a lag in the kind of feedback that serves to correct initial misperceptions or errors traceable to the establishment perspective and the selective use of sources. To this degree, the symbolic reality becomes self-confirming. It forces those who would participate in public life to orient themselves to the media, even while trying to change the media definition of what is happening. In fact, the public definition of any event is the collective product of the many efforts, from different vantage points, to control—to exploit and facilitate as well as to impede—the flow of information to the public about such an event. These efforts are a major part of politics.

The press plays a pivotal role in this process of social construction. Most of what people know about public life reaches them secondhand, which is to say by way of the various news media. Despite the advent of television, it remains a fact that very little of what people know of politics is based on direct observation. News that comes from television, like news that comes from other media, is mediated. Most people simply have no way of knowing for sure that reports of remote events faithfully convey what is there to be conveyed. However distrustful of the media, including television, they may appear to be (or say they are), there is little they can do but to accept at face value much that is reported.

This is not to say that the public behaves like a herd of sheep. Most people do approach the news with some skepticism. Generally they fall back on one (or both) of two means for testing the likely truth, or validity, of what they hear and see. There is the test of *affective congruence*—whether the report agrees with one's own feelings and/or wishes—and the test of *consistency*—how the report checks out against information from other sources. Affective congruence tends to reinforce any prior misconceptions inasmuch as persons pay more attention to reports that are congenial with ideas they already hold. On the other hand, the power of the consistency test is severely limited to the extent that other sources, useful for comparison, are limited. While the information to which people have access is abundant, its diversity is deceptive. There is considerable duplication insofar as news media often pool sources and borrow heavily from each other. In this respect, the relatively recent network practice of rotating responsibility for the televising of major news events, especially protracted deliberations, is restrictive. Still, is it more restrictive than the reliance on formal wire service arrangements and the informal trading of information within the press corps? News personnel themselves are among the heaviest consumers of news, constantly checking what they have learned against what others report, so that different sources of information may not be based on independent observation but actually have the same origin.

The Television Perspective

Does live television, compared to other media, provide a truer image of events, as even some who most criticize its coverage still tend to believe, or does it merely repeat and thereby reinforce any refraction introduced by the supporting communication networks on which its camera crews rely? Our studies pointedly suggest that television, like other media of mass communication, produces a refracted image of events it covers. There is, however, one major difference: Television journalists regard their technology as an ally in their effort to capture reality. To the extent that the camera can be relied on to bring the facts into focus, news staffs extricate themselves from responsibility for any false impression. Objectivity resides in the actuality provided by the picture.

Still, the idea of letting the picture speak for itself is taken far less literally today than when cameras were first used to broadcast congressional hearings to a fascinated nation in the infant days of video. Even when newer more mobile equipment was introduced, as during the 1952 nominating conventions, the camera alone could not guarantee a faithful rendering of reality. All journalists recognized that commentary was necessary to link what was shown to developments that could not be seen and to provide the viewer with a context for the correct encoding of the picture. But there is a risk, and a price that television pays, in supplementing the picture with the spoken word. The more extensive the use of contextual information and the more explicit the interpretation meant to guide the viewer, the more similar television reporting becomes to print reporting and the more open to the suspicion that it may be slanted. It is no coincident that the coverage of the impeachment hearings came to be considered one of TV's finest hours: How could viewers doubt that they saw for themselves when the journalists had so little to say?

In their construction of complex political events, television follows by now established codes that help weave the diverse elements into a coherent structure, assimilating these to certain schemata or (if you will) stereotypes,[2] without which viewers would be confronted with a meaningless kaleidoscope of images. Unless the production team is unusually self-searching, it will resort to an imagery already acceptable and familiar. Even when the unexpected happens, as it did during the first debate between Carter and Ford (Chapter 7), news staffs will rely on the routine to report the extraordinary. Likewise on MacArthur Day, television did nothing to disappoint the viewer's expectations, however disappointing the occasion may have been for the participant along the parade route (Chapter 2). In telling a story visually, cameras focus on what audiences can easily understand and spontaneously appreciate—the loyal wife intently gazing at her husband as he testifies before the Erwin Committee, the clusters of people at the airport to welcome home the hero. But is this adherence to the dictum that a "picture is worth a thousand words" necessarily the way to communicate the significance of the event?

The great appeal of the televised political event for most viewers is the opportunity to catch public figures in some kind of sustained close-up. Debates are followed not only "to hear what they say" but "to see how they say it." Both the Senate Watergate hearings and the impeachment hearings found viewers scrutinizing the cast of characters for clues as to "who was telling the truth." People still claim, however often they may have been fooled, that the camera "exposes the phony," that, on screen, public figures cannot help revealing their essential character. Yet even the sustained close-up can introduce an element of refraction. Do viewers in fact get a more revealing picture of the person than they can gain from other sources? Common sense answers yes, but such an answer has to be seriously qualified in the light of experience.

First, the opportunity to observe a speaker in close-up can distract from what is being said; it highlights how the speaker looks, whether he or she is nervous or relaxed, seems friendly or distant. But does the radio listener, lacking a picture, pay more attention to what is being said? Does the reader have more opportunity to weigh the words of a text than the viewer (or listener) who, once a speech is over, turns to the instant analysis that follows or to next day's news column to understand what has been witnessed? Now that most major speeches, though carried simultaneously on radio and TV, are mainly seen, it is difficult to carry out controlled comparisons of real-life reactions. Still, all the scanty evidence suggests how different may be the responses to the same speech. For instance, the dramatic improvement in Kennedy's personal image following his first debate with Nixon did not extend to radio listeners. The relatively few who had listened (mostly on car radios) were apt to have scored that debate a draw. They had no opportunity to witness Kennedy's drive and energy and Nixon's all too apparent discomfort.

Our study of the first Carter-Ford encounter further suggests that initial viewer reactions were significantly modified by media reporting of its outcome. Perhaps this is no problem, since commentators, knowing what viewers have seen, are forced to hue reasonably closely to what has actually transpired on television. But other questions remain. Can we be sure that a televised picture of two candidates locked in this kind of debate will correct previous conceptions of their real character, ability to lead, or what have you? Anxiety lest a close-up reveal some trait best kept hidden acts as a restraining influence. Most such television appearances lack spontaneity, except for those memorable occasions when the candidates momentarily forget themselves—and may even be caught wiping their perspiring faces or smirking at the wrong time. A skillful actor, like President Reagan, can give the appearance of spontaneity even when reading a prepared speech. Those who compel public figures, including the President, to submit routinely to sharp questioning by the press corps or to endure the ordeal that is the televised debate invite and tacitly encourage the semi-fake, a form of publicity that puts a premium on stage management in a way that a radio transcription or the printed stenographic record does not.

By 1984 debates between would-be nominees and candidates for public office at every level had become routine, even pro forma. In one sense, the format only follows a long-standing journalistic practice of juxtaposing opposing views that is meant to assure objectivity. The TV forum supplies each candidate with the chance to cut through the other's facade, unmask any pretensions, and expose the ill-founded view. In the coverage of other events, a similar confrontation pattern is achieved by employing media commentators with clearly divergent outlooks or soliciting the views of spokespersons representing different sides. So balanced, the presentation assumedly offers the viewer an opportunity to choose among competing versions of the event. Yet this approach, too, has its built-in sources of distortion. Presenting the two sides of every story—even where there is only one—can exaggerate the amount of conflict. Particularly when TV, in search of drama, publicizes deviant or irresponsible comments, as sometimes happens during controversies where self-appointed leaders posture for the cameras, it makes what they have to say more important and popular than it is. Some protest leaders have been little more than creations of a sensation-hungry press.

More generally, television, being preeminently a national medium, has contributed to the nationalization of politics. This effect is intrinsically neither good nor bad, but it has been long in the making. As early as 1952, television provided the means whereby those seeking General Eisenhower's candidacy escalated an internal dispute in the Republican party of Texas into a national issue (Chapter 3). Later, as southern police were caught on camera harrassing civil rights workers peacefully intent on desegregating public facilities, more and more southern whites became conscious that the enforcement of discriminatory practices, though rooted in local tradition, could no longer be considered a strictly local problem. Why the fury of some among the crowds protesting school integration should have been vented on Northern reporters and camera crews seems obvious. On the other hand, images of unfair police harassment, when generalized, could make even a legitimate arrest appear to be an arbitrary attack, thereby supplying justification for the antipolice riots that scarred many cities, mainly in the North, in the mid 1960s. Mainly since 1964 television has contributed to a basic change in the way we choose our Presidents. Each year increasing attention has been given to the outcomes of early primaries in states that are, in terms of population size, not very important. Given top billing by the media, they are now regarded as national events, curtain raisers for those ready to follow the long nomination process. In 1984, the media focus on the decisions of a few thousand voters, amounting to less than one percent of the electorate and from two clearly atypical states, overnight transformed Senator Gary Hart, until that time hardly known to most of the electorate, into a national political figure and a leading contender for the Democratic nomination. Whatever else voters would later see in him, at the time his appeal was as the latest media celebrity—a new face with New Ideas.

Early in the history of televised politics, attention turned to the reciprocal effects phenomenon—the way the mere presence of the camera elicted reactions from those on whom it focused (Chapter 2). The reciprocal effects observed ranged from the minute and trivial—better decorum at political functions, the omnipresent family standing beside the gracious loser as well as the victorious nominee, the spontaneous demonstrations of enthusiasm staged for the benefit of television—to the more widespread and serious—the practice of would-be leaders without constituencies using television to appeal to a wide audience of potential supporters as well as the persistent efforts of institutions to accommodate to the demands of the medium.

The whole pace and style of national political campaigning has been adapted to television with campaign schedules designed to secure the best possible place on the news. It has even been said that there is no campaign in the old sense of taking to the political stump—the campaign exists for and on television. For example, to avoid sensational but unanswerable charges on election morning, it was once the custom to end campaigning before the eve of the election. Now candidates vie for prime television time up to the hour the polls open.

And even on election day, as we have seen (Chapter 5), the candidates or their managers are still issuing statements meant to offset such adverse effects as may come from the rapid dissemination of returns by television. But the single most important reciprocal effect on campaigns has been to make the politician's television personality a major determinant of electoral choice.

Reciprocal effects also extend to such time-honored institutions as the presidential press conference. When Eisenhower first allowed the television cameras in, there was some fear that this would reduce the amount of give-and-take between press and President. While some Presidents have been more reluctant than others to meet with the press, the amount of interchange at a typical press conference has not diminished. As to its quality, it may have been sharpened. During the Watergate years it was sometimes confrontational. In yet another sense the institution has changed drastically; it no longer serves as an occasion for the off-the-record briefing. No longer does the President, assured that he will not be quoted as the source, use these as his principal forum for frank discussion of certain problems. The real briefings take place in private, often in the form of leaks. The press conference now serves the chief executive mainly as a platform for announcements he wishes to give wide public play. He weighs his replies to questions carefully because inadvertent remarks cannot be stricken from the record. The mere attempt to do so would make headline news in the same way that any deviation in a speech from the previously released text catches the reporter's ear. In these and similar instances, the impact of the media on the event and the impact of the event cannot be easily separated.

Electronic Participation

The technological capability for instantaneous rendition of actuality as it happens is not an altogether unmixed blessing. Mobile cameras have put the imprint of television on our symbolic environment by bringing distant events closer. But the audience may not be sufficiently mobile *psychologically* to keep up with the fast-changing scenes and cast of political personalities appearing on the TV-screen. We have tried to illustrate in our analysis of the first television nominating conventions how complicated it was to find one's way through the confusion, how great a challenge it was to understand what was presumed to be readily understandable. To make sense of the more puzzling convention episodes, a viewer had to know something about the job of the convention chairman, know what a caucus was and how it functioned, who the gallery spectators were and what role they normally played, what it was like to be a delegate, and so forth. Any bewilderment on the part of the viewer was, however, balanced, perhaps even outweighed, by the anchorman's constant reminder that the audience was participating in the convention as a favored spectator, seeing all, glimpsing even that which was hidden from many delegates.

The coverage of a complex event such as a convention amounts to an electronic transport to "everywhere." Viewers, elevated to a position of omniscience, are shown the event from every possible vantage point. Not that television viewers are actually persuaded that they see and know *everything* that is going on. On the contrary, most retain at least a reserve of skepticism. This is based, in part, on a reluctance to take at face value that which counters their beliefs or goes contrary to wishes. Over the decades of political television, this skepticism has been reinforced by the knowledge that all that meets the eye is not exactly what it seems, that some events have been reorganized to adapt to the presence of the cameras. Even the most sophisticated viewer may have waved to the camera as it panned the crowd, perhaps not at a political rally but surely at a ball game or concert. Yet these same viewers also subscribe to the notion long promoted by television that they see for themselves, that they are directly involved in history, that television does indeed take them to the scene of the crime, and that they have a better feeling for what is going on than some of the people right *there*. Viewers may complain that commentators talk too much or too little, or that they are too partial and their remarks misleading, but ironically, their awareness of such flaws only convinces them that they need not depend on reporters for conclusions that they can draw for themselves. They are especially convinced that they also know whenever information is being withheld from them.

The gist of the evidence from studies of MacArthur Day, the political conventions, televised debates, and the events of Watergate is that what people see for themselves is influenced by what they are shown and what is explained to them, even though a good many people persist in believing otherwise. This belief is far from irrelevant. Its effect, despite a nationwide decline in the credibility of television, a downgrading it shares with Congress, the presidency and other major institutions, may be as important as any effect of television that can be objectively documented. A faith in television, or merely the habit of treating the experiencing of televised events and personalities as authentic, supplies a degree of self-confidence in one's political expertise that permits viewers to validate their prejudices. This effect is manifest in the increasing voter volatility, noted by public opinion analysts. Especially during early presidential primaries when preferences have not yet firmed up, a telegenic personality, a carefully crafted advertising slogan and/or a catchy campaign slogan can catapult an unknown or an expected loser to victory. Thus John Kennedy (in 1960) managed to outpoll Senator Hubert Humphrey, long a champion of the poor, in West Virginia, a state of economic adversity. Other candidates, like Eugene McCarthy (in 1968), George McGovern (in 1972), Jimmy Carter (in 1976), and Gary Hart (in 1984) managed to emerge out of nowhere during the early primaries to offer a serious challenge to, though not always defeat, the better known front-runner. Also in 1976, Ronald Reagan won almost enough primaries to wrest the nomination from Gerald Ford, the incumbent President. To be sure, none of these upsets and near upsets could have been achieved without organization, but it was the use of television to appeal to voters over the heads of party leaders that spelled the difference between the serious challenger and the also-ran.

Viewers often lack the background to comprehend everything that may be happening before their very eyes. But this need not destroy their confidence in their own judgments so long as they perceive only what appeals to them or, more strategically, limit their participation to what they think they understand. They can decline to follow the camera and limit the number of personalities and the range of actions they permit to cross their threshold of attention. In this way, they can overlook much of what goes on while assimilating the rest into stereotypes and schemata available to them.

The new openness of politics, with once privileged negotiations—including the most complex negotiations—made public paradoxically can promote a conception of these events and of politics, in general, as more highly manipulated than they actually are. Believing that they see for themselves, some viewers interpret what they cannot fully understand as *evidence* that information is being deliberately withheld from them. In 1952, one network's attempt, using a hidden camera but no mike, to let the viewer in on what was going on at a state caucus being held routinely behind closed doors, succeeded only in convincing some viewers that they were being deliberately excluded, that mysterious machinations were being hidden from them. One viewer, asked why he believed the convention had been rigged, told our interviewer

> I saw that caucus. They let us in on one state. I don't know which one now—South Carolina or Texas or one of those, I think. They wouldn't let the press in. It was down at the Hilton, led by the big bosses. You couldn't tell how the decisions were made. You couldn't hear anything. You could just see men standing around talking and saw just the backs of them.

Here is how another viewer proved that delegates were told how to vote by the bosses:

> Well, Michigan stood right up [when it was being polled] and said they had a caucus. That means that somebody was telling them what to do.

There is no reason to believe that today's viewers would respond with less suspicion. Politicians, more versed in the use of television, may be more adept in impression management, showing only what they want to be seen, but the point remains the same: One can never take for granted that all or even most viewers will have enough experience and knowledge to draw the expected conclusion from available clues. Many will approach esoteric deliberations in terms of their own restricted codes and, except for what they take over the commentary, derive from these televised events only those meanings they themselves read into them. We consider it highly probable that there is an inverse relationship between viewers' convictions about the validity of their viewing and their ability or willingness to learn from it. The more viewers believe that they see for themselves, the less they gain. If video coverage of events is to contribute toward a public with a keener sense of discrimination and better informed to exercise its franchise, then the clarification of the factual and symbolic content of televised events demands as much, if not more, of the industry's attention than the campaign for unrestricted access, whether it be to Congress, to the court room, or to the local assembly. Political telecasts that fail to clarify the reality of a situation but have a special ring of truth may do more to mobilize emotion and indignation than to strengthen voter rationality. This danger is inherent in the one-way flow of message characteristic of all mass media but probably greater in television.

Cumulative Effects

Observations such as those above underline the resiliency of preconceptions and prejudices. They helped to foster what has been described as the "not common tendency [among researchers] to go overboard in blindly minimizing the effects and potentialities of mass communication."[3] While this view of media effects no longer represents the conventional wisdom, there is certainly ample evidence that people view the political content of the media in a highly selective fashion, that their interpretations of this content are influenced by their prior beliefs and then reaffirmed in discussions with people who are similar in background and outlook.

Nevertheless, these observations on selective exposure and interpretation do not encompass the whole range of media effects. For one thing, they shed little light on a problem central to our studies, namely, how the media define a very real political environment that can be known, whether directly or indirectly, only through the media. Exposure to this mediated environment is almost as difficult to escape as contact with one's immediate world. The main events, the cleavages that develop from them, the lineup of leading personalities on the major issues, and ideas about their personal characteristics somehow get through—perhaps not literally to everyone but to the vast majority, including the many who pay little attention to news and politics. The very pervasiveness of the news media forces us to look beyond their immediate and direct impact to consider their cumulative influence.

The important point is that the televised event—the debate, the press conference, the candidate stumping the campaign trail—no matter how inauthentic or unrevealing of the real thing, becomes the shared experience. It gives people, as Elihu Katz likes to put it, a "sense of occasion." A major televised event will be talked about, written about, and critically evaluated by other news media. Similarly, when fast-breaking stories come to dominate the news and command national attention—as during the tragic days following the assassination of President Kennedy, during the Iran hostage crisis, during a hotly contested primary campaign with candidates posturing before television, as well as during some natural disasters—the day-to-day coverage of major developments becomes the prime source of information for people everywhere. Inherent in such events is a potential for generating their own momentum. Once an event has been made into a big TV story, the other media also focus on it through television, so that the image of the event as depicted by television becomes its authentic image. The reality that lives on is the reality etched in the memories of the millions who watched rather than the few who were actually there.

Small wonder, then, that the televised image of MacArthur Day, however much it contradicted the direct experience of participants, survives as the authentic collective memory of the event. More than 30 years after the event, the *Chicago Tribune* (September 4, 1983, as part of a series entitled "The Way We Were") looked back on the

> estimated 3 million people [who] lined MacArthur's winding route.... Sentiment overwhelmingly favored MacArthur, whose desire to expand the Korean War into China, against Truman's orders, led to his sacking.... MacArthur's relatively short speech in Soldier Field was interrupted by applause 19 times.... When he began a sentence of the speech by saying, "Although my public life is now closed," the crowd responded with a thunderous, "No!".... MacArthur's visit was seen through what the The Tribune's Larry Wolters [at the time] called the "magic eyes of television."

Thus the legend of one of the first televised spectacles persists; the reporter looking backward continues to impute to the celebration a political significance that simply never existed. When conservative Republicans, some 15 months after the welcome home, sought to exploit the MacArthur legend by selecting him to keynote their nominating convention, his speech was judged to have laid an egg. It did not, as they had hoped, sweep the delegates off their feet nor, as everyone knows, was MacArthur ever seriously urged to run for President.

In trying to understand the political effects of the media, few studies have been focused on televised political events that are not more or less directly connected with the electoral process. Only when a major confrontation shapes up—as during the Watergate crisis—are there many exceptions to this rule. Communication research has concentrated mainly on media treatment of campaigns and responses to this. Perhaps this is as it should be. After all, voting still is for most people the principal vehicle of direct participation in the political process.

Yet, in focusing on what happens during periods of intense electoral activity, something is lost. It is difficult to understand the effects of the media during periods of intense electoral activity without considering the impact of their coverage, in between elections, of politically relevant events.[4] Especially with the erosion of party loyalties and increasing voter volatility, it becomes imperative to pay more attention to the way in which media coverage of events during these seemingly politically quiescent times helps to build issues and shape the lines of cleavage along which politicians seeking office are forced to position themselves. Here we refer to "issues" not just in their more formal sense (economic, social, and so forth) but to the more general public perceptions of problems facing the country today, perceptions that reflect less articulated feelings of unease or optimism concerning how things are going. It is in this more indirect and cumulative way that the media contribute to the climate of opinion in which the electoral contest is fought out.

This influence of television on the depiction of public moods, documented on MacArthur Day, has been, especially since the 1960s, the subject of much conjecture. During the period when violence was erupting in American cities, a print journalist traveling around the country described the kind of mood no opinion poll could adequately depict: "There was an uneasy feeling that things were going wrong in the cities and abroad, but that people couldn't help it, even if they didn't quite understand it, and therefore had to tolerate it, because they had no alternative to it."[5] Television had made it possible for people to be both on the battlefields of Vietnam and the battlefields of the inner city ghettoes; yet they could do nothing about either. Later they would become similarly frustrated and even infuriated as night after night they watched the Iranian militants trampling on American rights by storming the U.S. Embassy, defiling the American flag, and defying international law by their insistence on keeping 53 Americans hostage.

Even the most carefully crafted polls, in soliciting reactions to campaign issues and campaign events, cannot always tell us what the election results mean in terms of what the electorate expects, or will stand for, from those it elects. Exactly what mandate has been given— even in a landslide—remains open to interpretation. Watergate provides a good illustration of the emergent character of media influence on public opinion. In the summer that followed the bungled burglary (Chapter 6), news coverage created an awareness of Watergate but, surfacing during an election campaign, it was regarded as a strictly partisan political issue. After McGovern was buried under a Nixon landslide, the issue was just about dead so far as the general public was concerned. Yet only six months later, the question of White House complicity in a major scandal was beginning to tear the country apart. Watergate had taken on a new meaning with implications for the integrity of the presidency and the democratic values of governance. The issue had escalated to a point where it could no longer be settled to almost everyone's satisfaction by the usual political bargaining, without recourse to the authority on which legal decisions are usually based.

The moving force behind the effort to get to the bottom of Watergate came neither from the media nor an aroused public opinion responding to evident wrongdoing. In fact, after the summer/fall of 1972, when the reporting of Woodward and Bernstein first linked the Watergate break-in to the Nixon campaign committee and uncovered other evidence hinting at its explosive potential, no part of the press was a prime mover in the investigation. In fact, after Nixon's decisive electoral victory, the press came close to abandoning Watergate. Events that pertained to the incident no longer made headlines, at least not for a while. Then, as things kept happening and the issue revived, carried by its own momentum, the press reported mainly what information political insiders were happy to furnish it.

Thereafter, the main contribution of the news media, and particularly television, was the extensive and live coverage of certain critical events—including presidential speeches, the Senate hearings (Chapter 6), and the sequence of developments surrounding Nixon's firing of Watergate Special Prosecutor Archibald Cox, remembered as the "Saturday Night Massacre." Change in public perceptions of the issue came about gradually through the media's day-to-day coverage of the controversy and their highlighting of crucial events. What mattered was the context within which the media framed these events, the language they used to track them, the way they linked their reports on them to familiar and significant symbols, and their singling out of persons as spokesmen for the several sides. In this way the coverage had a good deal to do with the way the public—and the politicians as well—thought about and defined the underlying issues.

That the controversy, much of which was argued over television, should have been so visible nevertheless helped more than anything else to *legitimate* the process by which Nixon was finally ousted from office. In addressing a large and heterogeneous audience, the proponents had to make themselves appear as other than politically motivated. The very openness of the debate forced it to a higher level. Television, too, had to maintain a stance of impartiality. It could hardly afford the kind of parochial and moralistic tone that had characterized the press during the impeachment and trial of President Andrew Johnson some 100 years earlier. Then, newspapers were much more openly partisan in their political comment, printing only such versions of events as conformed to the views of their editors. During Watergate, the coverage was less parochial and less moralistic, with an emphasis on the facts. Continuous polling and appeals for understanding from both Congress and the White House put the public in a position to perceive itself as a jury called upon to render a verdict based on the evidence.

What was so remarkable about Watergate was how little the legitimacy of the succession of Nixon by Ford was questioned. After the resignation, no more than about 15 percent believed that he had been wronged. But what if the public had had no opportunity to observe the movers of public opinion at first hand? What if elite negotiations had remained privileged, as they so often are? The end to Watergate might well have been the same but the mood of the country when it was all over would have been different. Nixon's resignation would not have been so universally accepted as the right thing had the public not come to view the impeachment process as fair and nonpartisan. The live coverage of some of the blockbusters of Watergate went a long way toward so convincing the public that the process was fair and, in so doing, helped to keep the nation from being polarized and torn apart.

On another level, it is fair to say there could have been no public opinion on Watergate without the news media. Television played its part by calling into being a mass audience of bystanders, whose opinions had to be taken into account. It was likewise the media, which, by reporting shifts in opinion, presented the cast of political actors in Watergate—the White House, the Congress, the prosecution force—with a measure of the public response to their every move. In spite of this, public opinion was never an active participant in the campaign against Nixon. It did not direct the course of events, except when the reaction to the Cox dismissal—the spontaneous outpouring of telegrams and letters and telephone calls following Cox's televised press conference—signaled those in power that the time had come to take steps towards impeaching the President.

Television plays a large role in shaping the *impression* of public support for public policies and public personalities. Is the public then helpless against the machinations of the powerful who make use of the media to build an *impression* of public support? To a certain extent it is. The media can direct attention to some issues while ignoring others. They can build images of political figures so that people feel they know them. They are forever suggesting, simply by what they play up, what persons everywhere should know about, think about, have opinions about. From this perspective, Watergate was, indeed, a media-generated issue and every popular candidate (from Kennedy to Ronald Reagan or from Kefauver to Gary Hart) a creation of the media. People are rightly apprehensive about this form of domination. They have a reason to be suspicious of undue influence and to be on the alert, comparing what the big media tell them by consulting other sources. Such caution hardly qualifies as distrust.

But there is a kind of distrust that goes beyond the skepticism demanded of every intelligent citizen. Its roots lie in the complexities of political life and the inability of people without expertise to analyze issues that require specialized expertise. Full coverage and openness do not always succeed (as they eventually did during Watergate) in allaying the suspicions of those whose view of politics as sinister derives from a projection of their own sense of incompetence. We have indicated that, for such people, opening events to television cameras can actually backfire by making them feel that something is deliberately being hidden from them.

Over the past two decades America has experienced a very marked decline in public trust and confidence in just about every major government institution. There are concrete reasons behind some of this distrust—among these, governmental duplicity over the conduct of the war in Vietnam, the broken promises over civil rights, environmental protection, and other matters that affect people intimately. There are also public scandals, such as the massive laundering of campaign funds during the 1972 campaign or the Abscam operation that entrapped several congressmen and one senator into the acceptance of payoffs, not to speak of general frustrations over the apparent inability of government to solve fundamental economic problems and over major foreign policy failures. But this general demoralization has also coincided with the rise of television as the dominant news medium. It may not be the direct cause of this demoralization but it has certainly brought into sharp focus events that help to reinforce such feelings of powerlessness and incompetence as already exist.

That television has directly contributed to the widely prevalent distrust is difficult to document.[6] There have been suggestions, so far on less than conclusive evidence, that heavy viewers tend to define the world as more frightening and dangerous than others less addicted to television. Viewer reactions to the medium range widely. They include the following paradoxical phenomenon: A generalized and exaggerated suspiciousness of politics and politicians often goes hand-in-hand with high reliance on and trust in one particular news source as someone who is somehow exempt from the contamination imputed to the news media and politics generally. Since everyone acts in terms of some (to the person) credible image of the political world, in their search for the truth people need to place their trust somewhere or in someone. Television, because of its actuality, becomes the medium through which people judge the trustworthiness of leaders who appeal for their support. The emphasis is on the personality.

TV tends to personalize politics through closeups that encourage viewers to scrutinize the faces and mien of people who appear on the screen. Without knowledge of where the *truth* lies, viewers are limited to making judgments on who can be *trusted*. Television allows them to circumvent the political party as a mediating institution. They need no ward heelers or union leaders to tell them how to vote. They pay more attention to style, to indications of honesty and sincerity than to past records and political associates. Even the more sophisticated viewers lean on television to assess the personalities of the candidates making direct appeals for their votes.

Undoubtedly, personalized politics preceded the arrival of television, but given the number of candidates now entering political primaries we have entered a new phase. Being a viable candidate depends less on support from a party organization than on the ability to sell oneself in a media campaign (preferably well-financed). Regardless of which is cause and which effect, the weakness of parties and the opportunity to use television interact. The greater the disarray of the parties, the more important is television as a means to short-circuit what used to be normal political channels. Conversely, television gives outsiders with sufficient resources a better chance than ever before to enter the fray.

To repeat: It is difficult to demonstrate through a single experiment, or even a series of convincing experiments, what the long-range political effects of television have been. Trying to demonstrate these effects is an effort foredoomed to failure. Yet, neither is the inability to "prove" the cumulative effects of television by the standard measurement techniques an acceptable "counterproof." We have tried to find some clues to these cumulative effects by looking at the way television transmits reality and affects the imagery of politics and political figures. The search for these effects extends beyond the audience reacting to a specific set of messages transmitted on video. It extends to the shared experience of politics provided by television to which individuals, political actors, and institutions somehow accommodate.

NOTES

1. *New York Times Magazine* (November 19, 1967): 145.

2. Walter Lippmann, *Public Opinion* (New York: Harcourt Brace, 1922).

3. Joseph T. Klapper, *The Effects of Mass Communication* (Glencoe, IL: Free Press, 1960): 252.

4. Kurt Lang and Gladys Engel Lang, "Mass Media and Voting," in Eugene Burdick and Arthur J. Brodbeck, eds. *American Voting Behavior*, (1959): 217-35.

5. James Reston, *New York Times* (August 1967).

6. Only Michael Robinson, as far as we know, has ever pursued this implication, which we drew from our earlier convention study. See his "Public Affairs Television and the Growth of Political Malaise: The Case of the *The Selling of the Pentagon*," *American Political Science Review* 70 (June 1976): 409-32.